D0023742

ANTHOLOGY *of* AUSTRALIAN ABORIGINAL LITERATURE

ANTHOLOGY *of* AUSTRALIAN ABORIGINAL LITERATURE

Edited by Anita Heiss and Peter Minter

General Editor: Nicholas Jose

McGill-Queen's University Press

Montreal & Kingston • London • Ithaca

This book was produced under the auspices of the Centre for the Macquarie PEN Anthology of Australian Literature at Macquarie University, Sydney, Australia. It is published under the title *Macquarie PEN Anthology of Aboriginal Literature* in Australia.

The editors would like to thank the following organisations for their contributions:

Australian Research Council

Australia Council, the Australian Government's arts funding and advisory body, through its Aboriginal and Torres Strait Islander Arts Board and the Literature Board

Nelson Meers Foundation

Koori Centre, the University of Sydney

Sidney Myer Fund

Black Words, Aboriginal and Torres Strait Islander Writers and Storytellers

Australian Institute of Aboriginal and Torres Strait Islander Studies (AIATSIS)

Deakin University

The Australian Academy of the Humanities

ABOUT THE EDITORS

Anita Heiss is a member of the Wiradjuri nation of central NSW and a writer, poet, activist, social commentator and academic. She is author of *Dhuuluu-Yala: Publishing Aboriginal literature*, *Not Meeting Mr Right* and *Who Am I?: The diary of Mary Talence, Sydney 1937*. She won the 2004 NSW Premier's History Award (audio/visual) for *Barani: The Aboriginal history of Sydney*. She is National Coordinator of AustLit's Black Words subset.

Peter Minter is an award-winning poet, editor and scholar. He is the author of several collections of poetry, including *blue grass*, *Empty Texas* and *Rhythm in a Dorsal Fin*, was the editor of the *Varuna New Poetry* series, a founding editor of *Cordite Poetry and Poetics Review* and co-editor of *Calyx: 30 Contemporary Australian Poets*. From 2000 to 2005 he was poetry editor of *Meanjin*, and guest editor of two special issues. He lectures in Indigenous Studies and Poetics at the Koori Centre, University of Sydney.

© Anita Heiss and Peter Minter 2008
Individual extracts are copyright of the individual authors

ISBN: 978-0-7735-3459-9

Legal deposit third quarter 2008
Bibliothèque nationale du Québec

First published in Australia by Allen & Unwin as part of the
Macquarie PEN Anthology of Literature Project

Library and Archives Canada Cataloguing in Publication

　　Anthology of Australian Aboriginal literature / edited by Anita Heiss and Peter
Minter ; general editor, Nicholas Jose.

Includes bibliographical references and index.
ISBN 978-0-7735-3459-9

　　1. Australian literature--Aboriginal Australian authors. 2. Aboriginal
Australians--Literary collections. I. Heiss, Anita II. Minter, Peter, 1967-
III. Jose, Nicholas, 1952- IV. Title: Anthology of Aboriginal literature.

PR9614.5.A94P46 2008　　　　　　820.8'089915　　　　　　C2008-901398-0

Internal design by Kirby Stalgis
Set in 10.5/12.5 pt Bembo by Midland Typesetters, Australia
Printed and bound in Australia by Griffin Press

10 9 8 7 6 5 4 3 2 1

CONTENTS

FOREWORD

The *Anthology of Australian Aboriginal Literature* is of great importance to many both within Australia and internationally. Rich in diversity and content, it brings together a range of works that any serious student of Aboriginal history, life and culture will find invaluable. It will also be useful for those interested in more than just scholarship and academic pursuits; this volume is extremely significant from an Indigenous cultural perspective, containing many works that afford the reader a treasured insight into the Indigenous cultural world of Australia. This is a cultural product as much as it is a literary text. The history of Indigenous publications in the past two decades has almost overflowed with Indigenous creativity and effort. Much of that creativity and effort has been understandably linked to the politics of Aboriginal Australia. This publication makes a fine contribution in that direction.

I was lucky to grow up reading—sadly, a lot of Indigenous kids don't—and literature has played a very influential role in my life. As I get older it seems there is just not a whole lot of time to read all the things I want to. I would hope that one day all Indigenous kids are able to read very early and read often and I'm sure a volume like this anthology would be an inspiration to many. It does give a glimpse of what Indigenous people are capable of doing.

Literature and its creation are so important to the lives of everyone. It can be and is used as a powerful political tool by Aboriginal people in a political system which renders us mostly voiceless. It can give us confidence and pride to raise our voices through the silence.

This anthology contains work by some of the great Aboriginal writers, playwrights, novelists and poets. It is a wonderful encapsulation of their political and cultural activisms. I recommend it to all interested in the Indigenous literature of this country.

Mick Dodson

PREFACE

This transformative survey of Aboriginal writing presents the stories and patterns of Australian culture and society in new ways, foregrounding and celebrating Indigenous experience and expression. It introduces powerful and creative individual voices as it also reveals a larger history of struggle, suffering and strength. No doubt there are gaps and limitations. There are always more voices to be heard and other stories to be told. Yet in their gathering of literature the editors show that Aboriginal authors have created some of the best, most distinctive and most significant writing to come from this country.

Let me pay tribute to the vision of the editors, Dr Anita Heiss and Peter Minter, and the boundless dedication and good feeling they have brought to the enterprise. This work is part of a larger project managed by the Centre for the Macquarie PEN Anthology of Australian Literature at Macquarie University under the directorship of Professor Emerita Jill Roe and coordination of Dr Chris Cunneen. Their contribution, along with that of their colleagues Dr Geoff Payne, Terry Mangan, Jan Zwar and Jenny O'Brien, has been expert and invaluable. They have been sustained from the outset by Professor Christina Slade, Dean of Humanities, Macquarie University, whose support has been essential. Anita Heiss and Peter Minter are also members of the editorial team for the *Macquarie PEN Anthology of Australian Literature*, a companion volume to follow this one, with Dr David McCooey as deputy editor, Professor Elizabeth Webby, Dr Nicole Moore and Dr Kerryn Goldsworthy as contributing editors and myself as general editor. We have all benefited from the lively discussion and close collaboration that have characterised the editorial process.

The anthology project began with the Sydney Centre of International PEN, a world association of writers, in accord with PEN's charter to nurture literary heritage and make it available for contemporary audiences.

Mary Cunnane, former Sydney PEN vice-president, deserves special thanks for her indispensable role as advisory publishing editor. We are grateful to PEN, and to those members who contributed to the project, notably John Durack SC and Angela Bowne SC for legal advice. We have been no less fortunate in the unstinting support of our publishers, Allen & Unwin, as the project has grown. Elizabeth Weiss, Angela Handley, Pedro de Almeida, Ali Lavau and their colleagues have been a fount of enthusiasm, experience and good counsel. Nor would a major initiative of this kind have been possible without generous support from partner institutions and philanthropic bodies, particularly for help with copyright permission costs: the Australian Government through the Australia Council for the Arts, its arts funding and advisory body; the Myer Foundation; the Nelson Meers Foundation; the University of Adelaide; the University of Sydney, especially its Koori Centre; Deakin University; and AIATSIS. We are very grateful, too, for the Australian Research Council Linkage grant for 2007–09 that substantially funded our research and production costs. There are many individuals to thank as well, including Louise Walsh, director, Artsupport Australia; Imre Salusinsky, chair, Literature Board and Josie Emery, director, Literature Board; Iain McCalman, past president of the Australian Academy of the Humanities and John Byron, its current executive director, who were instrumental in providing financial support and encouragement at an early stage.

The editorial and research work required for such a project draws extensively on the scholarship and productivity of our predecessors and many present-day colleagues. We sincerely acknowledge the publications, compilations, reference works and resources (see Selected Reading and Sources and Permissions), as well as library and other institutional collections that have been available to us, especially the *Australian Dictionary of Biography*; AustLit: The Resource for Australian Literature; the National Library of Australia; and the State Library of NSW. We are also, and by no means least, grateful for the cooperation of the authors whose work is reproduced here, and of family members, literary estate holders, editors, publishers and agents. In summary, let me express the appreciation of all concerned for a remarkable set of partnerships with which we are proud to be associated in producing this anthology.

The *Anthology of Australian Aboriginal Literature* includes work produced in English by Australian Aboriginal authors published up to 2006. The works generally appear in the order of first publication or performance, with the date indicated at the end of each extract, and works by the same author are grouped together in order of publication, following the earliest published piece by that author. Poems or other items that appeared in journal form and were later collected for publication in book form are dated by first book publication. The date of a play's first performance is given in italics in the author biographies. The book is accompanied by a website which includes resources and links for teachers and students: www.macquariepenanthology.com.au

Nicholas Jose
Chair of Creative Writing
The University of Adelaide

ACKNOWLEDGEMENTS

The development of an anthology of this scope draws on the expertise, support and goodwill of a large number of individuals and institutions. We firstly wish to thank Professor Nicholas Jose, General Editor of both the *Anthology of Australian Aboriginal Literature* and the *Macquarie PEN Anthology of Australian Literature*, whose enthusiasm and guidance has encouraged our steadfast desire for excellence. We are also privileged to be part of an editorial team whose professionalism and good humour have been central to our shared vision, and we extend our gratitude to deputy editor Dr David McCooey, Professor Elizabeth Webby, Dr Kerryn Goldsworthy and Dr Nicole Moore. We would also like to thank our colleagues at Macquarie University, particularly Dr Chris Cunneen and Dr Geoff Payne for their tireless work behind the scenes. We are also grateful for the dedication and invaluable expertise of Elizabeth Weiss, Angela Handley and Pedro de Almeida at Allen & Unwin, and the insight and advice of Mary Cunnane.

We would also especially like to thank the following organisations and individuals for their generous assistance and advice: the Aboriginal and Torres Strait Islander Arts Board and the Literature Board of the Australia Council; Professor Mick Dodson and the National Centre for Indigenous Studies at the Australian National University; AIATSIS; the Koori Centre, University of Sydney; Warawara Department of Indigenous Studies, Macquarie University; Kerry Kilner and her colleagues at Black Words: the Aboriginal and Torres Strait Islander Writers and Story-tellers subset of the AustLit database; Professor Albert Wendt, University of Hawaii; Professor Larissa Behrendt, University of Technology, Sydney; Associate Professor Chadwick Allen, Ohio State University; Associate Professor Tracey Bunda, Flinders University; Dr Irene Vernon, Colorado State University; Dr Penny van Toorn, University of Sydney; Dr Kate Fagan, University of Sydney; Phillip Morrissey, University of Melbourne; Adrian Atkins, University of

Sydney; Sandra Smith, Museum Victoria. We also gratefully acknowledge the use of the following electronic sources for biographical information on authors: *Barani: Aboriginal history of the City of Sydney*; the *Australian Dictionary of Biography*; the National Archives of Australia; Gary Foley's *Koori History* website; Kev Carmody website; Magabala Books; Monash University; and HREOC.

We would finally like to thank our families, friends and communities for their unflagging support, and for sharing our belief that literature can tell it how it is.

Anita Heiss and Peter Minter

LIST OF ABBREVIATIONS

AIATSIS: Australian Institute of Aboriginal and Torres Strait Islander Studies

AIF: Australian Imperial Force

ANZAC: Australia and New Zealand Army Corps

APA: Aborigines Progressive Association

ATSIC: Aboriginal and Torres Strait Islander Commission

AustLit: The Australian Literature Resource (www.austlit.edu.au)

FCAATSI: Federal Council for the Advancement of Aborigines and Torres Strait Islanders

HREOC: Human Rights and Equal Opportunity Commission

NAIDOC: National Aborigines and Islanders Day Observance Committee

NSW: New South Wales

NT: Northern Territory

RSL: The Returned Services League of Australia

SA: South Australia

WA: Western Australia

WRANS: Women's Royal Australian Navy Service

ABORIGINAL LITERATURE

This anthology presents, for the first time in a single volume, the range and depth of Aboriginal writing in English from the late eighteenth century to the present day. Our selection begins with Bennelong's letter of 1796, the first known text in the English language by an Aboriginal author. At the time of the letter's composition, Bennelong had recently returned home from three years in England, where he had met King George III and only just survived as a racial curiosity. Bennelong's short, disarming inquiry after the wellbeing of his sponsor, Lord Sydney, and his slightly melancholic petition for shipments of fine clothes and shoes, speaks of one man's experience at the cusp of a sudden transformation in the human condition of all Aboriginal peoples. This anthology records the history of that transformation as it was witnessed in writing ranging from the journalism, petitions and political letters of the nineteenth and early twentieth centuries, to the works of poetry and prose that are recognised widely today as significant contributions to the literature of the world.

Our primary consideration has been to chronologically document literature written in English by Aboriginal authors. We also aim to introduce readers to the power, eloquence and beauty of a remarkable tradition within Australian writing, a set of stories, poems, plays and political works that, with all their grief and suffering, demand attention and celebration. Such a project necessarily begins with the fact of colonisation and the sudden arrival of the English language amidst Aboriginal societies and their modes of exchange. On 22 August 1770, Lieutenant James Cook raised the flag at Possession Island and declared Britain's acquisition of the east coast of Australia. This grandiose assertion was upheld eighteen years later by the tentative but nevertheless permanent British settlement of the continent at Sydney Cove, where on 26 January 1788 a crew of convicts and naval officers disembarked from the ships of the

First Fleet, establishing under Governor Arthur Phillip the colony of New South Wales. With them came not only the hopes and fears of a remote and tenuous European settlement; this moment also marks the arrival of English amongst Aboriginal people as an unexpected, perhaps unwanted, but eventually prevailing language.

With this in mind, we can address the development of Aboriginal literature not only from the perspective of history, but also with an awareness of the sudden appearance amongst Aboriginal people of a new set of linguistic and rhetorical conditions. At its inception, Aboriginal literary writing grew directly from a complex and ancient wellspring of oral and visual communication and exchange. It is generally agreed that at the end of the eighteenth century there were many hundreds of distinct Aboriginal societies in Australia, each of which possessed rich cultural, mercantile and day-to-day languages and forms of expression that had been intact for tens of thousands of years. But just as the Crown's acquisition of 1770 had made sovereign Aboriginal land *terra nullius*, it also made Aboriginal people *vox nullius*. It took only a few generations for almost two-thirds of the pre-contact Aboriginal languages to be made extinct. During the nineteenth century, Aboriginal people were dispossessed of their lands and many were interned on reserves and missions, institutions in which common human rights were rigorously limited by legislative machinery and ideological imperatives to 'smooth the pillow of a dying race'. Particularly in the eastern and southern parts of the continent, Aboriginal people were unable to live traditionally and were prevented from speaking their native languages.

For Aboriginal people, the use of English became a necessity within the broader struggle to survive colonisation. From the early days, writing became a tool of negotiation in which Aboriginal voices could be heard in a form recognisable to British authority. Aboriginal men and women were highly motivated by the duress under which they and their communities lived, and it is in their transactions with colonial administrations that the principal characteristics of the early literature were forged. Aboriginal authorship, as a practice and a literary category, first appears in genres that are common to political discourse: letters by individuals to local authorities and newspapers, petitions by communities in fear of further forms of dispossession or incarceration, and the chronicles of those dispossessed. In the first part of this anthology we have collected a range of moving and persuasive voices which are all the more valuable for their scarcity. These works reveal modes of performativity that are central to literary writing. They also demonstrate one of the persistent and now characteristic elements of Aboriginal literature— the nexus between the literary and the political.

The federation of the Commonwealth of Australia in 1901 did little to advance the social and political conditions of Aboriginal people. The new constitution specifically restricted the capacity of the Commonwealth to legislate in Aboriginal affairs, responsibility for which remained with each of the states and territories. From the late nineteenth century so-called 'Protection Acts', such as the 1869 *Act for the Protection and Management of the Natives of Victoria*, had evolved in each colony, and during the first decade of the twentieth century state and territory bureaucracies consolidated their authority over nearly every aspect of Aboriginal life. While the federal constitution had determined that Aboriginal people were effectively non-citizens, the Protection and later Aboriginal Welfare Acts saw lower tiers of government intensify control over what are generally considered to be fundamental human rights. For instance, Aboriginal people were forced to seek permission from authorities to exercise freedoms of movement and association, to enter into employment, or to marry. Governments and Protection boards acquired authority over the welfare of Aboriginal children, removing thousands from their families. Many of these children were placed in institutions and trained to work in menial, labour-intensive occupations. Aboriginal people were systematically disenfranchised from their traditional lands, their cultural practices and their languages.

The Aboriginal literature of the first decades of the twentieth century is characterised by a concerted and unmistakably public struggle against the overtly assimilationist legislative regimes endured by Aboriginal people. Between Federation and the 1960s, as had occurred in the nineteenth century, Aboriginal authorship appeared in letters and petitions to authorities—but now also in the political manifestos and pronouncements of Aboriginal activist organisations that had begun to coordinate resistance to government control. Organisations such as the Australian Aboriginal Progressive Association, the Australian Aborigines League and the Aborigines Progressive Association united Aboriginal men and women from across the south-eastern states between 1925 and 1938, focusing their shared confrontation with mainstream Australia. William Cooper's 'Petition to the King' and the APA's manifesto 'Aborigines Claim Citizen Rights!' are representative of writing at this time. In such texts we see responses to the extreme disadvantages suffered by Aboriginal communities denied access to land, property, education and health care, and a strong clarification of arguments against the various regimes of Protection. Demonstrations such as the 'Aboriginal Day of Mourning & Protest', held in Sydney on 26 January 1938 as the Commonwealth celebrated 150 years of British settlement, deepened the bond between political protest and Aboriginal writing.

The 1929 publication of *Native Legends*, David Unaipon's collection of his people's traditional stories, was a similarly significant development in Aboriginal writing. Unaipon was born and educated at the Point McLeay mission in South Australia during the early years of the assimilationist era, but as a gifted scholar, inventor, public speaker and writer he was able to successfully negotiate the complexities of life inside and outside the mission. His slim volume, produced by a metropolitan publisher for a white, middle-class readership in Australia and England, marks the arrival of a new genre of Aboriginal literature in English. Unaipon's *Native Legends* draws directly from the living wellspring of his traditional culture, but is also literary in its adaptation of his cultural imagination to particular modes of authorship and narration. Unaipon's achievement in publication, like that of his peers, was of course also political in nature. In writing *Native Legends*, Unaipon preserved in the English language something of his traditional Aboriginal culture, which he feared was already disappearing under the weight of colonisation. His legacy is fortunately twofold: Unaipon also gave subsequent Aboriginal writers a significant precedent by which to imagine their authorship of a culturally grounded future literature.

It would be another generation, however, before the next authored volume of Aboriginal writing appeared. Following the Second World War, the attention of Aboriginal activists returned to the domestic struggle for Aboriginal citizenship and the removal of state-based Protection and Welfare boards. During the 1950s and 1960s organisations such as FCAATSI coordinated the first nationwide movements agitating for Aboriginal rights and constitutional transformation. We have collected a number of letters, reports and petitions from a period in which the winds of change helped give Aboriginal political writing greater impetus and focus. Inspired by the worldwide radicalisation of Black politics and writing during the 1960s, particularly the American civil rights and the South African anti-apartheid movements, Aboriginal writing was at the forefront of a renewed and partially successful resistance to state authority. Aboriginal writer-activists such as Kath Walker helped lead the fight for full citizenship while producing the early poetry and political pieces that became major contributions to Aboriginal literature. Walker's first book of poetry, *We Are Going*, was—in 1964—only the second volume of Aboriginal literature published following Unaipon's work of 1929, and the first by an Aboriginal woman. Like Unaipon, Walker drew deeply from the traditional sources of her cultural imagination, however her literature's political aspirations were far more explicit. Directed to both her own community and to an enthusiastic mainstream audience, *We Are Going* marks the arrival of Aboriginal poetry as one of the most important genres in contemporary Aboriginal political and creative literature.

Key political texts were also produced during the escalating struggle for land rights. Having been on the Aboriginal rights agenda for many decades, demands for land rights took shape in the mid-1960s when tribal councils in the Northern Territory began taking on governments in their fight for the recognition of traditional land rights. Aboriginal stockmen and their entire communities walked off cattle stations and went on strike for equal pay and the return of their traditional lands. The 'Yirrkala Petition to the House of Representatives, August 1963' (Yirrkala Bark Petition) and the Gurindji Petition led by Vincent Lingiari in 1967 are both representative. The Yirrkala Bark Petition remains especially significant. Authored by tribal elders at a pivotal moment in the expression of Aboriginal autonomy, it is written in Yolngu with an English translation, and is bordered by traditional Yolngu designs that express Yolngu law and rights to land. It was the first traditional document prepared by Aboriginal authority that was recognised by the Commonwealth Parliament, and is thus the first recognition of Aboriginal people and language in Australian law.

Aboriginal literature as we know it today had its origins in the late 1960s, as the intensification of Aboriginal political activity posed an increasing range of aesthetic questions and possibilities for Aboriginal authors. Momentum for change took a significant turn with the success of the 1967 constitutional referendum. However practical changes were slow to come, and the period between 1967 and the election of the reformist Whitlam government in 1972 saw a new radicalisation in Aboriginal politics. With the political agenda focused on land rights and cultural self-determination, Aboriginal literature began to play a leading role in the expression of Aboriginal cultural and political life. New and challenging works of modern poetry and prose combined the traditions of protest established during the nineteenth and early twentieth centuries with the energy of the 'Black Power' movement. The period between 1967 and the mid-1970s is particularly significant for the sudden growth in Aboriginal authorship across a broad range of genres. Aboriginal writers began publishing volumes of poetry and fiction with both mainstream and grassroots presses, works for the theatre were successfully produced, published and widely read, and around the country Aboriginal journalists were contributing to the pamphlets, newsletters, newspapers and magazines from which an independent Aboriginal print media has since grown and flourished. The growing confidence of Aboriginal people throughout Australia, most of whom still lived in poor and ideologically isolated communities, was frequently demonstrated on the streets in marches and protests, the most prominent of which was the Aboriginal Tent Embassy built in 1972 on the lawn outside the capital's Parliament House. The literature of the 1970s, inspired by the broad push for political and territorial self-determination, demonstrates a fusion of political and creative energies. As new forms of agency were articulated in Aboriginal social and political life, new categories of authorship were explored and invented. We have collected work by writers such as Kath Walker, Jack Davis, Kevin Gilbert, Monica Clare, Gerry Bostock and Lionel

Fogarty, all of whom were active in the political sphere while simultaneously catalysing a nascent Aboriginal publishing industry and writing their own vanguard pieces of creative literature.

Following the uncertain political gains of the 1970s, many Aboriginal communities continued to suffer severe social and economic hardship, and political fights for social equity, land rights and cultural expression were intensified. During the 1980s, Aboriginal people around Australia sought to consolidate gains made in Commonwealth land rights legislation and the promise of self-determination. Aboriginal writers also maintained the rage, as was seen during the lead-up to the Commonwealth Bicentenary celebrations of 1988 when Aboriginal people and their supporters held nationwide demonstrations drawing attention to the Aboriginal rights agenda. They were often led by Aboriginal authors and activists such as Kath Walker, who, in protest against the Bicentenary, returned her MBE and readopted her traditional name, Oodgeroo Noonuccal. Noonuccal's defiant recovery of her true name is a defining moment in the evolution of contemporary Aboriginal literature, reflecting both an individual and a collective resurgence in the confidence of Aboriginal culture. In the final two decades of the twentieth century, the reach and impact of Aboriginal literature grew exponentially, attracting large mainstream audiences that were increasingly sympathetic to Aboriginal cultural and political demands. Behind the scenes, a new generation of Aboriginal authors, editors and publishers were working alongside elders to consolidate a vigorous and commercially independent network of Aboriginal literary presses. Mainstream publishers also took a strong interest in Aboriginal authors, and by the end of the 1980s Aboriginal writing was firmly established as a major force in Australian letters.

The recognition in Australian law of Aboriginal rights to land was significantly advanced in the High Court of Australia's 1992 Mabo decision, in which Eddie Koiki Mabo's claim of uninterrupted ownership of his people's traditional land at Mer Island was accepted by the court's full bench, thus finally admitting the falsehood of the assumption that Australia was *terra nullius* in 1788. This event foreshadowed a period of great potential during which government policy and public sentiment were broadly supportive of the recognition of the impacts of colonisation and the need for reconciliation between Aboriginal and mainstream Australia. Aboriginal voices gained widespread public attention as their stories were heard in national inquiries and reports, such as the Royal Commission into Aboriginal Deaths in Custody and the 'Bringing Them Home' report on the separation of Aboriginal children from their families (the stolen generation). While the worst years of the assimilation period were over, the expression of its legacies in the stories of communities, families and individuals was at the forefront of the recovery of Aboriginal cultural memory and the articulation of contemporary Aboriginal life and aspirations. Autobiographical narratives and testimonial fiction became the key storytelling genres of the late 1980s and 1990s, particularly for the growing number of Aboriginal women who found in literary writing a vehicle for both authorial independence and cultural responsibility. The growth in Aboriginal media also saw Aboriginal voices in film, television and music gain increased popularity, their political messages more frequently heard in everyday Australian life. The confidence and reach of recent Aboriginal literature has also been reflected in the work of a vigorous community of Aboriginal scholarly and critical writers, and in the essays, lectures and speeches by political voices who remind us that Aboriginal literature remains grounded in the shared experiences of contemporary Aboriginal men and women.

The anthology ends its survey in the middle of the first decade of a new century, perhaps a fortuitous moment at which to observe a body of literature that is now just over two centuries in the making. As is always the case with compiling anthologies, however, it has not been possible to include everything. The sheer range of available material made our editorial tasks both rewarding and difficult. Our guiding principle has been to seek out work that is not only eminently representative of a significant event, author or genre, but that is also clear and strong writing of the highest quality. We also sought texts in a variety of forms, such as the early letters, petitions and political manifestos, and contemporary works such as the song lyrics of Kev Carmody, Archie Roach and Bob Randall. Due to considerations of space, we have been unable to collect more than just a few excerpts from the rich number of available plays, and scripts for film and television have not been represented at all. At the time of writing, new texts of outstanding quality in poetry and prose have already made their marks but were published too late for us to include. Decisions were also made regarding the eligibility of some texts and authors. For example, we chose not to include translations of sacred Aboriginal 'songs' by anthropologists and poets, which rest more broadly within Australian literature than Aboriginal literature as we have interpreted it. We also decided against the inclusion of some authors who, while having made significant contributions to Australian literature and Aboriginal advancement, were in dialogue with local communities regarding ancestry and identity.

The resurgence of Aboriginal writing in recent years has taken place during a widespread and vigorous renewal in Aboriginal culture. In the visual arts, performance, film, photography and music, Aboriginal practitioners and their critical communities produce highly significant works that speak to audiences around the world. This anthology attempts to make a central contribution to the appreciation and study of a literature that over 200 years has borne witness to lives that were articulate, resolute and sensitive to their cultural and political milieus. Their voices are a challenge and an invitation.

Anita Heiss and Peter Minter

BENNELONG
c. 1764—1813

A senior man of the Wangal people, captured near Sydney in November 1789, Bennelong became one of the first Aboriginal people to be introduced to English culture—learning English, adopting European ways and dress, and helping Governor Arthur Phillip learn the local language and traditions. He gave Phillip an Aboriginal name, which located him in a kinship relationship and thus enabled the communication of customs and relationships to the land. Bennelong travelled to England in 1792, and in 1795 returned home in poor health, unable to rebuild relations with his people and out of favour in the colony.

Letter to Mr Philips, Lord Sydney's Steward

Sidney Cove
New S. Wales Augst 29
1796

Sir

I am very well. I hope you are very well. I live at the Governor's. I have every day dinner there. I have not my wife: another black man took her away: we have had murry doings: he spear'd me in the back, but I better now: his name is now Carroway. all my friends alive & well. Not me go to England no more. I am at home now. I hope Sir you send me anything you please Sir. hope all are well in England. I hope Mrs Phillip very well. You nurse me Madam when I sick. You very good Madam: thank you Madam, & hope you remember me Madam, not forget. I know you very well Madam. Madam I want stockings. thank you Madam; send me two Pair stockings. You very good Madam. Thank you Madam. Sir, you give my duty to Ld Sydney. Thank you very good my Lord. very good: hope very well all family. very well. Sir, send me you please some Handkerchiefs for Pocket. you please Sir send me some shoes: two pair you please Sir.

Bannalong

1796

THOMAS BRUNE
c. 1823—1841

Born probably on Bruny Island, Van Diemen's Land (Tasmania), and educated at the Orphan School near Hobart, Brune was with George A. Robinson (1791–1866) on Flinders Island from 1836. Robinson, who had arrived from England in 1824, was commissioned in the 1930s to repatriate Indigenous Tasmanians to this camp on Bass Strait. Brune taught at the school and was apprenticed to the shoemaker. Among the few who could read and write English with any fluency, he and Walter George Arthur (qv) (who signs himself as Walter Juba Martin at the end of the following extract) produced and wrote the *Flinders Island Chronicle*. In 1839, Brune accompanied Robinson to Port Phillip (Melbourne). He died there after a fall from a tree.

The Aboriginal or Flinders Island Chronicle

UNDER THE SANCTION OF THE COMMANDANT

The object of this journal is to promote christianity civilization and Learning amongst the Aboriginal Inhabitants at Flinders Island. The chronicle professes to be a brief but accuate register of events of the colony Moral and religious. This journal will be published weekly on Saturday the copies to be in Manuscript and written exclusively by the Aboriginals the Size half foolcap and the price two pence.

The Profit arising from the Sale of the journal to be equally divided among the writers which it is hoped may induce Emmulation in writing excite a desire for useful knowledge and promote Learning generally.

Proof Sheets are to be Submitted to the commandant for correction before publishing. Persons out of the colony may Subscribe.

[Signed] Thomas Brune
[Signed] Walter Juba Martin

Prospectus
I Certify that this Copy was written by one of the Aboriginals at Flinders Island whose Signature is herewith attached.

[Signed] G.A. Robinson
Commandant
Aboriginal Settlement
Flinders Island
10th September 1836

1836

The Flinders Island Weekly Chronicle

17TH NOVEMBER 1837

Now my friends you see that the commandant is so kind to you he gives you every thing that you want when you were in the bush the commandant had to leave his friends and go into the bush and he brought you out of the bush because he felt for you and because he knowed the white men was shooting you and now he has brought you to Flinders Island where you get every thing and when you are ill tell the Doctor immediately and you get relief you have now fine houses. I expect that you will not vex one another.

To morrow there will be a Market my friends will you thank the Commandant for all that he done for you in bringing you out of the bush when you knew not God and knew not who made the trees that where before you when you were living in the woods yes my friends you should thank the Commandant yes you should thank the Commandant. There is many of you dying my friends we must all die and we ought to pray to God before we get to heaven yes my friends if we dont we must have eternal punishment.

The brig Tamar arrived this morning at green Island. I cannot tell perhaps we might hear about it by and by when the ship boat comes to the Settlement we will hear news from Hobarton. Let us hope it will be good news and that something may be done for us poor people they are dying away the Bible says some of all shall be saved but I am much afraid none of us will be alive by and by as then as nothing but sickness among us. Why dont the black fellows pray to the king to get us away from this place.

[Signed] Thomas Brune Editor and Writer Commandant office.

1837

Weekly Chronicle

21ST DECEMBER 1837

The people of Van Diemen's land is gone in the bush with Commandant the other side of the Island and Richard had a swan and [Uptra ?] took it away from him and Uptra put it on the fire and roast it and he give Richard only bone of the swan, and why did not you give the Commandant any thing to eat. No because you was so greedy.

Why Commandant give you every thing and why dident you give the Commandant a pice of a kangaroo. No you would not because you was so greedy you was like hogs eating away as fast as you can could you throwed it on the fire as quick as you can in case that the Commandant should want a pice of it he did not want your kangaroos and he did not want your ducks and he did not want your downs and you did not make his breackwind you was to laze and you did not make his bread and he had making it for his own self and his bread also.

You ought my freinds you must behaved yourselves better than you do or else the Commandant be so angry with you and he wont give you any thing no more. And the Commandant his very soon go away from you Natives and he will leave you alway and he will be so glad you must get another Commandant …

And now my freinds do Let us come to the Commandant with kindess and he now give you every thing what you want and obey him and look out what he says to you and not to be going on in the foolish ways that always carrying on …

And now my freinds let us love the Commandant and let him not be growling at us for our greed and let us love him …

[Signed] Thomas Brune
Aboriginal youth
Editor and writter.

1837

MARY ANN ARTHUR
c. 1819–1871

Mary Ann Cochrane was born in Van Diemen's Land (Tasmania), the daughter of Tarenootairer (Sarah Cochrane). One of the Palawa people removed from their homelands to Flinders Island by George A. Robinson, in March 1838 she married Walter George Arthur (qv). The couple accompanied Robinson to Port Phillip in 1839, and returned to Flinders Island in 1842 but soon fell out with the superintendent Henry Jeanneret. Both were literate and as unofficial leaders of their community were involved in writing a petition to the Queen of England. Later they lived at Oyster Cove where, after Walter's death, Mary Ann married Adam Booker.

Letter to Colonial Secretary, Van Diemen's Land

I thank my Father the Govr that he has told us black people that we might write him & tell him if we had any complaint to make about ourselves. I want now to tell the Govr that Dr. Jeanneret wants to make out my husband & myself very bad wicked people & talks plenty about putting us into jail & that he will hang us for helping to write the petition to the Queen from our country people. I send the Gov. two papers one from Dr. Milligan & one from Mr. Robinson of Port Philip to tell the Govr that they know us a long time & had nothing to say bad of us but Dr. Jeanneret does not like us for we do not like to be his slaves nor wish our poor Country to be treated badly or made slaves of. I hope the Govr will not let Dr. Jeanneret put us into Jail as he likes for nothing at all as he used he says he will do it & frightens us much with his big talk about our writing to the Queen he calls us all liars but we told him & the Coxswain who Dr. Jeanneret made ask us that it was all true what we write about him. I remain, Sir, Your humble Aborigine Child, Mary Ann Arthur.

1846

WALTER GEORGE ARTHUR
c. 1820–1861

The son of Rolepa, who was known to Europeans as 'King George', Walter was born in north-eastern Van Diemen's Land (Tasmania). Separated from his people as a child, he became a petty thief in Launceston, and was known as 'Friday'. In 1832, George A. Robinson took him to Flinders Island and then to the Orphan School near Hobart, where he was educated. Returning to Flinders Island in 1835, in January 1836 Friday was renamed in honour of the Governor (Sir) George Arthur. He became a teacher, worked as a carpenter and shoemaker and co-edited with Thomas Brune (qv) the settlement's newspaper, the *Flinders Island Chronicle*. After their marriage in 1838, Arthur and his wife Mary Ann (qv) worked as shepherds. From 1839 to 1842 they were with Robinson at Port Phillip (Melbourne).

Back on Flinders Island, Walter was briefly imprisoned for his outspokenness. In 1847 the few survivors of Robinson's experiment were moved to Oyster Cove, and again the Arthurs demanded improved conditions for their people. It is thought that in May 1861 Walter fell overboard while rowing home to Oyster Cove from Hobart; his body was never found.

Letter to Colonial Secretary, Van Diemen's Land

I send you with this letter a Statement which I have written of my Imprisonment here in Flinders Jail by Doctor Jeanneret for 14 days and nights will you please to give this letter and my statement to my good Father His Excellency the Governor please tell him His Excellency that I hope he will do for me as if I was a Free white man to send to Flinders two Magistrates to take my informations against Doctor Jeanneret and other People for falsely putting me into Jail—for refusing to take my Bail—for wanting to get £50 from me to let me out—for keeping in Jail without a Committal wanting me to sign a Petition to him to Call myself a bad wicked man—and allso for not sending to the Governor our original Letter about our Petition being true, which we gave him open to read first and ask him to send it to the Governor for us We sent the Duplicate of it among our other letters to the Colonial Sec^ty in June last—Neigther myself or my Wife can live here under Doctor Jeanneret he treats us so badly and wants to make such Slaves of us all and is always revenging what took place when he was here before. I pray his Excellency the Governor will take Care of us poor Black people and send us the Magistrates to whom we will tell our Pitiful Story of what we poor Creatures are suffering different from what Col. Arthur and Mr. Robinson told us when we gave them our own Countrys of Van Diemens Land—the People are now all so frightened from Doctor Jeanneret constant growl and threatenings to put them in Jail and telling them he has full power this time to do as he likes with us all and that his Excellency has no power either over him or the black people that they do not know what to do and they are so watched that they are afraid to write to his Excellency any more as their letters wont be sent by Doctor Jeanneret. they Black People had to send their letters to the Governor in another way than by the Mail. Doctor Jeanneret says we will all be hung for high treason for writing against him he is worst on me for he knows I can speak English and that I do not like to see my poor Ignorant Country people badly treated or made Slaves of. I send you Sir a Certificate for his Excellency to read that I got from Mr. Clark our Catechist for he knows my wife and myself from we were young; and he knows how badly we are all treated here and that I did nothing to make Doctor Jeanneret put me into Jail but because I was one of the people who signed the Letter for to be sent to the Governor and because my wife put her name down in it both Doctor Jeanneret and Mrs Jeanneret Called her a Villain and is making out plenty of bad things about my wife and myself which I can very soon prove are not true. All I now request of his Excellency is that he will have full Justice done to me the same as he would have done to a white man and a freeman and according to the agreement between both Col. Arthur the old Governor and us black people when we were free people and when we gave up our Country and came to live at Flinders Island. 6th June Since I wrote this much the Fortitude has arrived I am too much frighted for Doctor Jeanneret to send my statements which I have write out for to tell the Governor of how I have been treated I must keep it until the Governor writes me leave to send it. I must inclose this letter to a friend in Hobart town to put into the Post Office for me for Doctor Jeanneret says he will send no letters for us. I want to tell the Governor that plenty bad salt beef has Issued out for us all for the last month and some of the fresh beef was of the worst kind on Saturday the 1st August we all got for our Ration of meat Stinking Salt Mutton. But these we had to throw out for we must not refuse anything he gives us. I am sure the Governor will be sorry to hear that my poor Country-people cry out plenty that they are very hungry from the bad meat Doctor Jeanneret gives them. I again pray the Governor will do some thing for us and not let us be badly treated in the way we are if Governor would send down some person they would very soon find that all I have wrote is true I know Doctor Jeanneret write plenty about us black people to the Governor but I hope Governor will ask ourselves first for we know that he says plenty of things that is not true of us.

I remain, Sir, Your humble Aborigine Servant, Walter G. Arthur Chief of Ben Lomond Tribes.

Please will the Governor give me and my Wife Mary Ann Arthur leave to go up to Hobarttown with Mr. Clark our Catechist when he gose to Town.

1846

KITTY BRANGY
c. 1859–1918

Born probably in the Upper Murray area of Victoria, Kitty Brangy was the daughter of Brangie, leader of the Oxley Flats people, near Wangaratta. In 1881, Kitty Brangy wrote several letters from Wahgunyah to her sister Edith at Coranderrk, an Aboriginal reserve established in 1816 near Healesville, Victoria. These letters demonstrate the strength of Indigenous family and kinship ties at a time when authorities were systematically trying to break them down.

Letter to Edith Brangy

My dear sister I write these few lines hoping you are quite well as it leaves us All at present. My dear sister I am very sorry that I could not write before. Now my dear sister I must tell you that I am living in Wahgunyah and it is such a poor place you can hardly get anything to eat.

I should like to come down there very much but I can never get the money to go anywhere. My dear sister I wish that you would ask Mr Briggs to lend me one pound and I will soon come and see you All. My dear sister I must tell you that I have got such a nice Little Boy and he is called Willie. My dear sister will you tell Mrs Briggs that her Uncle is dead. Tommy Read is dead. Mary send her love to her aunty and says that she would like to see you very much. My dear sister I think that the drink must of killed him he died in Corowan. My dear sister I am with Tommy McCays[?] tribe and they all send their kind love to you and would All like to see you. My dear sister I have not seen our dear Father since last year. I know not where he has got to. I should like to know very much

My dear sister I hope you will write as soon as you can for I might not be here long and then I should not get it. My dear sister I have no more to say at present but next time I hope that I will have some more to say next time. No more at present from your Loving and true sister

Kitty Brangy	kisses to you my dear sister
XXXXXXXXXXXXXXXXXXXX	
XXXXXXXXXXXXXXXXXXX	
XXXXXXXXXXXXXXXXXXXXX	Address Kitty Brangy
XXX XXXXXXXXXXXXXXX	Wahgunyah
XXXXXXXX	Post Office

1881

WILLIAM BARAK
c. 1824–1903

An artist and elder of the Wurundjeri people, also known as 'the King of the Yarra Tribe', Barak was moved from his country when Melbourne was settled. He was educated at a mission school (1837–39) and was later a member of the Native Police Force. From 1863 he lived at Coranderrk, an Aboriginal reserve, where he undertook religious studies and was baptised and confirmed a Presbyterian.

Barak became a respected spokesman for his people in the late 1870s. Until his death he was the acknowledged leader at Coranderrk, and his petitions, public appearances and contact with leaders such as Alfred Deakin were important spurs to action between colonial authority and Aboriginal people.

Letter to the Editor by the Coranderrk Aborigines

Sir,—We beg of you to put our little column in you valuable paper please. We have seen and heard that the managers of all the stations and the Central Board to have had a meeting about what to be done, so we have heard that there is going to be very strict rules on the station and more rules will be to much for us, it seems we are all going to be treated like slaves, far as we heard of it,—we wish to ask those Managor of the station Did we steal anything out of the colony or murdered anyone or are we prisoners or convict. We should think we are all free any white men of the colony. When we all heard of it, it made us very vex it enough to make us all go mad the way they are going to treat us it seems very hard. We all working in peace and quiteness and happy, pleasing Mr. Goodall, and also showing Mr Goodall that we could work if we had a good manager expecting our wishes to be carried out, what we have ask for, but it seem it was the very opposite way. So we don't know what to do since we heard those strict rules planned out. It has made us downhearted. We must all try again and go to the head of the Colony.—We are all your

Most Obedient Servants, Wm Barak (X), Thos. Avoca, Dick Richard (X), Thos. Mickey (X), Lankey (X), Lankey Manto, Thos Dunolly, Robert Wandon, Alfred Morgan, Wm Parker. Coranderrk, August 29th, 1882.

1882

ANNIE RICH
c. 1859–1937

Born at Murat Station (Ceduna), SA, at ten Annie Rich was sent to Victoria by her white pastoralist father to work as a domestic servant. Made pregnant, probably by her employer Alexander Jeffrey, she took refuge at Lake Condah Mission Station in 1880, but after the birth of her baby the superintendent, Reverend Johann Stähle, refused to allow her to leave. Her plea to the Board for Protection of Aborigines rejected, she ran away but was captured and sent back to Lake Condah. Later she married Alf McDonald, with whom she had seven children.

Letter to Solicitor, for Captain Page, Secretary of the Victorian Board for the Protection of Aborigines

Mission Station
Lake Condah
April 5th 1882.

To
The Solicitor,
Echuca

Sir,

In reply to the letter that I received from Mr Jeffrey last month, requesting me to write to you myself.

I beg you if you can apply to the Board for me to leave the Mission Station, that I do not wish to stay here.

Two years ago I came to the Mission Station, not to settle down, but to visit some of my friends, & to return home again to Echuca after my visit.

But there was an Order in Council telling me to stay on the Mission Station to settle down, But I do not wish to stay here.

Therefore will you please to investigate into the matter to the Board if they can give me permission to leave.

I remain
Sir
Yours most sincerely
Annie Rich

1882

BESSIE CAMERON
c. 1851–1895

The child of a Noongar couple, Bessie Flower spent her childhood at an Anglican boarding school in Annesfield, WA. As a young woman she travelled to Sydney and furthered her education in English literature, history, scripture and music.

In a plan devised by the Reverend Hagenauer to ensure the maintenance of Christianity in Aboriginal belief systems, Flower travelled with a group of Aboriginal women from WA to Ramahyuck Mission, Victoria, in 1867. They were to be married to Christian Kurnai men; however Flower became the teacher at the Ramahyuck Mission school, a servant and tutor to the Hagenauer children.

Flower caught the attention of a white man who asked Hagenauer for her hand in marriage. Hagenauer disapproved, and in 1868 he quickly married Flower to Donald Cameron, a Jupagilwournditch man. The marriage was not entirely successful and, after losing the favour of Hagenauer, the Camerons moved in 1883 to Cameron's traditional lands near Ebenezer in western Victoria for some time, before returning to Gippsland, though not to the Ramahyuck or Lake Tyers missions where Bessie Cameron would have preferred to be. She wrote numerous letters requesting permission to live at Lake Tyers and in 1884 was allowed to return.

Her letters were published in the *Church of England Weekly*, *Gippsland Mercury* and *Argus*.

Letter to the Editor

Having read in the Australasian of the 27th of March an account of 'The Vagabond's' impression of the people of Lake Tyers, I was moved to write a letter in defence.

In the first place, I will not say much on his style of calling us niggers, as he told us in his address that he was an American. Now, all respect to Mr Vagabond, but I know the way the niggers have been treated in America.

Secondly, Mr Vagabond says it was related to him that the Rev. F.A. Hagenauer knocked down a loafing blackfellow three times. Now, I have lived on Ramahyuck many years, and never in my time did it happen, nor before as I was told. Mr Hagenauer is not [of] a fighting nature; he managed us by kindness.

Thirdly, Mr Vagabond said he 'did not find the houses particularly clean and well kept.' He forgot that he went around inspecting at 9 o'clock on Saturday morning, just in the middle of cleaning.

If Mr Vagabond was a Benedict he would know all about the business of house-cleaning on a Saturday; but, then, in his own house there would be a room set apart for visitors, and we have only two rooms, so he must excuse us at not finding that houses clean and tidy at 9 o'clock Saturday morning.

In conclusion, I must say the words, 'Very lazy and useless is my summary of the Lake Tyers blackfellow,' are very sad, as there is some truth in them, yet still there is some work done, or else the station could not go on as it has done. But, as Mr Vagabond asks himself, 'Would I, in this place' and goes onto say, 'As I am a truthful judge of my own character I am compelled to admit I would not,' so we will take courage from that, and go on our way, trying what is in our power to bring up our children to earn their own living, and be useful members of society, and ourselves to be grateful to the board and our missionaries for all their kindness and patience to us aboriginals.

Hoping, Sir, you will excuse my taking up a little of your valuable time, as I am writing this in the name of all my coloured brethren and sisters of Lake Tyers.

1886

MAGGIE MOBOURNE
c. 1872–1917

Maggie Mobourne was a Keerrupjmara woman from the Lake Condah region, Victoria. She married Ernest Mobourne in 1893, and together they vigorously protested against Reverend Johann Stähle's treatment of Aboriginal people at the Lake Condah Mission. She wrote many letters, including one published in the *Hamilton Spectator*, and as a result of their protests Mobourne and her husband were removed from Lake Condah Mission by the Victorian Board for the Protection of Aborigines in 1900.

In 1907, Mobourne eloped with Henry Albert, but she returned to Ernest in 1910. They moved back to Lake Condah Mission but Mobourne was again forced to leave. She spent her remaining years near Lake Tyers. Although she was in poor health the Board for the Protection of Aborigines refused to allow her to return to Lake Condah.

Petition to D.N. McLeod, Vice-Chairman of the Victorian Board for the Protection of Aborigines

Mission Station
Lake Condah
February 27th, 1900
D.N. McLeod, Esqre. M.L.A.
and Vice Chairman

Sir

Having returned in September last to the Mission Station with the object of endeavouring to live in peace and in accordance with the rules of the Station I am sorry to inform you that Mr Stahle seems to take every opportunity to find fault with us, and it seems as if our efforts to live peacefully are of no use here because Mr Stahle seems determined to annoy us and to take every opportunity of reporting us to the Board for insubordination.

On the 18th inst. Mr Stahle spoke in a threatening manner to me and stopped our rations, which he denies and I say that _he is a liar and has always been_. (See full particulars in another letter). _and he doesn't treat us justly._ I would ask you to get up an impartial Board of Inquiry to investigate and see fairness and justice.

I am prepared to substantiate my statements to be true and also can get the majority here as witnesses to prove that we have been living peacefully.

I am
Sir
Yours respectfully
Maggie Mobourne

(We the following corroborate the statements given above)
Signatures

Ernest Mobourne	Isaac McDuff his X mark	
Robert Turner	his X mark	Bella Mobourne
Thomas Willis	his X mark	
James Cortwine	his X mark	
Jenny Green	her X mark	
Albert White		
Fred Carmichael		
Louisa White	her X mark	
Edward P Cortwine		

1900

DAVID UNAIPON
1872–1967

David Unaipon was a gifted Ngarrindjeri man born at the Point McLeay (Raukkan) Mission, SA. He attended the mission school until 1885, then worked as a servant for a family that encouraged his interest in philosophy, science and music, returning to the mission in 1890, where he continued to read widely, practise music and learn practical skills for employment. He married in 1902.

Unaipon was known as 'Australia's Leonardo' because of his intellectual capacity and inventions, which included a modified handpiece for shearing and nine other patents. Becoming a prominent Aboriginal voice in state and Commonwealth politics, he appeared as his people's spokesperson before government commissions and inquiries into the treatment of Aborigines, arguing throughout his life that Aboriginal people should be extended the benefits of education and Christianity.

From the early 1920s, Unaipon studied western mythology and began to compile his own people's myths and legends. He wrote for the Sydney *Daily Telegraph* from 1924 and, with the assistance of the Aborigines' Friends Association, began publishing his collected myths from 1927. His *Native Legends* (1929) is considered to be the first book authored by an Aboriginal person. Without Unaipon's permission, publisher Angus & Robertson onsold the copyright to his stories to William Ramsay Smith, who published *Myths and Legends of the Australian Aborigines* in London without acknowledging their original author.

Unaipon continued to travel widely, speaking and lecturing in schools and churches on traditional Aboriginal legends and contemporary Aboriginal affairs. He received a Coronation medal in 1953. Returning to Point McLeay Mission, he worked on inventions and his lifelong quest for the key to perpetual motion.

Since 1988, the David Unaipon Award, an annual literary competition, has honoured his memory with a prize for an unpublished manuscript by an Aboriginal or Torres Strait Islander author. Unaipon's portrait appeared on the Australian $50 note in 1995. His manuscript of Aboriginal legends was edited and published as *Legendary Tales of the Australian Aborigines* (2001), adopting his original title and finally acknowledging his authorship.

Aborigines, Their Traditions and Customs: Where Did They Come From?

[…] Since coming to Australia thousands of years ago, there has been probably little or no change in the habits and the customs of my people. They have kept the balance of Nature; for centuries they have neither advanced nor retrogressed. Our tribal laws and customs are fixed and unchangeable. Generation after generation has gone through the same rigid tribal training.

Every race has had its great traditional leader and law-giver who has given the race its first moral training, as well as its social and tribal customs. Narroondarie was our great traditional leader. The laws of Narroondarie are taught to the children in their infancy. The hunting-grounds were given out to the different families and tribes by Narroondarie. The boundaries of the tribal hunting-grounds have been kept the same from remotest time. Whilst the children of the tribes are hearing from their elders all the traditions and legends of our race, they are learning all the knowledge and skill of bush craft and hunting, as well as undergoing the three great tests or initiations, to Kornmund (full manhood) and Meemund (full womanhood), which is generally completed at the age of eighteen.

The first test is to overcome the appetite, by doing a two-day walk or hunt without food, and then to be brought suddenly before a fire, on which is cooking some choice kangaroo steak or other native delicacy. The next test is to overcome pain. The young boys and girls submit to having their noses pierced, their bodies marked, and to lying down upon hot embers, thinly covered with boughs. The third test is to overcome fear. The young people are told fearful and hair-raising stories about ghosts and the Muldarpi (Evil Spirit or devil-devil). After all this, they are put to sleep in a lonely place or near the burial-places of the tribe. During the night the elders, made hideous with white clay and bark head-dresses, appear, making weird noises. Those who show no signs of having had a disturbed night are then admitted as fully initiated members of the tribe.

No youth or maiden is allowed to marry until he, or she, has passed through these tests. The marriage is talked over first by all the old members of the tribe, and it is always the uncle of the young man who finally selects the wife. The uncle on the mother's side is the most important relative. The actual marriage ceremony takes place during the time of festivals. The husband does not look or speak at his mother-in-law, although he is husband in name to all his sisters-in-law. Under native conditions, the sex-laws are very strict.

A fully developed Aboriginal has, in his own way, a vast amount of knowledge. Although it may not be strictly scientific learning, still it is a very exact knowledge, and his powers of physical observation are developed to the utmost. For instance, an Aboriginal living under primitive life knows the habits and the anatomy and the haunts of every animal in the bush. He knows all the birds, their habits, and even their love, or mating, notes. He knows the approach of the different seasons of the year from various signs, as well as from the positions of the stars in the heavens. He has developed the art of tracking the human footprint to the highest degree. There is a whole science in footprints. Footprints are the same evidence to a bush native as fingerprints are in a court of law.

He knows the track of every individual member of the tribe. There is as much difference and individuality in footprints as in fingerprints. Of course, it will be readily understood that the Aboriginal language and customs vary a great deal according to the nature of the country the tribes are living in, although there is a great common understanding running through us all. Our legends and traditions are all the same tales, or myths, told slightly differently, with local colouring, etc. […] There is not the slightest hint in any of our traditions that there were any other previous inhabitants in Australia.

The greatest time of the year, to my people, is the Par bar rarrie (springtime). It is then that all the great traditional corroborees take place. All our sacred traditions are then chanted and told.

All the stars and constellations in the heavens, the Milky Way, the Southern Cross, Orion's Belt, the Magellan Cloud, etc., have a meaning. There are legends connected with them all. We call the heavens the Wyerriewarr and the ruler of the heavens Nebalee.

From time immemorial we have understood the subtle art of hypnotic suggestion. Our medicine men (the Mooncumbulli) have used charms, etc. to drive out pain.

It will be seen from the foregoing account, and from other sources, that my race, living under native and tribal conditions, has a very strict and efficacious code of laws that keeps the race pure. It is only when the Aborigines come in contact with white civilisation that they leave their tribal laws, and take nothing in place of these old and well-established customs. It is then that disease and deterioration set in.

1924

Hungarrda

JEW LIZARD

Thus and thus spake Nha Teeyouwa (blackfellow). Nhan-Garra Doctor: Children, I have many strange stories to tell you. All came to me whilst I slumbered in deep sleep.

Enfolding itself from its appointed place my Spirit Self gently stepped outside my body frame with my earthly body subjective consciousness. And this is my experience.

First I stood outside my mortal frame undecided what to do, and my Spirit consciousness revealed to me that I was encased within a bubble substance and as frail. Now if my bubble frame did burst, I'd be still within that Spirit World.

Then a vapour enclosed me round about like a shroud. And I moved away from my body and the earth upon the wings of a gentle breeze, towards the deep blue sky, far beyond the distant clouds. Then my progress ceased, suspended for awhile. With my earthly mind which I still retained, I thought of my body, home and environment, with Spirit vision clear, far excelling the King of Birds.

I looked toward the earth, sought my body frame, and saw its heaving breast still breathing deep in sleep. Then I thought of loved ones, kindred and my tribes. The aged honourable Ah Yamba and my people Harrunda. The landscape west, south and east, a radius of two hundred miles from the Mountain Ah Yamba. In panoramic order lay Ellureecha, Kokacha, Hunmajarra, Deiree and Allu Wharra Tribes. All under the swaying influence and Laws of the Harrunda.

Then by some unseen, compelling force I was carried swiftly onward until the bright sunlight grew dim, as I went through period after period of ten thousand, thousand years of ages past.

In the Early Dawn of Life, I stood upon the bounds and coastline of a slimy sea, and transparent. In wonderment I gazed into its depth, and saw a state of infinitesimal rippling. And yet the surface was undisturbed.

Suddenly out of the silent, slimy sea myriads of living creatures came pushing, jostling and struggling up the rugged incline, eager to reach the sunlight that shone with threadlike ray, twinkling in the distance through the misty age, beckoning them onward to the million years ahead to accomplish that life for which they were designed.

Up and up along the winding pathway of the Gulf of Time, like pilgrims this great mass moves o'er the earth in a living stream, until ten thousand years arrive, when some living species reach their appointed span and silently pass from the rank and file and die by the wayside. Embalmed and preserved by the kindly hand of Time, they were buried in a tomb of strata for a thousand years.

Thus Life with the world moved on, with seasons ever changing all living forms and creatures adapting themselves to conditions and seasons and environment too.

As we approached to the realm of the Day-light, all the great living creatures passed into the Land of the Dead, and a new order of Creatures came to take possession of the Earth.

They were strange living forms, ridiculously shaped, some with human body, legs and arms, with head, eyes and mouth of birds, reptile and fish, some with body of fish and human head.

But what amazed me most, the intelligence they possessed was like the culture of our present day.

I was interested in one particular being. As I approached him I saw that he returned the interest, and came toward me, and when about ten paces away he placed his right hand upon his belly, then closing the fingers, as if extracting something. Quickly extending his arm toward my stomach and opening his hand, a sign of offering of goodwill.

And then we sat upon a ledge of rock. He spake unto me in my tongue, Harruna, explaining the secret code of initiation. The origin and the adoption of Totemism and its laws that marriage custom must obey. And in parting said, Speak unto your neighbouring tribes the things I have told you. It is the word of Hungarrda, the great prophet who came out of the slimy sea, the Land of Mist.

In remembrance of our meeting take this stone; on it is inscribed the song I sang to the Kangaroo, Emu, Goanna, Snakes, and Insect Tribes.

THE SONG OF HUNGARRDA

Bright, consuming Spirit. No power on earth so great as Thee,
First-born child of the Goddess of Birth and Light,
Thy habitation betwixt heaven and earth within a veil of clouds dark as night.

Accompanied by furious wind and lashing rain and hail. Riding majestically upon the storm, flashing at intervals, illumining the abode of man.

Thine anger and thy power thou revealest to us. Sometimes in a streak of light, which leaps upon a great towering rock, which stood impregnable and unchallenged in its birth-place when the earth was formed, and hurls it in fragments down the mountain-side, striking terror into man and beast alike.

Thus in wonder I am lost. No mortal mind can conceive. No mortal tongue express in language intelligible. Heaven-born Spark, I cannot see nor feel thee. Thou art concealed mysteriously wrapped within the fibre and bark of tree and bush and shrubs.

Why dost thou condescend to dwell within a piece of stick?
As I roam from place to place for enjoyment or search of food,
My soul is filled with gratitude and love for thee.
And conscious, too, of thine all pervading spirit presence.

It seems so strange that thou wilt not hear or reveal thyself nor bestow a blessing unless I pray.

But to plead is not enough to bring thee forth and cause thy glowing smiles to flicker over my frame.

But must strive and wrestle with this piece of stick pressing and twirling into another stick with all the power I possess, to release the bonds that bind thee fast.

Then shall thy living spark leap forth in contact with grass and twig.
Thy flame leaps upward like waves that press and roll.
Radiant sister of the Day, I cannot live without thee. For when at twilight and in the depth of midnight; before the morning dawns, the mist hangs over the valley like death's cold shroud, And dewdrops chill the atmosphere. Ingee Too Ma.

Then like thy bright Mother shining from afar,
Thy beaming smiles and glowing energy radiates into this frail body.
Transfusing life, health, comfort, and happiness too.

1929

Narrinyeri Saying

Like children at play we begin Life's journey,
Push our frail bark into the stream of Time,
That flows from snow-capped Mountain.
With no care; Singing and laughing as our boat glides
Upon the tide wending its way through steep rocky banks,
And meadows with bushes and plants all abloom, with sweet fragrant flowers.
Until we arrive in the Great Ocean where we are battled and tossed by the
    angry waves. Onward and onward.
For three score years and ten. Then we are cast forlorn and shipwrecked upon
    the shore of a strange land.

1929

The Voice of the Great Spirit

It is interesting to learn how all races of men have wrestled with the problem of good and evil. The Australian Aborigines have a greater and deeper sense of morality and religion than is generally known. From a very early age the mothers and the old men of the tribe instruct the children by means of tales and stories. This is one of the many stories that is handed down from generation to generation by my people.

In the beginning, the Great Spirit spoke directly everyday to his people. The tribes could not see the Great Spirit but they could hear his voice, and they assembled early every morning to hear him. Gradually, however, the tribes grew weary of listening to the Great Spirit and they said one to the other: 'Oh, I am tired of this listening to a voice I cannot see; so let us go and enjoy ourselves by making our own corroborees.'

The Great Spirit was grieved when he heard this, and as the tribes did not assemble to hear him but went and enjoyed themselves at the corroborees, the Great Spirit said: 'I must give the people a sign that they will understand.'

He sent his servant Narroondarie to call all the tribes together again once more. Narroondarie did so, saying: 'The Great Spirit will not speak again to you but he wishes to give you a sign.'

All the tribes came to the meeting. When every one was seated on the ground, Narroondarie asked them all to be very silent. Suddenly a terrific rending noise was heard. Now, Narroondarie had so placed all the tribes that the meeting was being held around a large gum tree. The tribes looked and saw this huge tree being slowly split open by some invisible force. Also, down out of the sky came an enormous Thalung (tongue), which disappeared into the middle of the gum tree, and the tree closed up again.

After this wonderful performance Narroondarie said to the tribes: 'You may go away now to your hunting and corroborees.'

Away went the tribes to enjoy themselves. After a long time some of them began to grow weary of pleasure and longed to hear again the Great Spirit. They asked Narroondarie if he would call upon the Great Spirit to speak to them again.

Narroondarie answered: 'No, the Great Spirit will never speak to you again.'

The tribes went to the sacred burial grounds to ask the dead to help them but the dead did not answer. Then they asked the great Naboolea [...], who lives in the Milky Way, if he would help them but still there was no answer and the tribes at last cried aloud with sorrow and regret. They cut their bodies with sharp stones and painted themselves white. They began to fear that they would never get in touch again with the Great Spirit.

The tribes finally appealed to Wy young gurrie, the wise old blackfellow who lives in the South Cross. He told them to gather about the big gum tree again. When all were there, Wy young gurrie asked: 'Did you not see the Thalung go into this tree?'

'Yes,' answered the tribes.

'Well,' said Wy young gurrie, 'take that as a sign that the Thalung of the Great Spirit is in all things.'

Thus it is today that the Aborigines know that the Great Spirit is in all things and speaks through every form of Nature. Thalung speaks through the voice of the wind; he rides on the storm; he speaks out from the thunder. Thalung is everywhere, and manifests through the colour of the bush, the birds, the flowers, the fish, the streams; in fact, everything that the Aboriginal sees, hears, tastes, and feels—there is Thalung.

1930/1959

NORMAN HARRIS
c. 1898–1968

Norman Harris was born at Mount Helena, WA, and became a Noongar activist. His family were pioneer farmers in the Morawa region. In 1926, with his uncle, the civil rights leader William Harris, he formed an Aboriginal union, protesting against the treatment of Aboriginal Australians by state authorities. In 1934 he gave evidence before the Moseley Royal Commission. A farmer, gold miner and, later, a property owner in Perth, Harris married Eva Mary Phillips. Their children continued the family tradition of community leadership.

Letter to Jim Bassett

We have been looking out for you some time now but I don't think you are much of a swimmer and I know that you haven't got a boat and now that the lakes are running you can't come per road or water and perhaps not by train, so I don't expect to see you this winter.

Now, Jim, we are trying to get some of the natives and half-castes together has a deporation to the Premier has you know what for.

So we can get a vote in the county also one law for us all that is the same law that governs the whites also justice and far play.

I suppose you know that Perth is a prohibiterd around Perth for natives and half cast it is in Saturdays pappie of March 19th, 1927, and last year Tindale Cpt. said that the Government ought to put all the natives out of Australia onto a island out from Kimberly thats rotten what do you say Jim.

Last year in Parliament House they disgust where they should give halfcasts a vote or not anyhow their was hell to pop over that so they would not let them have it.

They are afraid of the native wanting the same has the halfcast why shouldn't he if he is respectable or any person.

Now you see yourself where is the Abo. got a fare go.

He is not alowed in a Pub, not to have a gun, not to camp on revers because squatters stock are there, he is not to have dogs near stock. He is not to grow grapes because he may make wine and get drunk. They bar him in football and cricket must not be in town to long after dark. All Police are in the bush a sort of proctor I have never heard of them protecting the native yet.

In the North has you know they were never given wages just work for kick in the sturn and a little tucker such has it is, and still the same.

A native can't leave this state without getting the permission from the Proctor (Mr. A.O. Neville) a rotten B. The white Police can do just has they like. The native is a prisiner wherever he is. He can be brought from any part of the State put in a Compond such has Mogumber, a rotten prison for alsorts just fancy young girls and boys brought up among them sort and for a certain they dont learn them much *and no moral trainning atal*. Thoes children are there being brought up among all the black cut throats the Police can lay their hands on from all parts of the country. They say they are trying to send them out in the world to do good for themsselves. How cant they when this Aboriginal Act is over them if a girl or boy goes out to work they get the money, if the girls have the misfortune to have a kidie she is got by the Police and sent strait back to Mogumber in most case death release them. So Jim you see they are blocked whatever way they go.

Now it is comonly known that while girls were in Carolup they were tired up floged some time four and five at a time. All thoes that were in Carolup Mission were brought to Mogumber. They never got payed for the work they done their. Now this is the question who got that land and place if it were sold what hapend the money I dont know does anyone know I never heard of any natives getting a holiday out of the money.

Now Mogumber, a native name Bob Lookenglass tryed to run away from that prison, he was caught near Moora belted by the Black Police of Mongumba. Then he got or was brought back to Mongumber he was tired to a tree and was belted by the white officer in charge put into the boob that they have ther I think of cause we cant say for a certain he was brought out of the boob *dead* or nearly.

Yet their are hundreds of halfcast send their children there for schooling and trainning think they are doing good if they only stop and think they can see enough. Then again if they dont send them the Police come along and sends them along to Mongumba or the Prison I should say The Police can take the children without a warrant or ask their perants permission. They are quite within the Act to take any Aborinal or Halfcast.

Someone goes up North getting all the half cast girls and boys off all the stations nitives to if they want them. They have got a motor truck with seats along the sides and big rings bolted to the centure chains from rings to natives.

The South Australian League for Natives are trying for a native State up in the Northern Territory that will be no good because they will have to keep them their that is the same has Mongumba only on a biger scale.

Mr. Neville gave a lecture in Perth and he said that it was no good giveing natives land because they would not work it they only use it for camping ground and he went on to say that he could not name a single native where he has got land and done good. So you see they will not let the native have land next. Not letting have land is quite easey when they make Perth Prohibited against natives and halfcast.

I have got a headache thinking about this Act. Uncle Bill has just gone from here in to Morawa I am at Dads place now but will be going back to my place next week. Uncle Bill is going down to Perth at about the end of the month he is going to Yalgoo now. Uncle Bills is going to have a go at the Aborigal Department. I think he will smash it up also all these Componds of cause he wants help from all the natives and h.c. He is not setting their for his own good because we all can do alright there are some halfcast yourself and us we get not a bad deal but it not the think we dont want to be under that Act atal, the one law is quite enough so if all the natives and halfcast pay a little in to him for a lawyer if we can get every one it will only run into a few shillings, anyhow thoes who dont pay what do you think ought to be done to them. So think this is enough about this question.

How are you getting on with your cropping, we haven't started putting any in yet. I was doing some rolling before that rain it settled the burn, although I set it alight last Sunday I may be able to plough it in. We are all doing alright has regards health my little fellow has got two teeth also walking about now so I think I have told you all the news this time hoping I will see you before I die and that you will get a good crop.

Questions within the meaning on the Act[1]

Why should the abo. Act be over us, it is only a By Law?
Isnt the one law good enough it is hard enough to live under?
Why shouldn't a native have land?
The country belongs to him?
Why segregation in his own land?
Why can't he be alowd in a public Hotel?
Why is he a prisnor in any part of the State?
He can be arrested without a warrant.
Why shouldn't he have a voise in the making of the Laws?
How do they suppose keeping natives in a big reserve?
Why shouldn't a native mother demand Freedom for her child?
Why should the Aboriginal Department put quadroons in Morgumba?
How many schollars have they turned out of Morgumba?
Why is it that the fairest are to the blackest?
Why is it that all letters are opened before going and out to?
Is it so that all girls and boy are found a job by the Dept?
Is it so that all from their have to send their money back?
Is it so that girls are lock up in Dormotorys?
Does children have to work?
There are about 300 people in Morgumba what do they do?
Do they get any money for their work?
What dose their food consist of, I bleave Billy Goats?
Do they encourage young people to come their?
Do they stop card playing or gambling their?
Why does anyone who leaves their have to report his movements?
Why is the Act still over anyone who comes from Morgumba?
Why was thoes people shifted from Carrollup to Morgumba?
Who has got Carrollup now how much was it sold for?
Who has got the money for it?
I bleave that girls were tied with chains to get punished.

---

1 Attwood and Markus (1999) note that these questions were undated and bundled together with this and other letters between the correspondents.

I bleave that girls were made bend forward while the kick them from behind Jist
    fancy that.

Why was the name change to Aboriginal Department from a Chief Proctor of
    Aborigines?

Where does the money go to that is set aside for the Aborigines?

In the early day a white person who married a native woman was aword a bit
    of land and never lost cast.

Now a white man who is caught near a camp is heavily find or imprisoned.

I could write a lot more but I have got to go on to home this afternoon so will
    ring off.

Burn this when you are finished with it or send it back to me.

1927

WILLIAM COOPER
c. 1861 – 1941

Born in Yorta Yorta country in Victoria, William Cooper spent his early life working in
the pastoral industry. He was married four times and had several children, including a
daughter who was matron of the first Aboriginal Hostel in Melbourne, a son who fought
and died in the First World War, and another who was a gifted sprinter. As a member
of the Australian Workers' Union in the late 1920s, Cooper became a spokesperson
for the Aboriginal peoples of central Victoria and western NSW. In 1933, he moved
to Melbourne where he became secretary of the Australian Aborigines League and a
leader in the 1930s campaigns against state Protection Acts and for constitutional change.
He began a petition for change, and in 1935 led a delegation to the Minister of the
Interior, the first Aboriginal meeting with a Commonwealth Minister. With members
of the Aborigines Progressive Association, Cooper led the first Aboriginal delegation
to a Prime Minister in 1938. Their claims rejected, and having collected over 1814
signatures from Aboriginal Australians, Cooper addressed his petition to King George VI.
The Commonwealth refused to forward his petition or to change the status quo. Cooper
was a leader of the Aboriginal Day of Mourning Conference and Protest in Sydney
on 26 January 1938. In 1940 he established National Aborigines Day, a forerunner to
NAIDOC week celebrations.

Petition to the King[1]

Whereas it was not only a moral duty, but also a strict injunction included in
the commission issued to those who came to people Australia that the original
occupants and we, their heirs and successors, should be adequately cared for;
and whereas the terms of the commission have not been adhered to, in that
(a) our lands have been expropriated by your Majesty's Government in the
Commonwealth, (b) legal status is denied to us by your Majesty's Government
in the Commonwealth; and whereas all petitions made in our behalf to your

---

1   This petition was produced by Cooper and the Australian Aborigines League and published during the
    reign of King George V. In 1937 a version was presented to the Commonwealth during the early reign of
    King George VI.

Majesty's Government in the Commonwealth have failed: your petitioners therefore humbly pray that your Majesty will intervene in our behalf and through the instrument of your Majesty's Government in the Commonwealth grant to our people representation in the Federal Parliament, either in the person of one of our own blood or by a white man known to have studied our needs and to be in sympathy with our race.

1933

ANNA MORGAN
1874–1935

Anna Morgan spent her early childhood in north-west Victoria and worked in domestic service from the age of eleven. In her twenties she moved near Cummeragunja Aboriginal Reserve, NSW, where she met and married Caleb Morgan in 1899. They had three children. Early in her marriage Morgan needed assistance but was rejected by the Board for the Protection of Aborigines. Later her application for a Commonwealth pension was also rejected. Morgan was a member of the Australian Aborigines League, and promoted Aboriginal women's education when part of the 1935 delegation to the Minister of the Interior.

Under the Black Flag

What flag flies over the Australian Aborigines? Some say it is the British flag. We say that we live under the Black Flag of the Aborigines 'Protection' Board. We have not the same liberty as the white man, nor do we expect the same justice. For twelve years we lived on a mission station in New South Wales. My husband was given a 30-acre block of land; he cleared and fenced it, and then waited for implements to break it up. There were only two teams of horses to do all the work for ten such farms, and no assistance from outside was allowed. When at last we did get in a crop the Board took away the land from us. We wanted to remain on the land and make our living however we could. But, no; the Board would not have that; we must live on the mission station.

After the men had cleared and fenced about 90[0] acres of virgin soil the manager wrote to the Board, saying that the men were too lazy to work the land. Those who protested against this injustice were classed as agitators, an expulsion order was made out against them, and it was served by the local police. My husband was among the victims. Soon after, he went away, but because we had no way of removing our belongings, we left some at his father's place.

A few months later we came, prepared to take our belongings away. We stayed one night at his father's place, and the next day my husband got a summons for trespassing. He was taken and gaoled for fourteen days. Did he break any of the British laws? No. He broke the laws of the Black Flag. When a white man is charged with a crime, he is taken to court and judged. If innocent, he is allowed to go home to his family, and there the matter ends. A black man is expelled from the mission—the land reserved for him and his people—and can never go back to his own people again. Perhaps the family, unwilling to be separated from him, shares his exile until it pleases the mighty

'Protectors' of the aborigines, or their managers, to give them a gracious pardon, and allow them to return home again. My husband and I have been expelled for all time.

Here we are! Taken from the bush, placed in compounds, told, 'This is your home and your children's as long as there is an aboriginal left'; put under managers, scarcely allowed to think for ourselves. We were suppressed. We were half-educated. We lived on what white people call 'sustenance'. We bought our own clothes. We cleared Crown lands. At the age of fourteen our girls were sent to work—poor, illiterate, trustful little girls to be gulled by the promises of unscrupulous white men. We all know the consequences. But, of course, one of the functions of the Aborigines' Protection Board is to build a white Australia. Those who pride themselves on 'British fair play' should think of us who live under the Black Flag. We want a home. We want education. You have taken our beautiful country from us—'a free gift'.

Even a worm will turn, and we, the down-trodden of the earth, at last raise a feeble protest, and dare to ask for better conditions and the abolition of the rule of the 'Black Flag'. Will you help us?

1934

WILLIAM FERGUSON and JOHN PATTEN
1882–1950   1905–1957

Trade unionist and Aboriginal activist William Ferguson was born in Darlington Point in the Riverina, NSW, and worked as a shearer from 1896, becoming shed organiser for the Australian Workers' Union. In 1916 he settled with his family in Gulargambone, where he reformed the local branch of the Australian Labor Party and was its secretary for two years. He moved to Dubbo in 1933, where he launched the Aborigines Progressive Association (APA) on 27 June 1938.

John Thomas Patten was born in Moama, NSW. Educated in both mission and public schools, he worked as a labourer and boxer. Patten became politically active from the early 1930s when he settled near Sydney and started organising political groups and protests, including his frequent Sunday lectures on Aboriginal rights at the Sydney Domain.

Patten joined the APA in October 1938 and with Ferguson began coordinating Aboriginal political protest. They first contributed to the NSW Legislative Assembly's inquiry into the Aborigines Protection Board, Patten visiting Aboriginal reserves to collect affidavits as evidence and Ferguson representing the APA at the inquiry. The failure of reform prompted them to co-write the pamphlet 'Aborigines Claim Citizen Rights!' and, with William Cooper (qv), organise the 1938 Day of Mourning. They later presented Prime Minister Joseph Lyons with a ten-point plan for national Aboriginal policy and Aboriginal equality. Ferguson and Patten's political relationship ended when Ferguson objected to an APA constitution published in the first issue of the newspaper *Australian Abo Call*, believing Patten was influenced by the non-Indigenous publisher, W.J. Miles.

Patten left the APA after Ferguson led a vote of no confidence, but continued to tour NSW reserves encouraging Aboriginal resistance to the Protection Board. Patten healed the rift with Ferguson by calling for Aboriginal unity at the APA annual conference in 1940. He served in the Australian army during the Second World War and was discharged injured in 1942, settling in Melbourne where he did clerical work and volunteered with the Australian Aborigines League.

During the 1940s, Ferguson's political interventions escalated but were consistently unsuccessful. In 1943 he was voted one of two Aboriginal members of the first NSW Aborigines Welfare Board, but was forced to resign in 1946 before being as quickly reinstated. In 1949, as vice-president of the NSW branch of the Australian Aborigines League, he drafted a number of reforms that were presented to the Commonwealth Minister for the Interior. Ignored, Ferguson resigned from the Labor Party and unsuccessfully contested the December federal election as an independent in Dubbo. He collapsed and died after delivering his final speech.

Aborigines Claim Citizen Rights!

ONE HUNDRED AND FIFTY YEARS

The 26th of January, 1938, is not a day of rejoicing for Australia's Aborigines; it is a day of mourning. This festival of 150 years' so-called 'progress' in Australia commemorates also 150 years of misery and degradation imposed upon the original native inhabitants by the white invaders of this country. We, representing the Aborigines, now ask you, the reader of this appeal, to pause in the midst of your sesqui-centenary rejoicings and ask yourself honestly whether your 'conscience' is clear in regard to the treatment of the Australian blacks by the Australian whites during the period of 150 years' history which you celebrate?

THE OLD AUSTRALIANS

You are the New Australians, but we are the Old Australians. We have in our arteries the blood of the Original Australians, who have lived in this land for many thousands of years. You came here only recently, and you took our land away from us by force. You have almost exterminated our people, but there are enough of us remaining to expose the humbug of your claim, as white Australians, to be a civilised, progressive, kindly and humane nation. By your cruelty and callousness towards the Aborigines you stand condemned in the eyes of the civilised world.

PLAIN SPEAKING

These are hard words, but we ask you to face the truth of our accusation. If you would openly admit that the purpose of your Aborigines Legislation has been, and now is, to exterminate the Aborigines completely so that not a trace of them or of their descendants remains, we could describe you as brutal, but honest. But you dare not admit openly that your hope and wish is for our death! You hypocritically claim that you are trying to 'protect' us; but your modern policy of 'protection' (so-called) is killing us off just as surely as the pioneer policy of giving us poisoned damper and shooting us down like dingoes!

We ask you now, reader, to put your mind, as a citizen of the Australian Commonwealth, to the facts presented in these pages. We ask you to study the problem, in the way that we present the case, from the Aborigines' point of view. We do not ask for your charity; we do not ask you to study us as scientific freaks. Above all, we do not ask for your 'protection'. No, thanks! We have had 150 years of that! We ask only for justice, decency and fair play. Is this too much to ask? Surely your minds and hearts are not so callous that you will refuse to reconsider your policy of degrading and humiliating and exterminating Old Australia's Aborigines? [...]

ABORIGINES PROTECTION ACTS

All Aborigines, whether nomadic or civilised, and also all half-castes, are liable to be 'protected' by the Aborigines Protection Boards, and their legal status is defined by Aborigines Protection Acts of the various States and of the Commonwealth. Thus we are for the greater part deprived of ordinary civil legal rights and citizenship, and we are made a pariah caste within this so-called democratic community.

The value of the Aborigines Protection Acts in 'protecting' Aborigines may be judged from the fact that at the 1933 census there were no Aborigines left to protect in Tasmania; while in Victoria there were only 92 full-bloods, in South Australia 569 full-bloods, in New South Wales 1,034 full-bloods.

The Aborigines of full-blood are most numerous, and most healthy, in the northern parts of Australia, where white 'protection' exists in theory, but in practice the people have to look after themselves! But already the hand of official 'protection' is reaching out to destroy these people in the north, as it has already destroyed those in the southern states. We beg of you to alter this cruel system before it gets our 36,000 nomadic brothers and sisters of North Australia into its charitable clutches!

WHAT 'PROTECTION' MEANS

The 'protection' of Aborigines is a matter for each of the individual States; while those in the Northern Territory come under Commonwealth ordinances.

This means that in each State there is a different 'system', but the principle behind the Protection Acts is the same in all States. Under these Acts the Aborigines are regarded as outcasts and as inferior beings who need to be supervised in their private lives by Government officials.

No one could deny that there is scope for the white people of Australia to extend sympathetic, or real, protection and education to the uncivilised blacks, who are willing and eager to learn when given a chance. But what can be said for a system which regards these people as incurably 'backward' and does everything in its power to keep them backward?

Such is the effect of the Aborigines Protection Acts in every State and in the Northern Territory.

No real effort is being made to bring these 'backward' people forward into the national life. They are kept apart from the community, and are being pushed further and further 'backward'.

'PROTECTION' IN NEW SOUTH WALES

We take as an example the Aborigines Protection Act (1909–1936) of New South Wales, the Mother State of Australia, which is now so proudly celebrating its 150th Anniversary.

This Act sets up a Board, known as the 'Board for Protection of Aborigines', of which the Commissioner of Police is *ex officio* Chairman. Other members— not exceeding 10 in number—are appointed by the Governor. The Board has power to distribute moneys voted by Parliament for the relief of Aborigines, and has power 'to exercise a general supervision and care over all Aborigines and over all matters affecting the interests and welfare of Aborigines, and to protect them against injustice, imposition and fraud'.

The arbitrary treatment which we receive from the A.P. Board reduces our standards of living below life-preservation point, which suggests that the intention is to exterminate us. In such circumstances it is impossible to maintain normal health. So the members of our community grow weak and apathetic, lose desire for education, become ill and die while still young.

ABORIGINAL WITHIN THE MEANING OF THE ACT

An 'Aborigine' is defined in the New South Wales Act as 'any full-blooded or half-caste Aboriginal who is a native of Australia, and who is temporarily or permanently resident in New South Wales'.

It will be noted that the Board's 'protection' extends to half-castes as well as to full-bloods.

Under certain provisions of the Act, the Board has power to control 'any person apparently having an admixture of Aboriginal blood', and may order any such person 'apparently' of Aboriginal blood (under a Magistrate's order) to live on an Aboriginal Reserve, and to be under the control of the Board.

By an amendment of the Act (1936) an averment that a person is an 'Aborigine' is regarded as 'sufficient evidence of the truth of such averment … unless the contrary is shown to the satisfaction of the Court'. The onus of disproof is thus on the accused, contrary to the traditional practice of 'British' law.

HALF-CASTES, QUADROONS AND OCTOROONS

The Aboriginal Protection Board, which has 'protected' the full-bloods of New South Wales so well that there are now less than a thousand of them remaining, has thus recently acquired the power to extend a similar 'protection' to half-castes, quarter-castes, and even to persons with any 'admixture' of Aboriginal blood whatever.

Its powers are so drastic that merely on suspicion or averment it can continue its persecuting protection unto the third, fourth and fifth generation of those so innocently unfortunate as to be descended from the original owners of this land.

POWERS OF THE BOARD

The Protection Act gives the Board an almost unlimited power to control the private lives of Aborigines as defined by that Act.

For example, the Board may order any Aboriginal into any Reserve or out of any Reserve at its own discretion.

The Board may prevent any Aboriginal from leaving New South Wales.

The Board may prevent any non-Aboriginal person from 'lodging or wandering in company' with Aborigines (thus keeping the Aborigines away from white companionship)!

The Board may prosecute any person who supplies intoxicating liquor to any 'Aborigine, or person having *apparently* an admixture of Aboriginal blood'.

The Board may cause the child of any Aborigine to be apprenticed to any master, and any child who refuses to be so apprenticed may be removed to a home or institution.

The Board may assume full control and custody of the child of any Aborigine.

The Board may remove any Aborigine from his employment.

The Board may collect the wages of any Aborigine, and may hold them in trust for the Aborigine.

The Board may order any Aborigines to move from their camp to another camp-site, and may order them away from towns or townships.

The Board may authorise the medical inspection of any Aborigine and may order his removal to any institution for treatment.

The Board may issue blankets, clothing and rations to Aborigines but blankets and other articles so issued are 'considered to be on loan only'.

The Board may make regulations to 'apportion amongst *or for the benefit of Aborigines*' the earnings of any Aboriginal living upon a Reserve.

DEPRIVED OF CITIZEN RIGHTS

The effect of the foregoing powers of the Aborigines Protection Board in New South Wales is to deprive the Aborigines and half-castes (and other 'admixtures') of ordinary citizen rights.

By a curious twist of logic, the Aborigines of New South Wales have the right to vote—for the State Parliament! They are considered worthy of the franchise, but not worthy of other citizen rights. They are officially treated either as a menace to the community (similar to criminals) or as incapable of looking after themselves (similar to lunatics)—but yet they are given a vote! [...]

ABOLITION OF THE A.P. BOARD

We, representing the Aborigines and half-castes of New South Wales, call for the abolition of the A.P. Board in New South Wales, and repeal of all existing legislation dealing with Aborigines.

We ask to be accorded full citizen rights, and to be accepted into the Australian community on a basis of equal opportunity.

Should our charges of maladministration and injustice be doubted, we ask for a Royal Commission and Public Inquiry into the conditions of Aborigines, to be held in public.

We can show that the Report of the Aborigines Protection Board omits to state relevant facts, bearing on the 'care and protection' which the Board is supposed to give our people.

The Aborigines themselves do not need or want this 'protection'.

NO 'SENTIMENTAL SYMPATHY', PLEASE!

We do not wish to be regarded with sentimental sympathy, or to be 'preserved', like the koala bears, as exhibits; but we do ask for your *real* sympathy and understanding of our plight.

We do not wish to be 'studied' as scientific or anthropological curiosities. All such efforts on our behalf are wasted. We have no desire to go back to primitive conditions of the Stone Age. We ask you to teach our people to live in the Modern Age, as modern citizens. Our people are very good and quick learners. Why do you deliberately keep us backward? Is it merely to give yourselves the pleasure of feeling superior? Give our children the same chances as your own, and they will do as well as your children!

We ask for equal education, equal opportunity, equal wages, equal rights to possess property, or to be our own masters—in two words: *equal citizenship!* How can you honestly refuse this? In New South Wales you give us the vote, and treat us as equals at the ballot box. Then why do you impose the other unfair restriction of rights upon us? Do you really think that the 9,884 half-castes of New South Wales are in need of your special 'protection'? Do you really believe that these half-castes are 'naturally backward' and lacking in natural intelligence? If so, you are completely mistaken. When our people are backward, it is because your treatment has made them so. Give us the same chances as yourselves, and we will prove ourselves to be just as good, if not better, Australians, than you!

Keep your charity! We only want justice.

A NATIONAL QUESTION

If ever there was a national question, it is this. Conditions are even worse in Queensland, Northern Territory and Western Australia than they are in New South Wales; but we ask New South Wales, the Mother State, to give a lead in emancipating the Aborigines. Do not be guided any longer by religious and scientific persons, no matter how well-meaning or philanthropic they may seem. Fellow-Australians, we appeal to you to be guided by your own common sense and ideas of fair play and justice! Let the Aborigines themselves tell you what they want. Give them a chance, on the same level as yourselves, in the community. You had no race prejudice against us when you accepted half-castes and full-bloods for enlistment in the A.I.F. We were good enough to fight as Anzacs. We earned equality then. Why do you deny it to us now?

EXPLOITATION OF LABOUR

For 150 years the Aborigines and half-castes throughout Australia have been used as cheap labour, both domestic and out-of-doors. We are to-day beyond the scope of Arbitration Court awards, owing to the A.P. Board system of 'apprenticeship' and special labour conditions for Aborigines. Why do the Labour Unions stand for this? We have no desire to provide coolie labour competition, but your Protection Acts force this status upon us. The Labour Parties and Trade Unions have given us no real help or support in our attempts to raise ourselves to citizen level. Why are they so indifferent to the dangers of this cheap, sweated labour? Why do they not raise their voices on our behalf? Their 'White Australia' policy has helped to create a senseless prejudice against us, making us social outcasts in the land of our ancestors!

COMIC CARTOONS AND MISREPRESENTATION

The popular Press of Australia makes a joke of us by presenting silly and out-of-date drawings and jokes of 'Jacky' or 'Binghi', which have educated city-dwellers and young Australians to look upon us as sub-human. Is this not adding insult to injury? What a dirty trick, to push us down by laws, and then make fun of us! You kick us, and then you laugh at our misfortunes. You keep us ignorant, and then accuse us of having no knowledge. Wake up, Australians, and realise that your cruel jokes have gone over the limit!

WINDOW-DRESSING

We appeal to young Australians, or to city-dwelling Australians, whose knowledge of us is gained from the comic Press or from the 'window-dressing' Aboriginal Settlement at La Perouse, to study the matter more deeply, and to realise that the typical Aboriginal or half-caste, born and bred in the bush, is just as good a citizen, and just as good an Australian, as anybody else. Aborigines are interested not only in boomerangs and gum leaves and corroborees! The overwhelming majority of us are able and willing to earn our living by honest toil, and to take our place in the community, side by side with yourselves.

RACIAL PREJUDICE

Though many people have racial prejudice, or colour prejudice, we remind you that the existence of 20,000 and more half-castes in Australia is a proof that the mixture of Aboriginal and white races are practicable. Professor Archie Watson, of Adelaide University, has explained to you that Aborigines can be absorbed into the white race within three generations, without any fear of a 'throw-back'. This proves that the Australian Aboriginal is somewhat similar in blood to yourselves, as regards inter-marriage and inter-breeding. We ask you to study this question, and to change your whole attitude towards us, to a more enlightened one. Your present official attitude is one of prejudice and misunderstanding. We ask you to be proud of the Australian Aboriginal, and to take his hand in friendship. The New Zealanders are proud of the Maoris. We ask you to be proud of the Australian

Aborigines, and not to be misled any longer by the superstition that we are a naturally backward and low race. This is a scientific lie, which has helped to push our people down and down in to the mire.

At worst, we are no more dirty, lazy, stupid, criminal, or immoral than yourselves. Also, your slanders against our race are a moral lie, told to throw all the blame for your troubles on to us. You, who originally conquered us by guns against our spears, now rely on superiority of numbers to support your false claims of moral and intellectual superiority.

A NEW DEAL FOR ABORIGINES!

After 150 years, we ask you to review the situation and give us a fair deal—a New Deal for Aborigines. The cards have been stacked against us, and we now ask you to play the game like decent Australians. Remember, we do not ask for charity, we ask for justice.

J. T. PATTEN,
> President,
> La Perouse.

W. FERGUSON,
> Organising Secretary,
> Dubbo.

1938

PEARL GIBBS
1901–1983

Pearl Gibbs (Gambanyi) was born near Sydney and grew up near Yass, NSW. She became politically active, supporting Aboriginal workers affected by the Depression and gathering information against the NSW Aborigines Protection Board. Gibbs joined the Aborigines Progressive Association (APA) and assisted in organising the 1938 Day of Mourning, becoming APA secretary until 1940. With William Ferguson (qv) she established the Dubbo branch of the Australian Aborigines League. During the 1950s, she co-founded the Australian Aboriginal Fellowship with Faith Bandler and was the only Aboriginal member of the NSW Aborigines Welfare Board. In later life Gibbs enjoyed great prominence as an Aboriginal spokesperson.

Radio Broadcast

Good evening listeners,

I wish to express my deepest gratitude to the Theosophical Society of Sydney in granting me this privilege of being on the air this evening. It is the first time in the history of Australia that an Aboriginal woman has broadcast an appeal for her people. I am more than happy to be that woman. My grandmother was a full-blood Aborigine. Of that fact I am most proud. The admixture of white blood makes me a quarter-caste Aborigine. I am a member of the Committee for Aboriginal Citizenship.

My people have had 153 years of the white man's and white woman's cruelty and injustice and unchristian treatment imposed upon us. My race is fast vanishing. There are only 800 full-bloods now in New South Wales due to the maladministration of previous governments. However, intelligent and educated Aborigines, with the aid of good white friends, are protesting against these conditions. I myself have been reared independently of the Aborigines Protection Board now known as the Aborigines Welfare Board.[1] I have lived and worked amongst white people all my life. I've been in close contact with Aborigines and I have been on Aboriginal stations in New South Wales for a few weeks and months at a time. I often visit them. Therefore I claim to have a thorough knowledge of both the Aboriginal and white viewpoints. I know the difference between the status of Aborigines and white men. When I say 'white man' I mean white women also. There are different statuses for different castes. A person in whom the Aborigine blood predominates is not entitled to an old-age, invalid or returned soldier's pension. There are about thirty full-blooded returned men in this state whom I believe are not entitled to the old-age pension. A woman in whom the Aborigine blood predominates is not entitled to a baby bonus.

Our girls and boys are exploited ruthlessly. They are apprenticed out by the Aborigines Welfare Board at the shocking wage of a shilling to three and six per week pocket money and from two and six to six shillings per week is paid into a trust fund at the end of four years. This is done from fourteen years to the age of eighteen. At the end of four years a girl would, with pocket money and money from the trust, have earned £60 and a boy £90. Many girls have great difficulty in getting their trust money. Others say they have never been paid. Girls often arrive home with white babies. I do not know of one case where the Aborigines Welfare Board has taken steps to compel the white father to support his child. The child has to grow up as an unwanted member of an apparently unwanted race. Aboriginal girls are no less human than my white sisters. The pitiful small wage encourages immorality. Women living on the stations do not handle endowment money, but the managers write out orders. The orders are made payable to one store in the nearest town—in most cases a mixed drapery and grocery store. So you will see that in most cases the mother cannot buy extra meat, fruit or vegetables. When rations and blankets are issued to the children, the value is taken from the endowment money. The men work sixteen hours per week for rations worth five and six-pence. The bad housing, poor water supply, appalling sanitary conditions and the lack of right food, together with unsympathetic managers, make life not worth living for my unfortunate people.

It has now become impossible for many reasons for a full-blood to own land in his own country. On the government settlements and in camps around the country towns, the town people often object to our children attending the school that white children attend. This is the unkindest and cruelest action I know. Many of the white people call us vile names and say that our children

---

1   The *New South Wales Aborigines Protection Act* (1909) was amended in 1940, and the Board for the Protection of Aborigines was replaced by the Aborigines Welfare Board.

are not fit to associate with white children. If this is so, then the white people must also take their share of the blame. I'm very concerned about the 194 full-blooded Aboriginal children left in this State. What is going to happen to them? Are you going to give them a chance to be properly educated and grow up as good Australian citizens or just outcasts? Aborigines are roped off in some of the picture halls, churches and other places. Various papers make crude jokes about us. We are slighted in all sorts of mean and petty ways. When I say that we are Australia's untouchables you must agree with me.

You will also agree with me that Australia would not and could not have been opened up successfully without my people's help and guidance of the white explorers. Hundreds of white men, women and children owe their very lives to Aborigine trackers and runners—tracking lost people. Quite a few airmen owe their lives to Aboriginals. I want you to remember that men of my race served in the Boer War, more so in the 1914–18 War and today hundreds of full-bloods, near full-bloods and half-castes are overseas with the AIF. More are joining each day. My own son is somewhere on the high seas serving with the Australian Navy. Many women of Aborigine blood are helping with war charities. Many are WRANS. We the Aborigines are proving to the world that we are not only helping to protect Australia but also the British Empire. New South Wales is the mother State and therefore should act as an inspiration to the rest of Australia. So we are asking for full citizenship and the status to be granted to us. We are asking that the 800 full-bloods in New South Wales be included in the claim—all those who are deprived of all federal social services to be granted, through the state, the old age pension and the maternity bonus until this injustice can be reformed by a federal law. We want an equal number of Aborigines as whites on the Welfare Board.

My friends, I'm asking for friendship. We Aborigines need help and encouragement, the same as you white people. We need to be cheered and encouraged to the ideals of citizenship. We ask help, education, encouragement from your white government. But the Aborigines Welfare gives us the stone of officialdom. Please remember, we don't want your pity, but practical help. This you can do by writing to the Hon. Chief Secretary, Mr. Baddeley, MLA Parliament House, Sydney and ask that our claims be granted as soon as possible. Also that more white men who understand my people, such as the chairman, Mr Michael Sawtell, be appointed to the Board—not merely government officials. We expect more reforms from the new government. By doing this you will help to pay off the great debt that you, the white race, owe to my Aboriginal people. I would urge, may I beg you, to hand my Aboriginal people the democracy and the Christianity that you, the white nation of Australia, so proudly boast of. I challenge the white nation to make these boasts good. I'm asking your practical help for a new and better deal for my race. Remember we, the Aboriginal people, are the creditors. Do not let it be said of you that we have asked in vain. Will my appeal for practical humanity be in vain? I leave the answer to each and every one of you.

1941

OODGEROO NOONUCCAL
1920–1993

Describing herself as an educator and storyteller, Oodgeroo (meaning 'paperbark tree') of the Noonuccal tribe of Minjerriba (North Stradbroke Island, Queensland) was an Aboriginal poet, environmentalist and leader in the struggle for Aboriginal rights.

She was educated at Dunwich State School, became a domestic servant at thirteen and joined the army during the Second World War. In 1942 she married her childhood friend Bruce Walker. She had two sons. In 1988, Kath Walker readopted her tribal name as a protest against Australia's Bicentenary celebrations and a symbol of her Aboriginal pride.

Oodgeroo was politically active from the late 1940s and became one of the most prominent Aboriginal voices. She joined the Communist Party of Australia, the only political party opposed to the White Australia policy at the time, and from the early 1960s held key positions in the Aboriginal civil rights movement. She was a founding member and Queensland state secretary of FCAATSI, and a leader of the successful 1967 referendum campaign. She later chaired the National Tribal Council, the Aboriginal Arts Board, the Aboriginal Housing Committee and the Queensland Aboriginal Advancement League.

We Are Going, the first book of poetry by an Aboriginal writer and the first book by an Aboriginal woman, was published in 1964. In the following years Oodgeroo wrote numerous volumes of poetry, books for children, a play, essays, speeches and books illustrated with her own artworks, including *The Dawn is at Hand* (1966), *My People: A Kath Walker collection* (1970), *Stories from Stradbroke* (1972), *Kath Walker in China* (1988), *The Rainbow Serpent* (1988) and *Australia's Unwritten History: More legends of our land* (1992). She travelled widely overseas, representing Aboriginal writing and culture. For many years Oodgeroo lived at Moongalba ('sitting-down place'), her home on Minjerriba, where she established the Noonuccal-Nughie Education and Cultural Centre and for over two decades shared her culture and way of life with thousands of visitors. The grandmother of Aboriginal poetry was buried on Minjerriba with great ceremony.

Speech Launching the Petition of the Federal Council for Aboriginal Advancement

[…] I feel now that I must bring in two very important words, they are integration and assimilation. There seems to be much confusion around these two words, the policy of the government up till now has been that of assimilation for my people. Now, boiled down, assimilation means the swallowing up by a majority group of a minority group. My people, the Aboriginal people, are the minority group and they can only be assimilated by the final wiping out of this minority group. Now it is not our desire to have this happen, they have tried hard to do this, but it has not been successful and we feel that this is the most inhuman way of bringing my people forward, we feel that something must be done about it, so picture if you can, in my attempt to explain to you these two very important words, picture if you can a river which we will call the river of ignorance with two banks, the one on the right side we shall call the civilisation side of the bridge, the other side—stone age. Imagine a span from the civilised side of the bridge up and we shall call that span assimilation. Now my people on the stone age side of the bridge have to jump the big gap to the assimilation side span of the bridge. Some made it, I was fortunate enough to be one of them, to have made this big jump, but there are thousands of my people who did not, and they fell to the river bank below and were forced to live like scavengers on the rubbish dumps of the white race. These are our fringe dwellers, they have come too far and cannot climb back to what used to be, but they have not yet reached the stage where they can stand side by side with the white race. Of all my people, I'm most upset about the fringe dwellers. Much help is needed for them. How then, can we help the fringe dwellers?

Now then, let us put the other span of the bridge in, the span from the stone age side of the bridge, and we'll call it integration. Integration means the bringing forward of a race of people with their own identity and their own pride intact. They would come forward onto the integration side of the bridge with such things as their culture and their language. No doubt the old people would want to stay at the integration side of the bridge, so let it be. Let the choice be that of my people, they should be allowed to stay there. But the young people who are forever pushing on, would no doubt cross to the assimilation side of the bridge and so on to the assimilation side of the river. But when they crossed this bridge, the young people would do so, proud of the fact that they were of Aboriginal blood, happy to be what they are, and not going forward as replicas of the white race. Assimilation can only bring us forward as replicas of the white race; this is not what we desire, we desire to be Aboriginals, proud of this fact, and when they stood on the other side of the bridge amongst the civilized people, the white people, they would stand there as a friend and neighbour alongside the white man, respecting his way of life and expecting him in return to respect the Aboriginal's way of life. Now I find in my tour through, that the Aboriginal's knowledge is much greater than that of the white man in one respect. He knows more about the white man than the white man knows about us, and this is something that we must get together and rectify. We took time off, we, the Aboriginals took time off to understand what the white man wanted and to respect his views, this has not happened on the white man's side of the bridge and now the time has come when he himself must get to know us and understand us and respect us for what we want. I know that the present generation is not responsible for the past, I cannot blame the present white man or woman nor will I hold him or her responsible for what has happened in the past. I care not about the past, but the future I am worried about. The future is what we want, a bigger and brighter future for both races. I will however, and I feel I'm justified, I will hold the present white man and woman responsible for what happens to my people in the future. This I feel is their responsibility as well as mine.

1962

Aboriginal Charter of Rights

We want hope, not racialism,
Brotherhood, not ostracism,
Black advance, not white ascendance:
Make us equals, not dependants.
We need help, not exploitation,   5
We want freedom, not frustration;
Not control, but self-reliance,
Independence, not compliance,
Not rebuff, but education,
Self-respect, not resignation.   10
Free us from a mean subjection,
From a bureaucrat Protection.
Let's forget the old-time slavers:
Give us fellowship, not favours;
Encouragement, not prohibitions,   15
Homes, not settlements and missions.
We need love, not overlordship,
Grip of hand, not whip-hand wardship;
Opportunity that places
White and black on equal basis.   20
You dishearten, not defend us,
Circumscribe, who should befriend us.
Give us welcome, not aversion,
Give us choice, not cold coercion,
Status, not discrimination,   25
Human rights, not segregation.
You the law, like Roman Pontius,
Make us proud, not colour-conscious;
Give the deal you still deny us,
Give goodwill, not bigot bias;   30
Give ambition, not prevention,
Confidence, not condescension;
Give incentive, not restriction,
Give us Christ, not crucifixion.
Though baptized and blessed and Bibled   35
We are still tabooed and libelled.
You devout Salvation-sellers,
Make us neighbours, not fringe-dwellers;
Make us mates, not poor relations,
Citizens, not serfs on stations.   40
Must we native Old Australians
In our own land rank as aliens?
Banish bans and conquer caste,
Then we'll win our own at last.

1964

The Dispossessed
For Uncle Willie McKenzie

Peace was yours, Australian man, with tribal laws you made,
Till white Colonials stole your peace with rape and murder raid;
They shot and poisoned and enslaved until, a scattered few,
Only a remnant now remain, and the heart dies in you.
The white man claimed your hunting grounds and you could not remain, 5
They made you work as menials for greedy private gain;
Your tribes are broken vagrants now wherever whites abide,
And justice of the white man means justice to you denied.
They brought you Bibles and disease, the liquor and the gun:
With Christian culture such as these the white command was won.   10
A dying race you linger on, degraded and oppressed,
Outcasts in your own native land, you are the dispossessed.

When Churches mean a way of life, as Christians proudly claim,
And when hypocrisy is scorned and hate is counted shame,
Then only shall intolerance die and old injustice cease,   15
And white and dark as brothers find equality and peace.
But oh, so long the wait has been, so slow the justice due,
Courage decays for want of hope, and the heart dies in you.

1964

We are Going
For Grannie Coolwell

They came in to the little town
A semi-naked band subdued and silent,
All that remained of their tribe.
They came here to the place of their old bora ground
Where now the many white men hurry about like ants.   5
Notice of estate agent reads: 'Rubbish May Be Tipped Here'.
Now it half covers the traces of the old bora ring.
They sit and are confused, they cannot say their thoughts:
'We are as strangers here now, but the white tribe are the strangers.
We belong here, we are of the old ways.   10
We are the corroboree and the bora ground,
We are the old sacred ceremonies, the laws of the elders.
We are the wonder tales of Dream Time, the tribal legends told.
We are the past, the hunts and the laughing games, the wandering
        camp fires.
We are the lightning-bolt over Gaphembah Hill   15
Quick and terrible,
And the Thunderer after him, that loud fellow.
We are the quiet daybreak paling the dark lagoon.

We are the shadow-ghosts creeping back as the camp fires burn low.
We are nature and the past, all the old ways   20
Gone now and scattered.
The scrubs are gone, the hunting and the laughter.
The eagle is gone, the emu and the kangaroo are gone from this place.
The bora ring is gone.
The corroboree is gone.   25
And we are going.'

                                                                           1964

Assimilation—No!

Pour your pitcher of wine into the wide river
And where is your wine? There is only the river.
Must the genius of an old race die
That the race might live?
We who would be one with you, one people,   5
We must surrender now much that we love,
The old freedoms for new musts,
Your world for ours,
But a core is left that we must keep always.
Change and compel, slash us into shape,   10
But not our roots deep in the soil of old.
We are different hearts and minds
In a different body. Do not ask of us
To be deserters, to disown our mother,
To change the unchangeable.   15
The gum cannot be trained into an oak.
Something is gone, something surrendered, still
We will go forward and learn.
Not swamped and lost, watered away, but keeping
Our own identity, our pride of race.   20
Pour your pitcher of wine into the wide river
And where is your wine? There is only the river.

                                                                           1966

Integration—Yes!

Gratefully we learn from you,
The advanced race,
You with long centuries of lore behind you.
We who were Australians long before
You who came yesterday,   5
Eagerly we must learn to change,
Learn new needs we never wanted,
New compulsions never needed,

The price of survival.
Much that we loved is gone and had to go,   10
But not the deep indigenous things.
The past is still so much a part of us,
Still about us, still within us.
We are happiest
Among our own people. We would like to see   15
Our own customs kept, our old
Dances and songs, crafts and corroborees.
Why change our sacred myths for your sacred myths?
No, not assimilation but integration,
Not submergence but our uplifting,   20
So black and white may go forward together
In harmony and brotherhood.

                                                          1966

The Dawn is at Hand

Dark brothers, first Australian race,
Soon you will take your rightful place
In the brotherhood long waited for,
Fringe-dwellers no more.

Sore, sore the tears you shed   5
When hope seemed folly and justice dead.
Was the long night weary? Look up, dark band,
The dawn is at hand.

Go forward proudly and unafraid
To your birthright all too long delayed,   10
For soon now the shame of the past
Will be over at last.

You will be welcomed mateship-wise
In industry and in enterprise;
No profession will bar the door,   15
Fringe-dwellers no more.

Dark and white upon common ground
In club and office and social round,
Yours the feel of a friendly land,
The grip of the hand.   20

Sharing the same equality
In college and university,

All ambitions of hand or brain
Yours to attain.

For ban and bias will soon be gone,   25
The future beckons you bravely on
To art and letters and nation lore,
Fringe-dwellers no more.

1966

No More Boomerang

No more boomerang
No more spear;
Now all civilized—
Colour bar and beer.

No more corroboree,   5
Gay dance and din.
Now we got movies,
And pay to go in.

No more sharing
What the hunter brings.   10
Now we work for money,
Then pay it back for things.

Now we track bosses
To catch a few bob,
Now we go walkabout   15
On bus to the job.

One time naked,
Who never knew shame;
Now we put clothes on
To hide whatsaname.   20

No more gunya,
Now bungalow,
Paid by higher purchase
In twenty year or so.

Lay down the stone axe,   25
Take up the steel,
And work like a nigger
For a white man meal.

No more firesticks
That made the whites scoff.   30
Now all electric,
And no better off.

Bunyip he finish,
Now got instead
White fella Bunyip,   35
Call him Red.

Abstract picture now—
What they coming at?
Cripes, in our caves we
Did better than that.   40

Black hunted wallaby,
White hunt dollar;
White fella witch-doctor
Wear dog-collar.

No more message-stick;   45
Lubras and lads
Got television now,
Mostly ads.

Lay down the woomera,
Lay down the waddy.   50
Now we got atom-bomb,
End *every*body.

                                              1966

Ballad of the Totems

My father was Noonuccal man and kept old tribal way,
His totem was the Carpet Snake, whom none must ever slay;
But mother was of Peewee clan, and loudly she expressed
The daring view that carpet snakes were nothing but a pest.

Now one lived right inside with us in full immunity,   5
For no one dared to interfere with father's stern decree:
A mighty fellow ten feet long, and as we lay in bed
We kids could watch him round a beam not far above our head.

Only the dog was scared of him, we'd hear its whines and growls,
But mother fiercely hated him because he took her fowls.   10

You should have heard her diatribes that flowed in angry torrents
With words you never see in print, except in D.H. Lawrence.

'I kill that robber,' she would scream, fierce as a spotted cat;
'You see that bulge inside of him? My speckly hen make that!'
But father's loud and strict command made even mother quake;   15
I think he'd sooner kill a man than kill a carpet snake.

That reptile was a greedy-guts, and as each bulge digested
He'd come down on the hunt at night as appetite suggested.
We heard his stealthy slithering sound across the earthen floor,
While the dog gave a startled yelp and bolted out the door.   20

Then over in the chicken-yard hysterical fowls gave tongue,
Loud frantic squawks accompanied by the barking of the mung,
Until at last the racket passed, and then to solve the riddle,
Next morning he was back up there with a new bulge in his middle.

When father died we wailed and cried, our grief was deep and sore,   25
And strange to say from that sad day the snake was seen no more.
The wise old men explained to us: 'It was his tribal brother,
And that is why it done a guy'—but some looked hard at mother.

1966

DOUG NICHOLLS
1906–1988

Pastor Doug Nicholls of the Yorta Yorta people was born on Cummeragunja Mission in NSW, and was schooled according to strict religious principles. At the age of eight he saw the police forcibly remove his sixteen-year-old sister Hilda from the family to take her to the Cootamundra Training Home for Girls.

Nicholls worked as a tar boy and a general sheep hand before becoming a professional footballer. He was recruited by the Carlton Football Club but because of the players' racist attitudes did not compete with the team. In 1932 he joined Fitzroy Football Club where, in 1935, he became the first Aboriginal player to be selected to play for the Victorian Interstate Team. Nicholls also boxed with Jimmy Sharman's Boxing Troupe, and earned an income running races, preparing him for the role of inaugural chairman of the National Aboriginal Sports Foundation.

Nicholls was a social worker, the pastor of the first Aboriginal Church of Christ in Australia, and a field officer for the Aboriginal Advancement League. He edited their magazine, *Smoke Signals*, helped set up hostels for Aboriginal children and holiday homes for Aboriginal people at Queenscliff, and was a founding member and Victorian secretary of FCAATSI.

In 1968 Nicholls became a member of the new Ministry of Aboriginal Affairs in Victoria. In 1976 he was appointed Governor of South Australia and in 1991 the Canberra suburb of Nicholls was named after him.

Letter to the Editor

In expressing our appreciation of Dr. Donald Thomson's[1] public statement (*The Age*, 23/5) of the position we have known he maintains, may I give some illustrations from my own experience.

Our birth place means much to our people.

Whenever possible I return to my home at Cummeroogunja, on the Murray. Like the people of Lake Tyers, we, too, wished to develop our land.

On each visit as I walk across the small part of the reserve still available to us, I see again the fine old people who were our parents, I remember the pride they had in their flourishing wheat fields, grown on land they had cleared.

Many families owned their own horse and jinker. We were proud of our homes, our church and our school.

Gradually the N.S.W. Government made it clear we had not titled right to the land. White neighbours were leased sections of the reserve.

We became dispirited and depressed. As the station commenced to break up the blame was put on to the people and it was said we were lazy and irresponsible.

Destroyed.

It was the Government's policy and bad administration which destroyed us.

A self-respecting, independent people became dependent on charity and hand-outs.

Many families, refusing to live under the Government's system, attempted to make their way in the white community. Descendants of these folk now walk the streets, live on the fringes of nearby towns and the banks of the Murray.

Other families who put up with conditions were ultimately offered homes in the nearest country centre, where, it was alleged, employment would be available and their children would receive a better standard of education.

The three families who accepted the offer found how difficult life is for unskilled aboriginal labourers in white society, in spite of assistance from well-intentioned people.

They became demoralised and disintegrated. Their children finished up in Government institutions.

This is what I have seen and I will fight to the end to prevent it happening to the Lake Tyers families.

The retaining of Lake Tyers as a basis for creation of employment through community development must be seen as a practical humane plan which can offer security, shelter and stability to family life.

1963

YIRRKALA PEOPLE

Situated in Arnhem Land on the north-eastern tip of the NT, Yirrkala is a small community of predominantly Yolngu people. In 1963, Prime Minister Robert Menzies

---

1 An anthropologist who worked with the Yolngu people in Arnhem Land.

announced that 390 square kilometres of Yirrkala land would be leased to a bauxite mining company. The Yirrkala people protested the lease by presenting a petition to the Commonwealth Parliament signed by seventeen elders. Typed on paper in both Yolngu and English, the petition was glued to a sheet of stringy-bark bordered by paintings expressing Yirrkala law. The petition protested the government's secrecy and failure to consult, and requested an inquiry into the lease. A parliamentary committee acknowledged the Yirrkala people's moral rights to their land, but failed to stop the mine. As the first traditional document by an Aboriginal community to be recognised in the Australian Parliament, the Yirrkala Bark Petition represents the first recognition in Australian law of Aboriginal language and culture.

Yirrkala Bark Petition

The Humble Petition of the Undersigned Aboriginal people of Yirrkala, being members of the Balamumu, Narrkala, Gapiny and Miliwurrwurr people and Djapu, Mangalili, Madarrpa, Magarrwanalinirri, Gumatj, Djambarrpuynu, Marrakula, Galpu, Dhaluaya, Wangurri, Warramirri, Maymil, Rirrtjinu tribes, respectfully sheweth.

1. That nearly 500 people of the above tribes are residents of the land excised from the Aboriginal Reserve in Arnhem Land.

2. That the procedures of the excision of this land and the fate of the people on it were never explained to them beforehand, and were kept secret from them.

3. That when Welfare Officers and Government officials came to inform them of decisions taken without them and against them, they did not undertake to convey to the Government in Canberra the views and feelings of the Yirrkala aboriginal people.

4. That the land in question has been hunting and food gathering land for the Yirrkala tribes from time immemorial; we were all born here.

5. That places sacred to the Yirrkala people, as well as vital to their livelihood are in the excised land, especially Melville Bay.

6. That the people of this area fear that their needs and interests will be completely ignored as they have been ignored in the past, and they fear that the fate which has overtaken the Larrakeah tribe will overtake them.

7. And they humbly pray that the Honourable the House of Representatives will appoint a Committee, accompanied by competent interpreters, to hear the views of the people of Yirrkala before permitting the excision of this land.

8. They humbly pray that no arrangements be entered into with any company which will destroy the livelihood and independence of the Yirrkala people.

And your petitioners as in duty bound will ever pray God to help you and us. (English translation)

Bukudjulni gonga'yurru napurrunha Yirrkalalili Yulnunha malanha Balamumu, Narrkala, Gapiny, Miliwurrwurr nanapurru dhuwala mala, ga Djapu, Mangalili, Madarrpa, Magarrwanalinirri, Djambarrpuynu, Gumaitj, Marrakula, Galpu, Dhabuayu, Wangurri, Warramirri, Maymil, Ririfjinu malamanapanmirri djal dhunapa.

1. *Dhuwala yulnu mala galki 500 nhina ga dhiyala wananura. Dhuwala wanga Arnhem Land yurru djaw'yunna naburrungala.*

2. *Dhuwala wanga djaw'yunna ga nhaltjana yurru yulnungunydja dhiyala wanga nura nhaltjanna dhu dharrpanna yulnu walandja yakana lakarama madayangumuna.*

3. *Dhuwala nunhi Welfare Officers ga Government bungawa lakarama yulnuwa malanuwa nhaltjarra nhuma gana wanganaminha yaka nula napurrungu lakarama wlala yaka'lakarama Government-gala nunhala Canberra nhaltjanna napurruga guyana yulnuyu Yirrkala.*

4. *Dhuwala wänga napurrungyu balanu Iarrunarawu napurrungu näthawa, guyawu, miyspunuwu, maypalwu nunhi napurru gana nhinana bitjarrayi näthilimirri, napurru dhawalguyanana dhiyala wänganura.*

5. *Dhuwala wänga yurru dharpalnha yurru yulnuwalandja malawala, ga dharrpalnha dhuwala bala yulnuwuyndja nhinanharawu Melville Bathurru wänga balandayu djaw'yun nyumukunin.*

6. *Dhuwala yulnundja mala yurru nhämana balandawunu nha mulkurru nhämä yurru moma ga darangan yalalanumirrinha nhaltjanna dhu napurru bitjara nhakuna Larrakeahyu momara wlalanguwuy wänga.*

7. *Nuli dhu bungawayu House of Representatives djaw'yn yulnuwala näthili yurru nha dhu lakarama interpreteryu bungawawala yulnu matha, yurru nha dhu djaw'yun dhuwala wangandja.*

8. *Nunhiyina dhu märrlayun marrama'-ndja nhinanharawu yulnuwu marrnamathinyarawu. Dhuwala napurru yulnu mala yurru liyamirriyama bitjan bili marr yurru napurru hha gonga' yunna wangarr'yu.*

(Australian *matha* original)

1963

NARRITJIN MAYMURU
c. 1916–1981

A prominent member of the Maymuru family, Manggali clan—bark painters, printmakers and sculptors of north-eastern Arnhem Land, NT—Narritjin (Narrijin) was active in developing relationships between the Yolngu and outsiders. He worked for a pearler and for the missionary Wilbur Chaseling and produced paintings for the anthropologist Ronald Berndt. In the 1950s he lived in Darwin. Narritjin helped to paint the Yirrkala Bark Petition presented to the House of Representatives in 1963. After mining was established at Nhulunbuy in 1971, he worked with film-maker Ian Dunlop to document Yolngu life. In 1978, with his son Banapana, Narritjin was offered a Visiting Artistic Fellowship at the Australian National University. He played a major role in encouraging women to produce sacred paintings and his daughters became well-known painters.

Letter to Mr H.E. Giese, Director of Aboriginal Welfare, NT

Mr Gise who looking after for all the Aborigines in the N.T. We want to help us belong to this country Yirrkala, please Mr Gise? Because the Maining campany will be here soon. All the Aborigines in Yirrkala are wondering about this country. What we are going to do Mr Gise? You think us a funny? or you think

us a good people. You going to help us Mr Gise? or no. These maining people will chasing us to other places, we don't like that. Please sir? We like Yirrkala best. This is a word for all the people in Yirrkala. We want Yirrk. open country. So we may go hunting for meat. We don't like the maining campany will come close to the Mission area, please Mr Gise? Our children are in school. They will grow up belong to this country. They may us what they were learned in school. They will help the fathers, mothers, sisters, brothers, or their relations about the white man laws, white man way to living, white man ways to eat. White man way to cook, and wash our plates. This time we don't understand about the white man ways yet. We going to ask you for this country Yirrkala. We are don't like to come near to the Mission. If the maining people like to use this country, alright they will stay away from the Mission, Mr Gise? This is a words for Narrijin and all the Aborigines in Yirrkala Mission, says this.
Thankyou Mr Gise, Goodbye.

1963

VINCENT LINGIARI
1919–1988

Vincent Lingiari was the 'Kadijeri man' (leader) of the Gurindji people, Kalkaringi, NT. In 1966 he led the Wave Hill walk-off, protesting against poor conditions and pay for Aboriginal workers on the cattle station, owned since 1914 by the British pastoral company Vesteys. Lingiari's thumbprint was the first signature on the petition to the station owner, and he successfully expanded the protest to include a claim for traditional land rights. After years of struggle, the Gurindji were handed inalienable title to their land in 1975 by Prime Minister Gough Whitlam, who, in an iconic gesture, poured sand from his hand into Lingiari's. The Gurindji success was further reflected in the *Aboriginal Land Rights (Northern Territory) Act* 1976 (Cth). Lingiari is remembered in the song 'From Little Things Big Things Grow', by Paul Kelly and Kev Carmody (qv).

Gurindji Petition to Lord Casey, Governor General

MAY IT PLEASE YOUR EXCELLENCY

We, the leaders of the Gurindji people, write to you about our earnest desire to regain tenure of our tribal lands in the Wave Hill–Limbunya area of the Northern Territory, of which we were dispossessed in time past, and for which we received no recompense.

Our people have lived here from time immemorial and our culture, myths, dreaming and sacred places have evolved in this land. Many of our forefathers were killed in the early days while trying to retain it. Therefore we feel that morally the land is ours and should be returned to us. Our very name Aboriginal acknowledges our prior claim. We have never ceased to say amongst ourselves that Vesteys should go away and leave us to our land.

On the attached map, we have marked out the boundaries of the sacred places of our dreaming, bordering the Victoria River from Wave Hill Police Station to Hooker Creek, Inverway, Limbunya, Seal Gorge, etc. We have begun to build our own new homestead on the banks of beautiful Wattie Creek in the Seal Yard area, where there is permanent water. This is the main place of our dreaming only a few miles from the Seal Gorge where we have kept the bones of our martyrs all these years since white men killed many of our people. On the walls of the sacred caves where these bones are kept, are the painting of the totems of our tribe.

We have already occupied a small area at Seal Yard under Miners Rights held by three of our tribesmen. We will continue to build our new home there (marked on the map with a cross), then buy some working horses with which we will trap and capture wild unbranded horses and cattle. These we will use to build up a cattle station within the borders of this ancient Gurindji land. And we are searching the area for valuable rocks which we hope to sell to help feed our people. We will ask the N.T. Welfare Department for help with motor for pump, seeds for garden, tables, chairs, and other things we need. Later on we will build a road and an airstrip and maybe a school. Meanwhile, most of our people will continue to live in the camp we have built at the Wave Hill Welfare Centre twelve miles away and the children continue to go to school there.

We beg of you to hear our voices asking that the land marked on the map be returned to the Gurindji people. It is about 500 square miles in area but this is only a very small fraction of the land leased by Vesteys in these parts. We are prepared to pay for our land the same annual rental that Vesteys now pay. If the question of compensation arises, we feel that we have already paid enough during fifty years or more, during which time, we and our fathers worked for no wages at all much of the time and for a mere pittance in recent years.

If you can grant this wish for which we humbly ask, we would show the rest of Australia and the whole world that we are capable of working and planning our own destiny as free citizens. Much has been said about our refusal to accept responsibility in the past, but who would show initiative working for starvation wages, under impossible conditions, without education for strangers in the land? But we are ready to show initiative now. We have already begun. We know how to work cattle better than any white man and we know and love this land of ours.

If our tribal lands are returned to us, we want them, *not* as another 'Aboriginal Reserve', but as a leasehold to be run cooperatively as a mining lease and cattle station by the Gurindji Tribe. All practical work will be done by us, except such work as bookkeeping, for which we would employ white men of good faith, until such time as our own people are sufficiently educated to take over. We will also accept the condition that if we do not succeed within a reasonable time, our land should go back to the Government.

(In August last year, we walked away from the Wave Hill Cattle Station. It was said that we did this because wages were very poor (only six dollars per week), living conditions fit only for dogs, and rations consisting mainly of salt beef and bread. True enough. But we walked away for other reasons as well. To protect our women and our tribe, to try to stand on our own feet. We will never go back there.)

Some of our young men are working now at Camfield, and Montejinnie Cattle Stations for proper wages. However, we will ask them to come back to our [own] Gurindji Homestead when everything is ready.

These are our wishes, which have been written down for us by our undersigned white friends, as we have had no opportunity to learn to write English.

Vincent Lingiari. Pincher Manguari. Gerry Ngaljardji. Long-Johnny Kitgnaari. Transcribed, witnessed and transmitted by Frank J. Hardy. J. W. Jeffrey.

1967

JOE TIMBERY
1912–1978

Poet, storyteller and world champion boomerang thrower, Joe Timbery spent much of his life at La Perouse near Sydney. His ancestors included Timbere, King of the Five Islands, and his Dharawal grandmother, Emma, a gifted traditional shellmaker. Timbery was highly regarded for his boomerangs, which were decorated with carved images of animals and the Sydney Harbour Bridge. He demonstrated his boomerang throwing beneath the Eiffel Tower, and in 1954 presented Queen Elizabeth II with one of his boomerangs during her visit to Australia.

The Boomerang Racket

Boomerangs are now being manufactured by the thousand by people with very little (or no) experience of how such weapons should be made.

In Sydney, it will soon be hard to find a boomerang made by an Australian Aborigine. Some Aboriginals who really have the experience and can make good boomerangs are out of business, or soon will be. Most of the shops are to blame for this. They want boomerangs so cheap they don't care who makes them.

When an Aboriginal takes his boomerang to try and sell them as before, most of the shops say 'We buy our boomerangs from agents now'—but the agents haven't been handling boomerangs made by Aborigines. It doesn't matter to the shops if the boomerangs offered to them are good throwing types—they won't pay any more money for them. They don't even know what are good throwers. But if you go to buy a boomerang from them, they say the ones they have are good throwing boomerangs.

How can Aborigines compete with their genuine, quality boomerangs? No wonder some dark people live the way they do.

The public are being caught all the time. I feel sorry for them. They have been good to me—that is why I write this warning.

Now to try and help you, remember this—

The cross on one end of the boomerang, and the arrow at the other is often a gimmick to help sell it. Such marks don't always mean that a boomerang is a genuine throwing kind.

If shown how, almost any person can throw a boomerang and make it return, if it has been made right. But it does not matter how good a boomerang thrower may be, it won't return to you correctly if it has not been made right. The instruction on how to throw it is of no use to you—only a gimmick to help sell it.

If your boomerang is faulty, don't muck around with it unless you know the cause of the trouble. A boomerang is a weapon and could be dangerous when thrown.

If the boomerang is made from good natural coloured wood, and is about a quarter of an inch thick, in the first place it may be warped. A good boomerang should, when thrown correctly, spin very fast, and not lose its spin until it lands. If it does lose its spin, don't blame yourself, it's not made right. There could be many things wrong with it. For instance, the less angle the boomerang has, the harder it is to make it return.

More experience is needed in making a boomerang from heavy timber than making one from light wood.

There are very, very few living in Sydney today who have the kind of experience needed to make boomerangs correctly.

Your children would have a much better chance of throwing a good boomerang made by an expert, than the cheap, mass-produced ones sold in most shops. And when they are successful, they will have the fun of their lives. You will be happy too.

1968

CHARLES PERKINS
1936–2000

Charles Nelson (Charlie) Perkins was born at the Alice Springs Telegraph Station Aboriginal Reserve, NT. His parents were Arrente and Kalkadoon people. At the age of ten he was removed from the reserve and sent to a home for boys in Adelaide, where he completed his schooling. He qualified as a fitter and turner in 1952. A talented soccer player, Perkins played as a professional with English club Everton, and on his return to Australia with Adelaide Croatian and Sydney Pan-Hellenic.

While studying at the University of Sydney, Perkins became active in the Indigenous rights struggle and co-founded the group Student Action for Aboriginals. Inspired by the American civil rights movement, he led the 1965 Freedom Ride to NSW country towns, where he and fellow students protested against racial discrimination. That year Perkins was the first Aboriginal person to graduate from university.

In 1969 he joined the Commonwealth Office of Aboriginal Affairs. In 1975 he published his autobiography, *A Bastard Like Me*. By 1984 he was deputy secretary of the Department of Aboriginal Affairs. A well-known and controversial national figure, Perkins resigned in 1988 after a clash with his Minister over allegations of financial mismanagement that were later dismissed.

In later years Perkins lived in Alice Springs. His lifelong love of sport led him to mentor several Aboriginal athletes. In 1993 he was elected to ATSIC, serving as deputy chairman (1994–95). He was honoured as one of the *Bulletin*'s '100 Most Influential Australians' in 2006.

Letter to the Editor

I would like to enlighten E.J. Smith, who asked in a letter to *The Australian* on March 27 why part-Aboriginal people such as myself identify as Aboriginals.

Firstly we were usually born on Mission Stations, Government Reserves or shanty towns. We received aid only as far as it was convenient for the white people. We were therefore identifiable to ourselves as well as white people as 'the Aboriginals'.

Secondly we were related by kinship, blood and cultural ties to our full-blood parents or grandparents. This tie can never be broken merely because the degree of 'blood' may vary, or if white authority or individuals wish it so. An example of this is the Northern Territory where before 1956 an Aboriginal was any person with one drop of Aboriginal blood in his veins—the definition was reversed by law only some ten years ago. Very convenient for the law-makers, but imagine its effect on the Aboriginal family. Aboriginals are not like white people. They love their children, whatever shade. Generally, in the past, the white people never really wanted us. When they did it was usually on their terms for sexual, economic or paternal reasons.

Thirdly many thousands of our people were forced to carry passes—much like passports—if ever we wished to mix in the white community. This carried our photograph, plus character references. We were labelled as fit and proper Aboriginals to associate with white people. I was one of the few Aboriginals in Adelaide who refused to carry a pass or 'dog ticket' as we called it. All my life, before I graduated from the University of Sydney, I was categorised by law and socially as an Aboriginal. Now that I have graduated I am suddenly transformed by people such as Smith, into a non-Aboriginal.

This conveniently puts me into a situation where I must, according to official assimilation policy, forget my people, my background, my former obligations. I am now 'white'. I therefore am not supposed to voice an opinion on the scandalous situation Aboriginal people are in nor am I entitled to speak any longer as a 'legal Aboriginal'. All this because I have received my degree and am in a position to voice an opinion. Or could it be that I, and others like me, could influence the unacceptable social-racial status quo in Australia?

Fourthly there can be no real comparison between a nationality and race. A nationality is a mere political or geographic distinction between people. Race on the other hand goes much further into the biological (colour) and cultural (kinship, customs, attitudes) field.

The Aboriginal people in Australia today—full-blood and part blood—do not want the sympathy of white people with an attitude such as Smith's. We have had enough of this in the past.

What we want is good education, respect, pride in our ancestry, more job opportunities and understanding.

It seems people such as Smith carry a guilt complex of past mistreatment, and would want to now stop the truth from being revealed, and hence control Aboriginal advancement.

If Australians would delve into our social history in a truthful manner they would be horrified at the result of the investigation.

The story is not a nice one and Aboriginals have suffered as a consequence.

All our lives Aboriginals have lived in a secondary position to the white Australian.

I no longer wish for this situation. Therefore I, and approximately 250,000 others like me, claim our ancestry. We are Aboriginal Australians—proud of our country and our race.

1968

JACK DAVIS
1917–2000

The grandfather of Aboriginal theatre, Jack Leonard Davis grew up at Yarloop, WA. His many plays and poems were inspired by the experiences of his family and the Noongar people—his mother was forcibly removed from her parents, and on the death of his father Davis was sent to Moore River Native Settlement to learn farming at the age of fourteen. He left after nine months, having experienced the appalling conditions in Aboriginal reserves that would be the focus of much of his work.

The young Davis worked as a stockman, boxer, horse breeder, train driver and truck driver. While living at the Brookton Aboriginal Reserve he started to learn the language and culture of his people. He discovered the details of his mother's family history, and later spent time in tribal society while working as a stockman.

Davis's writing spans the genres of drama, poetry, short fiction, autobiography and criticism, reflecting a lifelong commitment to Aboriginal literature and activism. He was the director of the Aboriginal Centre in Perth from 1967 to 1971 and became the first chair of the Aboriginal Lands Trust in WA. His first book of poetry was *The First-born and Other Poems* (1970). In 1973 he moved to Sydney to join the Aboriginal Publications Foundation as editor of *Identity*, soon moving the magazine back with him to Perth. He published further books of poetry and wrote a series of groundbreaking plays, such as *No Sugar* (1985/1986), *Kullark* (1979/1982) and *The Dreamers* (1982/1982), defining modern Aboriginal theatre's exploration of colonisation and cultural dislocation, the search for identity and meaning by Aboriginal youth, and the clash of Aboriginal and white law. His works include *Jagardoo: Poems from Aboriginal Australia* (1977), *Honey Spot* (1987), *John Pat and Other Poems* (1988), *Barungin: Smell the wind* (1989), *A Boy's Life* (1991), *Black Life: Poems* (1992) and *Moorli and the Leprechaun* (1994).

Davis also made a significant contribution to Aboriginal literary life as a cultural activist and administrator. In the 1980s he co-founded the Aboriginal Writers, Oral Literature and Dramatists' Association, and was a member of the council of the Australian Institute of Aboriginal Studies and the Aboriginal Arts Board. Davis was named an Australian Living National Treasure in 1998.

The First-born

Where are my first-born, said the brown land, sighing;
They came out of my womb long, long ago.
They were formed of my dust—why, why are they crying
And the light of their being barely aglow?

I strain my ears for the sound of their laughter.   5
Where are the laws and the legends I gave?
Tell me what happened, you whom I bore after.
Now only their spirits dwell in the caves.

You are silent, you cringe from replying.
A question is there, like a blow on the face.   10
The answer is there when I look at the dying,
At the death and neglect of my dark proud race.

                                                                  1970

The Black Tracker

He served mankind for many a year
Before the jeep or the wireless.
He walked, he loped, no thought of fear,
Keen-eyed, lithe and tireless.

He led Eyre[1] to the western plains;   5
He went with Burke and Wills;[2]
He put Nemarluk[3] back in chains:
He found the lost in the hills.

He found hair and spittle dry:
He found the child with relief.   10
He heard a mother's joyful cry
Or a mother's wail of grief.

He found the lost one crawling south,
Miles away from the track.
He siphoned water, mouth to mouth,   15
And carried him on his back.

He heard the white man call him names,
His own race scoffing, jeering.
'A black man playing white man games,'
They laughed and pointed, sneering.   20

No monument of stone for him
In your park or civilized garden.
His deeds unsung, fast growing dim—
It's time you begged his pardon.

                                                                  1970

Warru

Fast asleep on the wooden bench,
Arms bent under the weary head,

---

1   Edward Eyre (1815–1901), English explorer of SA and WA.
2   Irishman Robert O'Hara Burke (1821–61) and Englishman William John Wills (1834–61) led an ill-fated
    expedition from Melbourne to the Gulf of Carpentaria (1860–61).
3   An Aboriginal warrior active in the NT during the early twentieth century.

There in the dusk and the back-street stench
He lay with the look of the dead.

I looked at him, then back through the years,   5
Then knew what I had to remember—
A young man, straight as wattle spears,
And a kangaroo hunt in September.

We caught the scent of the 'roos on the rise
Where the gums grew on the Moore;[1]   10
They leaped away in loud surprise,
But Warru was fast and as sure.

He threw me the fire-stick, oh what a thrill!
With a leap he sprang to a run.
He met the doe on the top of the hill,   15
And he looked like a king in the sun.

The wattle spear flashed in the evening light,
The kangaroo fell at his feet.
How I danced and I yelled with all my might
As I thought of the warm red meat.   20

We camped that night on a bed of reeds
With a million stars a-gleaming.
He told me tales of Noongar deeds
When the world first woke from dreaming.

He sang me a song, I clapped my hands,   25
He fashioned a needle of bone.
He drew designs in the river sands,
He sharpened his spear on a stone.

I will let you dream—dream on, old friend—
Of a boy and a man in September,   30
Of hills and stars and the river's bend—
Alas, that is all to remember.

1970

Integration

Let these two worlds combine,
Yours and mine.
The door between us is not locked,

---

1 The government of WA administered Moore River Native Settlement near Mogumber between 1918 and 1951.

Just ajar.
There is no need for the mocking   5
Or the mocked to stand afar
With wounded pride
Or angry mind,
Or to build a wall to crouch and hide,
To cry or sneer behind.   10

This is ours together,
This nation—
No need for separation.
It is time to learn.
Let us forget the hurt,   15
Join hands and reach
With hearts that yearn.

Your world and mine
Is small.
The past is done.   20
Let us stand together,
Wide and tall
And God will smile upon us each
And all
And everyone.   25
                                                                 1970

Walker

To Kath[1]

Fight on, Sister, fight on,
Stir them with your ire.
Go forward, Sister, right on,
We need you by the fire.

Your mind is no flat desert place,   5
But like serrated spears;
You must lead the talk, talk for our race
And help dispel our fears.

You were not born to walk on by
Or rest in sheltered bower,   10
But to fight until the ink is dry,
Until the victory hour.

                                                                 1978

---

1   Kath Walker, Aboriginal poet and activist also known as Oodgeroo Noonuccal (qv).

From *No Sugar*
Act 2, Scene 6

A clearing in the pine plantation. Moore River Native Settlement, night. A camp fire burns. JIMMY and SAM are painted for a corroboree. JIMMY mixes wilgi in tobacco tin lids, while SAM separates inji sticks from clapsticks. JOE arrives with an armful of firewood and pokes at the fire.

JOE: They comin' now.

BILLY: [*off*] Get no rain this place summertime.

[BILLY *and* BLUEY *enter and remove their shirts.*]

JIMMY: Eh? Where you fellas been?

BLUEY: Aw, we been pushing truck for Mr Neal.

BILLY: He goin' Mogumber.

BLUEY: [*miming taking a drink*] Doin' this fella.

JOE: He'll be *minditj* tomorrow.

[BLUEY *and* BILLY *paint themselves with wilgi.*]

BILLY: My word you fellas pr-retty fellas.

BLUEY: *Wee-ah,* plenty *wilgi.*

BILLY: Eh? You know my country, must be walk two, three days for this much. Your country got plenty.

[JIMMY *strikes up a rhythm on the clapsticks.* BLUEY *joins him.*]

JIMMY: [*singing*]
> Tjinnung nitjakoorliny?
> Karra, karra, karra, karra,
> Moyambat a-nyinaliny a-nyinaliny,
> Baal nitja koorliny moyambat a-moyambat moyambat,
> Moyambat nitja koorliny moyambat.
> Kalkanna yirra nyinny kalkanna,
> Yirra nyinniny, yirra nyinniny,
> Moyambat a-kalkanna moyambat a-kilkanna
> Yirra nyinniny, yirra nyinniny, yirra nyinniny,
> Karra koorliny kalkanna karra karra koorliny kalkanna.
> Karra koorliny, karra koorliny, karra koorliny,
> Woolah!

BLUEY: Eh, what that one?

JIMMY: That's my grandfather song. [*Miming with his hands*] He singin' for the *karra,* you know, crabs, to come up the river and for the fish to jump up high so he can catch them in the fish traps.

SAM: [*pointing to* BILLY'S *body paint*] Eh! Eh! Old man, what's that one?

BILLY: This one *bungarra,* an' he lookin' for berry bush. But he know that fella eagle watchin' him and he know that fella is cunnin' fella. He watchin' and lookin' for that eagle, that way, this way, that way, this way.

[*He rolls over a log, disappearing almost magically.* BLUEY *plays the didgeridoo and* BILLY *appears some distance away by turning quickly so the firelight reveals his painted body. He dances around, then seems to disappear suddenly. He rolls back over the log and drops down, seated by the fire.*]

BLUEY, SAM and JIMMY: *Yokki! Moorditj! Woolah!*

JIMMY: Eh? That one dance come from your country?

BILLY: Nah. That one come from that way, lo-o-ong way. *Wanmulla* country. Proper bad fellas.

SAM: Well, I won't be goin' there.

JOE: Me either!

[*JIMMY, JOE and SAM laugh. SAM jumps to his feet with the clapsticks.*]

SAM: This one *yahllarah!* Everybody! *Yahllarah!*

> [*He starts a rhythm on the clapsticks.* BLUEY *plays didgeridoo.* JIMMY, *and then* JOE, *join him dancing.*]

Come on! Come on!

> [*He picks up inji sticks. The Nyoongahs,* SAM, JIMMY *and* JOE, *dance with them.* BILLY *joins in. They dance with increasing speed and energy, stamping their feet, whirling in front of the fire, their bodies appearing and disappearing as the paint catches the firelight. The dance becomes faster and more frantic until finally* SAM *lets out a yell and they collapse, dropping back to their positions around the fire.* JIMMY *coughs and pants painfully.*]

[*To* JIMMY] Eh! Eh! [*Indicating his heart*] You wanta *dubakieny,* you know your *koort minditj.*

BILLY: This country got plenty good dance, eh?

BLUEY: *Wee-ah!*

JIMMY: Ah, *yuart,* not too many left now. Nearly all finish.

BILLY: No, no, no. You song man, you fella dance men. This still your country. [*Flinging his arms wide*] You, you, you, you listen! *Gudeeah* make 'em fences, windmill, make 'em road for motor car, big house, cut 'em down trees. Still your country! Not like my country, finish … finish.

> [*He sits in silence. They watch him intently.* JOE *puts wood on the fire. He speaks slowly.*]

BILLY: *Kuliyah.* [*Miming pulling a trigger, grunting*] *Gudeeah* bin kill 'em. Finish, kill 'em. Big mob, 1926, kill 'em big mob my country.

[*Long pause.*]

SAM: *Nietjuk?*

BILLY: I bin stop Liveringa station and my brother, he bin run from Oombulgarri. [*Holding up four fingers*] That many days. Night time too. He bin tell me 'bout them *gudeeah.* They bin two, three stockman *gudeeah.* Bin stop along that place, Juada Station, and this one *gudeeah* Midja George, he was ridin' and he come to this river and he see these two old womans, *koories,* there in the water hole. He says, what you doin' here? They say they gettin' *gugja.*

> [*He mimes pulling lily roots and eating.*]

Midja George say, where the mans? They over by that tree sleepin', and Midja George, he get off his horse, and he bin belt that old man with the stockwhip. He bin flog 'em, flog 'em, till that *gudeeah,* he get tired. Then he break the bottle glass spear, and he break the *chubel* spear.

> [*He grunts and mimes this.*]

And that old man, he was bleedin', bleedin' from the eyes, and he get up and he pick up that one *chubel* spear, and he spear that one *Midja George.*

[*He demonstrates violently.*]

And that *gudeeah*, he get on his horse, he go little bit way and he fall off … finish … dead.

JIMMY: Serve the bastard right.

BILLY: No, no, no bad for my mob. Real bad. That old man and his two *koories*, they do this next day.

[*He indicates running away.*]

Two *gudeeah* come looking for Midja George. They bin find him dead.

[*Silence.*]

[*Holding up a hand*] Must be that many day. Big mob *gudeeah*. Big mob politjmans, and big mob from stations, and shoot 'em everybody mens, *koories*, little *yumbah*.

[*He grunts and mimes pulling a trigger.*]

They chuck 'em on a big fire, chuck 'em in river.

[*They sit in silence, mesmerized and shocked by* BILLY's *gruesome story.*]

JIMMY: Anybody left, your mob?

BILLY: Not many, gid away, hide. But no one stop that place now, they all go 'nother country.

JOE: Why?

BILLY: You go there, night time you hear 'em. I bin bring cattle that way for Wyndham Meat Works. I hear 'em. Mothers cryin' and babies cryin', screamin'. *Waiwai! Wawai! Wawai!*

[*They sit in silence staring at* BILLY *who stares into the fire. Suddenly a night hawk screeches.*]

SAM: Gawd, I'm getting out of here.

JIMMY: Me too!

BLUEY: Hm, hm, hm, hm, *wee-ah, wee-ah!*

[*They quickly pick up their things and leave.* JOE *remains alone.*]

SAM: You comin'?

JOE: Go on, I'll catch you up. Go on!

JIMMY: You watch out.

[*He pinches his throat with thumb and forefinger.*]

JOE: I'll be all right.

SAM: Don't forget the *kaal*.

JOE: Okay.

[*They exit.* JOE *looks around, pokes the fire, stands and waits. The moon begins to rise. There is a low mopoke call. He replies with a similar call and gets a reply.* MARY *runs into the clearing. They embrace.*]

I didn't think you were gunna get here.

MARY: I bin watchin' youse for nearly half an hour.

JOE: *Kienya!*

MARY: I mean listenin', not watchin'.

JOE: It's all right, wasn't man's business. Did you have any trouble gettin' away?

MARY: Nah. Topsy's coverin' up for me. I'll just walk in the dinin' room in the mornin'. They won't miss me.

JOE: [*nervously*] Where you gunna sleep tonight?

[*They kiss.* MARY *withdraws from him and sits on the log. She begins to cry. He checks that they are alone and sits close beside her on the log.*]

JOE: Eh? What's up? Come on, tell me what's up. You been fightin' with someone?

[*She shakes her head.*]

Come on! Tell me what's the matter.

MARY: Mr Neal.

JOE: Yeah, what about him?

MARY: He's tryin' to make me go and work at the hospital.

JOE: Well, what's wrong with that?

MARY: Everything.

JOE: You get better tucker.

MARY: It's more than that, Joe.

JOE: What d'ya mean?

MARY: When Mr Neal sends a girl to work at the hospital, it usually means …

JOE: Means what?

MARY: That he wants that girl … for himself.

JOE: *What?*

MARY: Everyone know, even the *wetjalas.*

JOE: Rotten, stinkin', lowdown bastard. I'll kill him!

MARY: Joe …

JOE: I'll smash his head in with a *doak!*

MARY: Joe, listen!

JOE: Filthy pig. You not goin' anywhere near that hospital!

MARY: If I don't, he reckons he'll send me back home.

JOE: Home? Where?

MARY: Wyndham. He reckons he send me up home 'coz I'm a give girl.

JOE: Like hell you are.

MARY: I don't want to go up there to marry no old man.

JOE: You're meant to be gettin' married to me.

MARY: Mr Neal not gonna let us get married.

JOE: [*exploding*] Jesus! [*Indicating running*] We're doin' this tonight, right this fuckin' minute.

MARY: Joe, you'll get in big trouble!

JOE: I'll get in bigger trouble if I have to chip that walrus-faced bastard. I'll kill him.

MARY: Joe, listen! Where we gunna go?

JOE: Home, Northam.

MARY: What about your mum and dad?

JOE: We'll tell 'em now, come on, come on.

[MARY *just stands there.*]

Come on. I'm gunna show you my country. Got a big river, swans, beautiful white swans.

[JOE *picks up his shirt and a billy of water, which he tips on the fire. He leads* MARY *off into the darkness.*]

1986

JOHN A. NEWFONG
1943–1999

John Archibald Newfong was born in Brisbane and spent his early years on Stradbroke Island, his mother's traditional country. The first Aboriginal journalist to be employed in the Australian print media, he trained at the *Sydney Morning Herald* and enjoyed a long career writing for Australian newspapers. Newfong was also a highly respected Aboriginal political leader. In 1961 he joined the Queensland Council for the Advancement of Aborigines and Torres Strait Islanders and by 1970 had been elected general secretary of FCAATSI. An organiser and 'ambassador' for the 1972 Aboriginal Tent Embassy and an executive founding member of the National Aboriginal Conference (1977–79), Newfong was twice editor of the Aboriginal magazine *Identity*. From the 1970s he used his considerable experience to direct public relations for Aboriginal organisations and authorities, and later lectured extensively in Australian universities, teaching journalism, media studies, Indigenous health and government relations.

To Number One Fella Big White Boss

Since you become big fella number one white boss me bin thinkin'—before, when we bin goin' Canberra, we bin talkin' white fella way. Yous bin saying, when yous gettum gubberment, you come up our way and you gonna talk black fella way.

But you like all white cockies, when yous gotta pay our people big fella white man's wage, yous allas say we no work good. Then yous say our people not know 'bout da politics and dat none can work for you. Our people know 'bout politics 'cause dat's da only way we gonna live in dis white fella's world. Yous allas say you gonna help us do things black fella way but, in 1970 at da FCAATSI Conference, you bin turn aroun' an' vote against us like all da other white people. You reckon then dat we black fellas gotta lot to learn and now you still say we not learnin' fast enough to tell you what black fellas is all about. You gotta have white people and dese white people 'aven' bin near us 'cept now when day got big job with big white fella pay.

When you come up here we no get to talk to you. All you do is fly in aeroplane with all dem other white fellas and black fellas that we don' know. My people bin thinkin' 'bout dis other black fella down there that runnin' dis magazine all about us but you no bring 'im. 'Stead you bring all those white fellas. When we ask you 'bout dis black fella wid this magazine all about us, you say you got no room an' 'im gone walkabout. But you bring your sons and one of dem when 'im go back Melbourne, 'e laughs 'bout us black fellas' 'gripes and groans'. How you gonna change all those other white fellas down dere when you not able change own sons?

You say before you gett'm gubberment dat you gonna give us back da land. What you bin doin' since you gettum gubberment? All yous bin done is give da Gurindji what da last gubberment give dem. You no give us back da land you only tell us like those other white fellas in Parliament House before you dat we borrow the land.

You say you stop mining companies from takin' our land then why you no give it to us? Why you say we only borrow it? This mean when you want it back you come and take it. Then where we gonna go? You no better than all da others.

It because dem other Liberal–Country white fellas say we only borrow da land and not own it like we used to dat our fellas camp in front Parliament House in da first place. Now you say da same thing as those other fellas when they da boss so we think we gotta camp down your way again. You give some our people in Redfern in Sydney lot o' money for houses but they think dis only 'cause you want dem to forget 'bout us black fellas here in da bush. They think all dis money for houses still no good if we not gonna get back tribal land.

All you done since you bin made big fella boss number one is say we can have free lawyer, free dentist, and free pill. When we try to get lawyer they tells us dat we gotta ring you in Canberra but we got no money for dat. When we try to get dentist they tell us we not real Aboriginal. But when black woman gets sick they give her da pill whether she want it or not or they cut her with the knife so she no have any more black babies.

You bin talkin' 'bout dis for long time now you say black women havin' too many babies but you not bin doin' anything 'bout food for these babies—all you doin' is talkin'.

You tell us dat when you white fellas become boss dat we gonna be equal. You tell us dat some your tribe want to help us but some your tribe more equal than others. We bin tried to talk with these fellas for long time now but they not interested in us.

Before you fellas become boss of dis place last year you tell us Dr Cairns[1] him bin gonna make us equal like your other friends in the Labor Party but Dr Cairns never bin one to talk with us. You say yous all socialist and want us all equal but Dr Cairns just like all the rest of yous. Him still bullyman anyway.

Only few of you fellas bin showin' any interest in us. Dat Tom Uren[2] fellah him not bad bloke but dat Jimmy Keeffe[3]—him da fella. Dat Manfred Cross[4] fella 'im good bloke too. He pretty quiet but 'im don' go roun' talkin' 'bout what 'im bin doin' for us.

You not doin' anythin' yet. Anyone think you doin' us a favour when you talkin' 'bout us. You not doin' us any favours. When you start doin' somethin', you only payin' your rent.

1973

GERRY BOSTOCK
b. 1942

Playwright, poet and film-maker Gerry Bostock was born in Grafton, NSW, of Bundjalung descent. A founder of the Aboriginal Black Theatre in the 1970s, he

1   Jim Cairns (1914–2003), left-wing activist and Labor politician during the 1960s and '70s.
2   Tom Uren (b. 1921), left-wing activist and Labor politician from the late 1950s until 1990.
3   Queensland-based left-wing activist and Labor politician.
4   Labor member for the federal seat of Brisbane (1961–1975 and 1980–1990), member of FCAATSI and highly respected agitator for Aboriginal social justice.

co-directed the documentary film *Lousy Little Sixpence* (1981), which examined the employment conditions of children forcibly removed by the Aborigines Protection Board. *Here Comes the Nigger* was first produced by the Black Theatre in 1976.

From *Here Comes the Nigger*
Act I, Scene II

SAM *and* VERNA *can be heard coming up the stairs laughing and joking. The door opens.* VERNA *enters carrying the groceries. She crosses the room and puts the bag on the table and looks around the room.* SAM *enters, closes the door and takes a few paces and stops. He puts the suitcase down.*

SAM: [*smiling*] Well, don't just stand there. Go and put the tucker away, woman.

VERNA: [*She picks up the groceries and turns to him, smiling.*] Still the male chauvinist, hey, big brother?

SAM: Old Aboriginal custom.

VERNA: [*She crosses to the kitchen as* SAM *picks up the suitcase.*] You'll never change.

SAM: I hope not.

VERNA: So do I, big brother!

SAM: [*He crosses the room and places the suitcase down by the settee.*] Thanks kid. You made my day.

VERNA: [*from the kitchen*] Don't mention it. Do the same for a black-fella!

SAM: Oooh, you're all heart, kid. You're all heart.

VERNA: [*re-entering the room*] Well, how's my big-time brother, the poet?

SAM: [*grins*] Still struggling, sis. Still struggling. And how's my triple certificated nehse?

VERNA: Oh, Sam … [*She crosses the room and hugs him.*] Gee, it's good to see you, Sam. It's really good to be back home.

SAM: It's good to have you back.

VERNA: Miss me …?

SAM: I sure did … we both did. We missed you a lot. [*He holds her at arm's length.*]

VERNA: I missed you too. [*She kisses him. He hesitates and they both seem embarrassed.*]

SAM: How … anyway, how'd you like to hear some good, black music?

VERNA: Yeah … yeah, I'd like that … [*She regains her composure.*] How about something to drink … you want the usual?

SAM: Plenty o' pips in the lemon juice, hey!

VERNA: Sure thing, big brother. [*She crosses to the kitchen.* SAM *goes to the stereo.*]

SAM: Ya hear anything of Bobby Randall in Adelaide?

VERNA: Yeah. He's lecturing at the Torrensville School of Advanced Education.

SAM: Oh …? What's he doing there? [*He feels the records, searching for the one he requires.*]

VERNA: The Black Studies Course. He's teaching black kids about culture and identity.

SAM: Well, that's something ya don't get in the average school.

VERNA: Yeah. Not even the white kids can get it.

SAM: I'm glad somebody's gettin' through to our own kids … and if anyone can do it, it'll be someone like Bobby Randall. He's a really great guy.

VERNA: He sure is. And he's a real black-fella, too; not like some o' them coconuts!

SAM: Coconuts …? What do you mean?

VERNA: Brown on the outside and white on the inside.

SAM: [*finds the record and puts it on the turn-table*] I got Bobby's latest record the other day … listen to this.

VERNA: [*Enters the room with two drinks. She places one on the bookshelf and approaches* SAM *with the other as he plays the record.*] Gettin' any lately, big brother? [*She takes his right hand and places the drink in it. He gives her a smile.*]

SAM: I know love's suppose t'be blind … but I ain't found anyone that blind enough, yet!

VERNA: [*giving him a sexy hug*] Nemmine. Ah still loves ya, honey! [*He gives her a playful slap on the backside.*]

SAM: [*smiles*] Garn, ya gin. I bet ya say that t'all us handsome black-fellas!

VERNA: [*She snaps her fingers and wriggles her hips.*] Whell … white might be right, but black is beautiful! Anyway, I'd rather be a slack black than an uptight white!

SAM: [*grins*] All-a-tarm, baby. All-a-tarm! [*They both laugh.*] Come on. Let's sit down.

VERNA: Wait'll I get my drink, hey. [*She gets her drink and tastes it.*]

VERNA: Mmmm. I needed this. [*They cross to the settee.*] I see Billy's put up some new posters.

SAM: Yeah. He likes to change them now and again.

VERNA: How's he been? [*They sit down.*]

SAM: [*grins*] Bloody unbearable. Ya wouldn't believe it … [*She turns to him and smiles.*]

VERNA: I know what's wrong with him. He's sex-starved, the bastard!

SAM: This could be true!

VERNA: Too bloody right, it's true! But then, so am I.

SAM: You gins are all the same, hey?

VERNA: I don't see any of you black-fellas knockin' us back. [*They laugh as they sip their drinks.*]

SAM: By the way, I got a letter from the Aboriginal Publications Foundation yesterday.

VERNA: Yeah?

SAM: I sent them a couple o' the poems ya wrote out for me before ya went to Adelaide.

VERNA: What'd they say?

SAM: Aaagh, not much. They just sent me a cheque for fifty dollars.

VERNA: [*She smiles, then squeezes his hand.*] Gee, that's great, big brother. Fame and fortune at last, hey?

SAM: They can shove the fame. All I want's the fortune.

VERNA: Ya startin' t'sound like one o'them Black Bureaucrats from Canberra, now.

SAM: [*smiles*] How about that.

VERNA: I got me doubts about you, Sam. [*They smile warmly at each other.*]

SAM: How was South Australia, anyway?

VERNA: Why d'ya think I came home!

SAM: It's like that, hey?

VERNA: Yeah. It gave me the shits. It really did!

SAM: Billy said you were working with some black-fellas on a reserve … what were they like?

VERNA: The blacks were good. The whites were shit-house.

SAM: [*holds her hand*] Ya want t'talk about it, sis? [*She looks at him in silence.*]

SAM: Well, what about it, sis?

VERNA: Ya know, Sam, before I went to the Centre I use to think us Kuuris on the coast had it bad, but truly, you should see how some o' the country blacks have to live. It's really bad.

SAM: I thought you were suppose to be based in Adelaide?

VERNA: [*She regains her composure and sips her drink.*] I was there for a couple of weeks but then I went up to the Centre with a Medical team from Royal Adelaide.

SAM: [*smiles*] Learn a bit, did ya?

VERNA: You better believe it.

SAM: Yeah? What was it like?

VERNA: Bloody incredible! Jeeze, the whites out there reminded me of the Hitler Youth and the Pious Pioneer all rolled into one.

SAM: [*gives a short laugh*] Now that's laying it on a bit thick, isn't it?

VERNA: Oh, Sam. If only you could see, and could see just some of the kids I had to treat …

Ya know, big brother, I thought I was tough … I mean, really tough. I thought nothing, nothing at all could get under my skin until I saw our little Black babies out there.

Medical terminologies like trachoma, malnutrition, scurvy and scabies didn't mean a thing to me when I saw those kids out there. All I could think of when I saw them was that they were our future Black Nation; a Black Nation with pussed-up eyes, bloated bellies and bodies riddled with sores and bleeding scabs … if you could see something like that, Sam, you wouldn't forget it in a hurry.

SAM: But you're a trained nurse. You've seen worse things than that.

VERNA: Yes. And I tried to be cold-blooded about it at first, but seeing so many sick black babies in so many different areas just turned my gut. A person can only take so much …

SAM: What about the Department … what are they doing about it?

VERNA: Sweet F.A.! The bastards don't give a damn, and besides, the only way blacks can get anything out of the Department is to shack up with the mongrels who control the purse-strings.

SAM: But what about the blacks who work for the Department …?

VERNA: Them blacks in Canberra are all the same. They're nothing but Black Bureaucrats; Black puppets dancing to the white man's tune.

SAM: But surely some of them are at least trying to do something?

VERNA: Look brother, if by chance them Blacks in Canberra manage to get off their ahrse and go to an Aboriginal Reserve, they don't live with the grass-roots people and experience conditions for themselves; no, instead they go and stay in posh hotels where they can go to buffet luncheons and have room-service with hot and cold running women. Why should they worry about the Blacks? They've got it made.

SAM: [placing an arm around her] It's okay, sis. You're home now. [He sips his drink.] Mmmmm. You still fix a mean drop.

VERNA: [Recovering her composure, she lifts her head and kisses him on the cheek.] Thanks, Sam.

SAM: [He flips the lid of his watch and feels the dial for the time.] Well … Billy should be home soon.

VERNA: Mmmm. I might go and have a shower and get freshened up.

SAM: Good. When he comes in I'll get Billy to go up the pub and get something more to drink.

VERNA: [getting up and preparing to leave] Good thinking ninety-nine. And get him to pick up a flagon o' Red. [She goes toward the bathroom door and turns.] Ya know what they say about the Old Red Ned … puts lead in ya pencil!

SAM: S'no good having lead in your pencil if you got no bastard to write to … [They both laugh. A pause. Sam smiles.] Garn, peasant. Go and have ya shower.

VERNA: Okay bundji … I'm goin', I'm goin'.

[She enters the bathroom. SAM gets up and goes over to the lounge chair and feels for the guitar, finds it, picks it up and then sits down and begins to tune it. Sound FX of flushing toilet. VERNA comes out, picks up her suitcase and goes to the bedroom. SAM sings a song. VERNA enters the room with a towel wrapped around her and goes to the bathroom as the song ends. SAM again tunes the guitar. Sound FX of shower. The bathroom door is slightly ajar.]

VERNA: [from bathroom] How are your studies coming along? [SAM is lightly strumming the guitar.]

SAM: [smiles] Got meself a new tutor. [He stops strumming.]

VERNA: What happened to the last one ya had … that nice Mr Bates?

SAM: Yates!

VERNA: What?

SAM: [He puts the guitar aside and raises his voice.] My old tutor was Mr Yates; not Bates! He had to leave town for a while. [He gets up and goes to the table and pours himself another drink.]

VERNA: Who's ya new tutor?

SAM: It's a Miss Odette O'Brien. [*He sips his drink and smiles. Sound FX of shower turns off.*]

VERNA: Who did you say?

SAM: A Miss Odette O'Brien. She's comin' around t'morra afternoon. You can meet her then, if ya like? [*He goes back to the chair.*] Hope she's a good sort. But ya never know ya luck in a big city. [*He sips his drink and almost spills it at* VERNA's *next remark.*]

VERNA: Are you another one of these black-fellas who talk black and sleep white!

SAM: [*sitting down, and taking occasional sips*] What did ya say? A what?

VERNA: She a gubbah chic?

SAM: I dunno … yeah … I suppose she is … [*Sound FX of shower back on.* SAM *ponders.*] Billy asked me that too … but I wonder what makes Verna say something like that … [*Raising his voice*] Why did ya say that, Verna?

> [*Sound FX off. The bathroom door opens and* VERNA *pokes her head out. She has a towel draped around her body and a smaller one covering her wet hair. She has a worried expression on her face.*]

VERNA: I just don't want t'see ya get hurt, that's all. [*She goes back into the bathroom. Annoyed,* SAM *rolls a cigarette.*]

SAM: What are ya talking about? She's only going to tutor me; nothing else … anyway, what harm could a white girl do here … [*Looking hurt*] After all, I'm just a poor, helpless blind man.

VERNA: [*grinning, coming back to the door*] Helpless, my black foot! [*More tenderly*] Look, Sam. All whites want to do is to change you into a black version of themselves. They want to civilise the native, and when they've had their bit, when they've got what they wanted and ripped-off as much as they could, they'll piss you off. And what will you be then: just another screwed-up black-fella! [*She re-enters the bathroom.* SAM *is silent for a moment as he expresses disbelief at* VERNA's *comment. Sound FX back on.*]

SAM: [*chuckles*] What d'ya reckon she's gonna do? Come in here, get her gear off and say, 'Here I am, Darkie … let it all hang out!' [SAM *continues to chuckle.* VERNA *can be heard laughing in the shower.*]

VERNA: Hey, Sam! You better watch it, bud. You know what they say: 'If ya start mixing with white stuff too much it might rub off on ya!'

> [SAM *is about to answer when* BILLY *bursts into the room. He looks excited as he glances about. Startled,* SAM *looks toward him.*]

BILLY: Hey, Sam! Where is she?

VERNA: In here … waiting! [BILLY *gives a joyful yell.*]

BILLY: You little beauty! [*He strips off his shirt as he moves to the bathroom.* SAM *follows his every movement and smiles humorously, if somewhat uncomfortably. With a contemptuous grin to* SAM, BILLY *throws his shirt to the floor and enters the bathroom.* VERNA *squeals with laughter as* BILLY *wrestles with her.*]

BILLY: Hey, Sam! Come an' look at this! [*Both* BILLY *and* VERNA *are laughing.*]

VERNA: Billy … cut that out!

BILLY: Sam! Come on in … COME ON!

VERNA: Billy! Bill … OOoooohhh … EEeeeee … Billllly … stop that ya mongrel!

[SAM *walks across the room, feels the shirt, picks it up, folds it and puts it on the settee. He then goes to the table and begins to clear it. The laughter still continues in the bathroom.*]

Fade out

1977

MONICA CLARE
1924–1973

Born near Goondiwindi, Queensland, Monica was the daughter of an Aboriginal shearer and an English woman. Following the death of her mother in 1931, Monica and her brother Dan lived in various homes in Sydney before being fostered to the Woodbury family on a farm near Spencer, NSW. Although treated with affection by the Woodburys, the children were removed to a home by government officials in 1935 and separated. Monica worked in domestic service for numerous families before beginning work at a cigarette factory. Following this she became a waitress and studied at night school to become a secretary.

Her interest in Aboriginal social justice grew from the late 1940s when she became a regular visitor to the Bellwood Aboriginal Reserve while staying with the Woodburys, who had retired to Nambucca Heads. In 1953 she married and had a daughter, the marriage later ending in divorce. In 1962 Monica married union official and Aboriginal rights advocate Leslie Forsyth Clare and became actively involved in the union's women's committee. She and Les travelled around NSW, highlighting the appalling living conditions and racial discrimination inflicted upon Aboriginal people.

Prior to the 1967 referendum, Clare became secretary of the Aboriginal committee of the South Coast Labor Council, often writing to politicians and passing on complaints of discrimination. She helped to establish housing and low-interest loans for Aborigines, and in 1968, as secretary to the South Coast Illawarra tribe, led the campaign to re-house the Aboriginal communities there. A delegate to many FCAATSI conferences, she was also active on the International Women's Day, May Day and National Aborigines Day committees. Her autobiographical novel *Karobran: The story of an Aboriginal girl* (1978) was published posthumously.

From *Karobran*
Chapter 4

On the train, the woman welfare officer who was seated opposite Isabelle and Morris could do nothing to lessen the shock they were in, as the children stared backwards at the long shiny railway lines that were taking them further and further away from their Dad.

Days later in Sydney, the woman rang a bell that seemed to open a small gate in a high wooden fence at the girls' home. She handed Isabelle and her brother over to the Matron, who sternly told them that if they did not behave and stop their crying, she would send Morris to the boys' home.

Then the Matron rang a bell, and another girl much older than Isabelle appeared. Hand in hand, and bewildered at what was going on, Isabelle and

Morris were led down stone steps through another gate and into a big bathroom, where the bath was built up high. Standing beside it was a woman the children very quickly learned to call 'Nurse'.

'Come along!' Nurse said sharply to the older girl. 'Get those rags off them, and burn them at once.'

Then she looked down her nose at the two naked figures standing in front of her, and without a sound she made signs for them to climb the steps into the bath. She told the older girl to scrub them hard with the brush, while she stood stiffly by and watched them with disgust.

For most of the day, Isabelle had to go to the school that was built in the same grounds but sometimes she could look out the window, and see Morris and other smaller children being taken by an older girl for a walk around the huge lawn.

At mealtime the two children would be seated in the same dining room, but talking was forbidden and no one dared to ask for more than was put in front of them; and when the nurse who was always seated at a table near the door said, 'Start!' or 'Finish!' everyone obeyed immediately.

Never before had Isabelle and Morris been put to bed so early, so that when their beds were near each other, they would laugh and talk loudly, forgetting that there were others nearby who wanted to sleep, until they would either hear the stern voice of the nurse or feel her hand on their bottoms.

One day the nurse told Isabelle that she was to fetch Morris and take him around to Matron's office. Isabelle was frightened because she had heard other girls say that when anyone played up, they were sent to Matron's office for punishment. Hand in hand they were dawdling along, when Matron's white uniform flashed around the corner in front of them and she said, 'Come along now!'

'Please Matron, what have we done wrong?' asked Isabelle as Matron took hold of Morris's hand.

Matron looked down and smiled at Isabelle. 'You haven't done anything wrong, Isabelle!' she said. 'I just want you both to meet someone.' Then as Isabelle looked towards Matron's office, she could see a strange woman sitting in a chair smiling at them. Matron went and sat in her chair before telling the children:

'This lady's name is Miss Manbury, and she lives in the country and she would like to take both of you up there, to live with her.' Neither of the children spoke for a few seconds: then Morris asked in a shy voice, 'Yer got any sheep?'

The women smiled at each other. Then Miss Manbury said, 'No lad, but we have got cows, horses, ducks, chooks and dogs; and a big river that you can catch some fish in sometimes—if you're lucky—and we've got pigs, too.'

'That's great,' said Morris with a broad grin, and he felt for his sister's hand to get her approval.

'Mind you,' said Matron, 'you'll have to be good, otherwise Miss Manbury will bring you back here again.'

They talked more about it.

'Right,' said Matron, as she rose from her chair. 'Come along, and let's see what's in the store. We'll have to fit you out now, because Miss Manbury wants to leave early in the morning.'

Carrying smart new suitcases filled with new clothes, Isabelle and Morris were so excited as they sat in the train. When Miss Manbury led them from the railway station towards a broad river, they were anxious until she assured them that the launch was safe. Neither of them had even seen one before, but they soon settled down.

'Look Isabelle, look at the crayfish!' shouted Morris in the launch, getting excited again.

'No, lad, they're not crayfish,' Miss Manbury told him, 'they are called crabs. You can pick them up, but be careful, because they have nippers and they bite sometimes, so watch out.'

Morris leaned further over the side to get a better look, and Miss Manbury caught hold of him just in time to stop him from falling overboard.

Isabelle settled down beside Miss Manbury and smiled up at her, asking, ''Ave yer got any kids?'

Miss Manbury smiled back and said, 'Just you and Morris me girl, but there's only my brother and me, and it gets very lonely sometimes. So we are looking forward to both of you being with us for a long time. We do have a lot of visitors though, mostly relatives, and then the house is not big enough! But you'll find out all about that, when you start to help me clean it out.'

Isabelle felt contentment for the first time in a long while; and Morris, sliding closer to the other side of Miss Manbury, put a hand through her arm, asking: 'What's your name again?'

As she put a gloved hand on Morris's hand Miss Manbury said, 'Carmel's my first name, and Manbury's far too long isn't it? How would you like to call me Auntie?'

'Yeah, Aunt,' they shouted out together, so loud that the man who was driving the launch turned around and smiled. Then they settled back and enjoyed the scenery.

Isabelle looked about her, and thought how beautiful it all really was, with the wide river going on for miles and miles, and the tall mountains on both sides of them. Everything was lovely and green, and now and then they would go past a house with lots of fruit on the trees. She really had not seen anything like this before.

Aunt broke her silence and brought Isabelle's thoughts back to the present by saying:

'See that house up there, the one with the red roof on it? Well, that's your new home.'

'It's gone, it's gone!' shouted Morris, as he stood up in the launch, and for the second time Aunt saved him from falling overboard.

'No son, it's not gone, we just went round a bend in the river,' said Aunt, 'you'll see it again in a minute. Look, there it is now.'

'I can see it,' Morris shouted, then as he looked over at his sister, he asked, 'Isabelle, can you see it? It's on top of a hill.'

Isabelle had been looking in silence, but the only thing that she could really see was the verandah that went right around the house. She was still seeing the verandah even after they had left the launch and were walking up the hill towards it, but as she got closer, she could see the flower garden that was in front of it; and she smiled to herself. This verandah could not be sad for her, because the flowers were too beautiful.

A man came hurrying down the hill towards them. Isabelle liked him at once, and as he smiled, Aunt introduced them all affectionately.

'This is my brother, and your new Uncle,' she said.

'We'll have to feed them up, won't we?' said Uncle, as he ruffled Morris's hair. 'Come on, young man, let you and me go down to the wharf, and get your cases, and we can have a yarn about your trip.'

Then he and Morris hurried off chatting together as though they had always known each other. Aunt and Isabelle continued up the hill to the house; and as Isabelle was being shown from one room to the other she knew that she and Morris would be all right here, as she could feel the love in it.

The kitchen which was built separate from the house, was almost as big. The long dining table and stools that went with it suddenly reminded Isabelle of the ones that Ma had in the cook-house on the station, and her mind went back. Aunt, noticing that something was wrong, tried to cheer her up.

'See all these pictures on the walls, Isabelle, it's due to be papered again, and you can give me a hand just as soon as we get enough newspapers saved up.'

Isabelle could not help smiling at that. Then on the river side of the kitchen Aunt opened a small board window, and there at the bottom of the hill sat Uncle and Morris yarning away.

Just then Isabelle noticed under the window the lovely pink flowers growing along a small garden fence, and she said: 'Gee, Aunt, they're pretty.'

'Yes, Isabelle, I call them button roses,' replied Aunt, and she pointed out to Isabelle things that were growing in the garden. 'Over there is where I grow things I need for cooking, like parsley, sage and mint.'

All that afternoon was spent showing Isabelle and Morris over the farm. The dairy came first, where the cream was separated from the milk and made into butter, the shed where feed was kept and where pumpkins and gramma and melons were put to ripen, then to the orchard where almost every kind of fruit tree was laden with fruit; then to the cow bails and pig pens, the big patch of peas and beans that were growing from one side of the rise in the hill to the other. Above the vegetable garden Isabelle found a flat rock with a big hole in the middle of it, which still held water from the last rains. As she stood on top of it, she found out that she could see for miles and miles everywhere, almost to the top of the big mountain behind her.

She was reluctant to leave.

The two adults smiled at each other when they saw the happiness in Isabelle's face.

'Do you like that rock?' asked Uncle.

'Oh yes!' replied Isabelle. 'I can see everything from up here, and when I look down, I can see myself in the water.'

'You can have the rock, if you like,' said Uncle, still smiling at her, and he winked at Aunt.

'You mean it!' exclaimed Isabelle, sounding surprised.

'Yes: and we'll call it Isabelle's rock, if you like,' said Uncle.

Isabelle bounded off the rock, and pulled Uncle and Aunt down to her size and kissed them on the cheek, and they blushed. As they were walking back to the house, Isabelle kept turning back to look at her rock, when she heard Uncle say:

'We'll have to find you something now, won't we, Morris?'

'I know what he'd like,' said Aunt with a smile, as Morris, all excited, ran backwards down the hill in front of her.

'What's that?' asked Uncle.

'A bent pin, and some dough to go fishing with,' said Aunt.

1978

KEVIN GILBERT
1933–1993

Born in Wiradjuri country at Condoblin, NSW, Gilbert was a leading poet, playwright, essayist, editor and political activist. Raised by relatives and in welfare homes after he was orphaned at seven, he worked as a seasonal agricultural worker and station manager. In 1957 he was sentenced to life imprisonment when his wife was killed in a domestic dispute.

Gilbert learned to read while in prison and became interested in art and literature. He discovered a gift for lino printmaking and is considered to be the first Aboriginal printmaker. In 1968, while still in prison, he wrote the first play by an Aboriginal author: *The Cherry Pickers* (1971/1988). Gilbert was paroled in 1971 and *The Cherry Pickers* was performed in August that year in Sydney, the first production of an Aboriginal play. He disowned the 1971 publication of his poems, *End of Dreamtime*, as his editor made significant alterations without permission. The corrected volume, *People Are Legends: Aboriginal poems* (1978), is considered to be Gilbert's first authorised collection of poetry.

Gilbert joined the Aboriginal Black Power movement and played an important role in establishing the 1972 Aboriginal Tent Embassy in Canberra. Beginning with *Because a White Man'll Never Do It* (1973), he wrote and edited a number of political works arguing for Aboriginal land rights and the restoration of Aboriginal cultural and spiritual autonomy. His oral history *Living Black: Blacks talk to Kevin Gilbert* (1977) won the 1978 National Book Council Award. In 1988 he coordinated the Treaty '88 Campaign and wrote *Aboriginal Sovereignty: Justice, the law and the land*, promoting Aboriginal sovereignty and treaty.

Many of Gilbert's books combine art, photography and language. He helped to organise the photographic exhibition *Inside Black Australia*, and used this title for a groundbreaking anthology of Aboriginal poetry, which won HREOC's 1988 Human Rights Award for Literature. Gilbert refused the award, protesting that his people were still deprived of human rights in their own land. The Kevin Gilbert Memorial Trust was established in 1993 to advance his political, literary and artistic aspirations. His other books include *Child's Dreaming* (1992) and *Black from the Edge* (1994).

People *Are* Legends

Kill the legend
Butcher it
With your acute cynicisms
Your paternal superfluities
With your unwise wisdom   5
Kill the legend
Obliterate it
With your atheism
Your fraternal hypocrisies
With your primal urge of miscegenation   10
Kill the legend
Devaluate it
With your sophistry
Your baseless rhetoric
Your lusting material concepts   15
Your groundless condescension
Kill it
Vitiate the seed
Crush the root-plant
All this   20
And more you must needs do
In order
To form a husk of a man
To the level and in your own image
Whiteman   25
                                                          1978

From *The Cherry Pickers*
Act 3, Scene 2

At the old Cherry Tree—King Eagle.

King Eagle stands down stage, right of centre. He is a huge old cherry tree with twisted boughs wrought with life's growth. His leaves are plentiful but brown and dying off.

Lighting simulates a hot parched atmosphere. Tall sparse tussocks of grass are wilted and browned by the summer heat.

A breeze moves the leaves and small eddies of dust.

A whisper of Aboriginal tribal music is heard, didgerridoo and bullroarer. Faint voices moan in corroboree, spirits from the past.

TOMMLO enters. Looking directly at audience, he stares unseeing, discomfortingly hard at them. He glances around the orchard and stares again at audience with look of despair, pain, hopelessness, as his face reflects his inner loss and uncertainty. In his left hand is an old carved Churinga stone. Bullroarer sounds softly as he places the stone on the ground reverently. He faces King Eagle, rips at his clothes and discards upper sections.

He approaches King Eagle in small quick nimble steps, whirls around, facing audience, and angrily throws away his belt and trousers. He whirls around in several flexing leaps. Tempo and volume of tribal music ascends. He scoops up a handful of earth, swirls it towards base of tree, slaps leg with right hand in time to haunting didgerridoo and corroboree chants. As he faces audience, music fades.

TOMMLO: [*yelling*] ZEENA! Zeena—ZEEEENNNAAA!!!! What the bloody hell is taking you so long? ZEENNAAA!!!

ZEENA: [*off-stage*] Alright, ALRIGHT! I'm coming Tommlo.

    [*Enter ZEENA, carrying a cumbersome bundle: A sugar-bag, a brown paper parcel and two spears under her arms.*]

I get on OK in my rightful role as your gin and your wife Tommlo, but I am *not* accustomed to acting as a bloody myall bush donkey or workhorse for you!

TOMMLO: It's the woman's place to carry the family possessions, Zeena.

ZEENA: Since when has the woman have to carry the flamin' spears? You didn't carry any.

TOMMLO: Zeena, I had to carry the Bullroarer and the Sacred Churinga stone that I found on Corroboree Hill.

ZEENA: How do you know it *is* a Sacred Churinga? Just because you 'found' it in the old place?

TOMMLO: This is *not* the time—or the place to argue. I *know*—I—*feel* it, woman. I feel it an' recognise it for what it *is*!

ZEENA: Recognise it do you? *Your* feelings have been wrong before today. Remember Kathy and your feelings that you were *meant* for each other? That was until I smashed a wine bottle on your thick head for being so damned silly!

TOMMLO: OK OK!! I was wrong then—but that feeling sprung from my guts. This one is straight from my heart!

ZEENA: [*laughing*] Not your *guts* Tommlo, but from what hangs from it! I never realised that you'd grown so you could tell the difference between the heart and the other part of the body that makes you do the things you do!

TOMMLO: [*pained, accusing*] Zeena, Zeena, *our* People are dying. We've lost our way. Their hearts are breaking because they have been denied justice and human rights, because they have been denied their rightful place in this our land and—the only thing you can contribute is your silly laughter!!

ZEENA: [*hurt*] Tommlo? That's not right, Tommlo. I'll do anythin' to help them. I want to stop the starvation, the needless dyin', the endless pain too. I *do*!!

TOMMLO: Undress! Get those skirts off!

ZEENA: This is impossible! Tommlo, we can't go back in time!

TOMMLO: We can *change* things. We *have* to change things. It is our destiny to find our human way.

ZEENA: I *want* to help. I would do any thing Tommlo to have stopped our babies from dying. I would do anything to bring my babies back to life and make our living easier—*but we can't!! We can't go back. We can't change what has happened!!*

TOMMLO: We've got to. We've *got to find our place*!! Our rightful place. Not a 'place' where we've been kicked and trodden, smashed and starved, killed and conquered until we take the shape of whitemen—*imitation whitemen.* I'm a *man*!! I'm gunna *live* as a man, and by the livin' Jesus I'm gunna *die* as a man! I'm gunna *fight* for the right for my kids to *live*, and to live as *whole* human beings!!!

ZEENA: They were *my* babies too, Tommlo. Mine too!!!

[TOMMLO *springs towards the base of the huge tree, he pulls the tussocks of grass together then springs back and rips open the brown paper parcel. ZEENA sits slumped with head in hands, emotionally overcome, near the parcels and spears. TOMMLO tears a small decorated shield from parcel, picks up bullroarer, leaps to pile of grass. He rubs the bullroarer on the shield to spark off the fire. ZEENA has slowly, tiredly, risen and removed her blouse.*]

TOMMLO: Enough!! This *has* to be done!

ZEENA: [*defiantly*] If it *has* to be done, then why ain't you and I, two Australian Aborigines, dancing this Sacred Dance under an Australian gum-tree? A gum-tree with the Sacred Bora Ground symbols carved deep into its guts? *We* two are corroboreeing beneath a cherry-tree. Doesn't this prove that *some* advance has been made because 'cherry tree' means money—*and* food?

[TOMMLO *leaps up in fury and cuffs* ZEENA *across the head with his open hand.*]

TOMMLO: Shut up!!

[*He goes to the sugar-bag, picks up a wooden boondi and a glass jar containing gum 'blood'. He passes the boondi and jar to* ZEENA *and commands*]

Now!!

ZEENA: This blood has jellied together!

TOMMLO: Use it!

[*He kneels, facing audience, hands at side, head back.* ZEENA's *face twists as she dips the boondi applicator into the jar of 'blood' and taps it rapidly on his shoulders. As sufficient 'blood' flows on, she quickly presses featherdown onto the 'blood' to form patterns.*]

TOMMLO: [*pained*] *You* don't believe our culture should exist, either?!!

ZEENA: [*tremulous, positive*] I! Of *course* I believe our old culture should exist!—Culture is the development of man, it is the outward expression of man's inner beauty and is relevant to—and through *every* age!

[ZEENA *rapidly taps his arms, his thighs and decorates with down.*]

TOMMLO: Then *what* are you complaining about?

ZEENA: Oh, I'm not complaining. I am merely trying to tell you that we can't live, nor find a new life, by embracing a stone-age identity in this nuclear age. We should be rightfully proud of our old culture for it was the expression, the cry, the search for beauty by man. *This truth* we should hold and advance by, not revert to that cultural age. We must advance, must mature and must never, never revert back, for life is a constant process of growth.

TOMMLO: Our growth has been stopped—through this we can grow again! We have nothing save our culture. We *must* git back our culture!!

ZEENA: [*sorrowfully, gently*] Our culture, the age of our culture has passed for we have outgrown it! Man must go forward, must advance with the times, the age!

TOMMLO: We *must* keep our identity! Without it we have *lost all. Do* you see us advance?

[TOMMLO *attempts to light fire again.*]

ZEENA: [*listlessly*] I have some Federal safety matches here, Tommlo. They'll be much quicker.

TOMMLO: [*savagely*] *This* is how it *has* to be done. Now shut up and git undressed!!

ZEENA: *No. No!!* Not everything. *Not Everything!!*

TOMMLO: Everything! The lot! Git the bloody lot orf! Are you frightened that God made your body black, ugly and unclean so it can't face the clean air of day without shame!! *Are you ashamed of your black body?!*

ZEENA: I—No! It's not *that* but I—

TOMMLO: Then show yourself as you were made, woman!

> [TOMMLO *leaps to the hessian sugar-bag, pulls out rings of red, white, black feathered symbols placing them either side of the tussock at the base of the tree, parallel with a perpendicular blaze of a white feathered shaft, as* ZEENA *slowly, hesitantly undresses.*]

Help me. Come on woman, help me with these!

ZEENA: No woman is allowed to touch the Sacred Churinga symbols. To touch is to die.

TOMMLO: It is *different* now. There is no one left out of our tribespeople to help me!

> [TOMMLO *moves at a furious leaping pace, kicking aside sticks, leaves, grass and pushes the circlet symbols into the earth. He leaps to the paper parcel, grabs several feathers and forms arm-leg patterns on circlets, while* ZEENA, *in a leaping crouch, places the other symbols beside him. She squats on ground, hands between legs, and zig-zags in kangaroo hops between the symbols. Occasionally she sits up, scratches ribs with forepaws, nibbles at grass.* TOMMLO *has begun his corroboree. Aboriginal ghost music ascends.* ZEENA *sits upright, scratches rib in kangaroo pose.*]

ZEENA: This is wrong, only *learned* ones can do this!

TOMMLO: [*corroboreeing*] Uh—uh—gnhuuu—there are *no* Learned Ones left, therefore *we* must do it!!

> [ZEENA *moves again in the Kangaroo dance.*]

ZEENA: But I am a *woman* and the sacred ceremonies would not produce miracles if a woman was even present in the old days.

> [TOMMLO *leaps behind her, spear upraised as he stalks his sacrificial victim, corroboreeing, leaping thrusting the aim of the spear.*]

TOMMLO: The old days have *gone!*

> [TOMMLO *leaps forward, twirls, springs again toward her his spear ready to thrust—he stops, as if confused, as she glances up at him.*]

ZEENA: No!! No!!! What are you doing?? If the old days are gone, then what are you doin', what *are* we doin' here???

TOMMLO: It's alright! We're doin' what we *must*, now *shut up!!—Dance!!*

ZEENA: Six strong warriors and the Songman must attend these rites. You are no Songman an' I am no Warrior.

TOMMLO: Our Songmen have all died. Only you and I believe, and it is said: 'Where two or three are gathered together in *my* name ...'

ZEENA: God said that, *not* the Corroboree Men.

TOMMLO: This dance isn't for the Corroboree Men either. It's for *us*, a People. It's for us *blacks* and our right to live!!!

ZEENA: This is wrong, Tommlo. We can't go back in time and change things!

TOMMLO: We can't go back in time—but we can bring time back to us. Dance, dance!! Keep movin' or so help me Christ!!

[*Tribal music ascends.*]

ZEENA: [*afraid*] Those were cave-age days, the Stone Age. This—this is an anachronism! The truths from the beginning of time—the truth of two hundred years ago can't be given rebirth and become the truth applicable to today!

TOMMLO: *This* is not the time to argue! What are you trying to say?

ZEENA: I can't say it. Do you remember the poem that Bidjarng wrote? The one about true *truth* and each man's right being another's wrong?

TOMMLO: So what the hell does that mean?

ZEENA: [*reciting*]

> I *know* you're right—when you claim I'm wrong
> that I'm out of tune with your own sad song
> For you *believe* and to me, it seems
> that your feet of clay keeps your heart from dreams
> and away from a Nobler Truth.
> Yet you believe, and I know I know
> that man must crawl before he grows
> and man must *leap* and often fall
> yet aeons pass and *still* you crawl
> *still* you believe
> and I know, I grieve—I know.

[*The last words are uttered as a sob-sighing of spirit.*]

TOMMLO: What does all that supposed to mean?

ZEENA: It means the Jews shouldn't go and build a Golden Calf again, just because it belongs to a story in Moses' time. Nor should we attempt to imprison the spirit of man, nor his attempts to mature. Just because we *believe* something, doesn't necessarily mean it is right. It is little more than one hundred years ago since a high court in England tried a pig, yes, an animal on a charge of witchcraft. The pig had to stand in the dock—and the court found it guilty as charged and sentenced it to be burnt!!!

The poem means we should grow out of superstition. It means we should not crawl forever, nor leap, then crawl back into the protective past and become blinded by cowardice and bigotry, too afraid to grow again, to leap again. It means we should leap to our full height. We might fall, but we must be prepared to fall and leap again. We must hold to a truth only until such time as we can think it out and then supersede it by a higher truth.

TOMMLO: Zeena, this is not just for the old culture. This is for the goin' forward. This is our hope for a People. It means we find we're trapped—and we've *got to leap*. Without hope, without justice, without *true identity* a People die! *Come dance!! Dance!! Dance!!!*

[ZEENA *remains squatting.*]

Don't you understand, Zeena? I've looked at life, the world, the whiteman's way. I've looked through a whiteman's eyes and I was lost. [*Pause.*] I ain't lost anymore. I am a *nothing*. The trees, the grass, the river, the earth is life, is *everything*. I am *nothing*, a *nothing*. Now that tree is *me*. It is all of me. I am that tree. I am nothing, yet I am somethin' because the earth is me. These rocks are me and I am the movin' soul of them all. See, I looked at the tree and said that is a tree. I kept it all separate and alien, but now, like the old days, I am a nothing but that *tree* is me and I am a something and when I die I will flow into the creative essence that made *me*, the tree and all created life, for we are all inseparable. I have come home, Zeena. I am *me*, a nothing, that tree is *me*. I have come home because the infinite living immortal *essence* of all life is *me*. I am the moving soul and the truth of me is the truer truth that Our People will find.

It's not going back to the 'Stone Age', it's flowing our soul back to the Beginning, the Dreaming, being one with the Presence of the undying Spirit. Why did them Old People of ours sit in the ashes and chant their chants? Whitemen call it 'yuckaiing', but our Old Ones know it's calling the Spirit. You want to talk in poems, hey? Listen then to this:

> By my campfire at night with the heavens in sight
> with the Great Serpent Spirit a-star
> I sing songs of love to the Presence within
> as it plays with the sparks in my fire!

[*Silence.*]

That's what we had. That's what we have to regain. *Now dance!! Dance!! Dance!!!*

[TOMMLO *follows* ZEENA *with spear poised—she moves into a frenzied tempo— the kangaroo trying to evade its hunter—*TOMMLO *leaps to the small fire, picks up the Churinga stone, rubs the designs quickly. Background tribal music and chanting heightens.* TOMMLO *holds Churinga in left hand, pulls* ZEENA *back by grasping her hair. He cuts her upper arms in initiation, her breasts. He hauls her to her feet, springs away in a weaving corroboree midst the circlets—their tempo increases as* ZEENA *follows him in the dance. He now weaves in high stepping, feet stamping, kangaroo hopping motion.*]

TOMMLO: Yuck—aiee—Ba—ai—mee—Yulangarrah—God—Doungudieeee. Dance— dance—dance—dance. Zeena—dance!!

PHONSO: [*off-stage*] Johnollo—John-o-llo—John-o-llo—o—John-o-llo—

ZEENA: They are comin'! Oh, oh my dress!!

[*She snatches her dress.*]

TOMMLO: You spoke of Truth and the times, Zeena. Your body is not a shameful thing. This land is *our* Garden of Eden. We were created here in this land. We'll restore our place, we'll restore our place, we'll find *our* God again, a new and true way, Zeena, and no man will stop us!

[ZEENA *drops the dress, places her arms about him in a quick embrace. He caresses her hair, gently pushes her away. He picks up the bullroarer, the sacred circlets, places them quickly back on the ground, gathers his pants, leaps to pick up* ZEENA's *dress, clasps his spears.* TOMMLO *and* ZEENA *move slowly gracefully and exit.*]

1988

Me and Jackomari Talkin' About Land Rights

He said
Don't be like the rest of 'em bud
a big loose mouth or a pen
Who's gonna lead us ... and lead ya must
to git us our right place again   5
we're sick of the pain and the sneerin'
tired of bein' treated like dirt
we ain't fifth-raters—we're human
'cept they keep up the cripplin' an' hurt ...
say what is the *word* for us Blacks now   10
where are we goin' to turn
if you're like the rest Christ help us—

I replied
Men have died in less hope brother
LAND justice is our cause   15
don't tremble at the sound of drums
or cringe at thought of wars
stand yourself up fiercely
gather strength from all your grief
and terrorise injustice if you must   20
to cure the thief ...
and we'll stand there beside you
our land will glow applause
the big mouths too will join and lead
and pens turn into swords   25
our women with their eyes aglow
their suckling babes at breast
will MARCH AND BURN AND BLEED AND WEEP
AND WIN before we rest.

                                              1990

Redfern

In the savage streets of Redfern
where the 'cockatoo' and turk
peer from the doors of porno dens
while dealers do their work
dicing out a score or two   5
and wait with bated breath
the coins or coppers to descend
in thrills of sudden death

A country girl in fear subdued
reels bloodied from a lane   10

to strains of raucous laughter
boomeranging 'come again'
the crows with forks awaiting
thin strips of lusting meat
to pay the bill of vice-squad men   15
grown fat on Redfern street

In the ghetto streets of Redfern
prowls the battler on the dole
the Blacks still free come morning
who survived the night patrol   20
and paddy-wagon coffins
who only ply their trade
where politicians don't count votes
police training grounds are made

From the ghetto streets of Redfern   25
which abound with rats and mice
comes a wail—a human wailing
that is surging strong and nice
of people grown angry
tired of horror and the pain   30
marching to a bicentenary
armed to blow apart the chains
with a mop in hand
a bucket and something more besides
in the grandest celebration   35
for the 'free' door opening wide
In the savage streets of Redfern
coils a Taipan poised to strike
the fangs are readied, gleaming
in the alley-ways at night.   40
                                                     1990

Tree

I am the tree
the lean hard hungry land
the crow and eagle
sun and moon and sea
I am the sacred clay   5
which forms the base
the grasses vines and man
I am all things created
I am you and
you are nothing   10

but through me the tree
you are
and nothing comes to me
except through that one living gateway
to be free   15
and you are nothing yet
for all creation
earth and God and man
is nothing
until they fuse   20
and become a total sum of something
together fuse to consciousness of all
and every sacred part aware
alive
in true affinity   25
1990

Speech at the Aboriginal Tent Embassy, Canberra

It's twenty-five years since we Aboriginal People have had Australian citizenship imposed upon us, very much against the will of the Aboriginal People, for we have always been Australian Aborigines, not Aboriginal Australians.

We have never joined the company. We have never claimed citizenship of the oppressor, the people who have invaded our country.

Twenty-five years after this citizenship, which was supposed to give us some sort of rights and equality we see that instead of lifting us to any sort of degree of place or right it has only given us the highest infant mortality rate, the highest number of Aboriginal people in prison, the highest mortality rate, the highest unemployment rate.

And after twenty-five years we still have Aboriginal children and people dying from lack of clean drinking water, lack of medication, lack of shelter.

We have still had twenty-five years of economic, political and medical human rights apartheid in Australia. And it hasn't worked for Aboriginal People.

At the end of the twenty-five years, we have seen the Australian Government and the Australian people try and get off the hook of responsibility by saying, ten years down the track, we'll have Reconciliation.

And Reconciliation doesn't promise us human rights, it doesn't promise us our Sovereign rights or the platform from which to negotiate, and it doesn't promise us a viable land base, an economical base, a political base, or a base in which we can again heal our people, where we can carry out our cultural practices.

It is ten more years of death! There must be something better.

Australia is calling for a Republic and a new flag, a new vision. It cannot have a vision. It cannot have a new flag. It cannot have a Sovereign nation until it addresses the right of Aboriginal People, the Sovereign Land Rights of Aboriginal people.

You cannot build a vision, you cannot build a land, you cannot build a people, on land theft, on massacre, on continuing apartheid and the denial of the one group of Aboriginal people.

We have committed no crime, we have done no wrong except own the land which the churches and white society want to take from us.

It must change.

And we can never become, and we never will become, Australian citizens. For we are Aboriginal People. We are Sovereign Aboriginal People. [...]

1992

Song of Dreamtime

With our didgeridoos
in the heart of night
we piped to our God our song
our sacred chants filled the ever-Now
The Beginning covenant   5
The Essence of the presence
Our Dreaming Spirits Flow
and we held His hands
in the heart of night
and walked by His side at day   10
we rejoiced with His sacred angels
as they danced in the trees and clay
and leapt with love in the quivering stars
shimmered the trembling leaves
became a part of pirouetting waves   15
and the roar of the sea's great heaves.
Our sacred chants filled the ever-Now
we sang and danced with God
and loved with Him creation's gift
Our Dreaming Spirits Flow.   20
Hand in hand to the hunt were we
knee to knee in love
heart to heart in our sacred chant
all sacred our sacred mud
eye to eye in our testament   25
hand in hand the Son
we children of the one Great God
who fell to the vandals' gun.
Their poisoned flour sapped our lives
their greed stole our sacred land   30
but they couldn't change our chants to hate
our love to a less than grand
they could not steal our sacred song
nor make our God depart

nor raise His hand in vengeance   35
to those who kill our heart
while ever our pipes speak to His Being
while ever our camp-fires glow
He'll dance and laugh and cry with us
while His lost white children grow   40
and seek and learn to know His face
where the fire's red embers leap
He'll bring them yet to His covenant
and a Dreaming that they'll keep.

    1994

LIONEL FOGARTY
b.1958

Lionel George Fogarty is a respected poet and political activist, born on Wakka Wakka land at Barambah Mission, now known as Cherbourg Aboriginal Reserve, Queensland. He is of the Yoogum and Kudjela tribes and also has relations from the Goomba tribe. Educated to ninth grade at Murgon High School, he took various casual jobs, went ringbarking, worked on a railway gang and at sixteen moved to Brisbane.

In the early 1970s, Fogarty became increasingly aware of the injustices he had experienced on the reserve. Inspired by the growing Black Power movement, he combined writing poetry with a commitment to Aboriginal political struggles. He led protests against Aboriginal deaths in police custody. Fogarty has travelled in Australia and overseas as an ambassador for his Murri culture and Aboriginal causes; in 1976 he addressed the American Indian Movement of the Second International Indian Treaty Council in South Dakota, USA, deepening his commitment to the international fight for racial justice.

Fogarty's poetry powerfully challenges literary and political conventions by creating new possibilities for radical poetic expression. His poems demonstrate a commitment to Aboriginal social justice, his belief in land rights as the basis for an Aboriginal future without oppression, and convey his Murri beliefs, knowledge and experiences. His books include *Yoogum, Yoogum* (1982), *Kudjela* (1983), *Ngutji* (1984), *Jagera* (1990), *New and Selected Poems: Munaldjali, Mutuerjaraera* (1995) and *Minyung Woolah Binnung—What Saying Says* (2004).

As Fogarty's writing has become better known, he has continued to support local Aboriginal writing, and has passed on his stories in books for children, such as *Booyooburra* (1993), a traditional Wakka Wakka narrative published with the approval of his elders.

Shields Strong, Nulla Nullas Alive

Morning dawning stems that core
won't adore poor poor songs
potentially people quit easy
rarely having arts
personal solos move.   5
Stunning outrageous woomeras

flew spears that side cornered
Arnhem Lands
Clapsticks local long maybe
normal entrance   10
finger nail giving painting
sane once again.
Carvings came flying through didgeridoos
over Kimberley roots.
Timber prides   15
simple ornament like mulga wood crafted
Maningrida distinct types.
Finely grained boomerangs
miniatures proved adults
shaped and thrown in the desert life.   20
Weaving fabrics
entirely rich relaxed music
designs your ochre coiled of unique colours.
Landscapes
lovers relate   25
snakes, wild dingo, emus, birds, animals
just like fruit salad.
Traditional authentic coolamons
Yes makers earlier include all.
Fantastic lush property   30
pumped to a gallon of manure
could you believe that this we were told
was better than
what we had.
An intact society based on quality of life.   35
How sad for you.
Or shields are strong
Nulla nullas alive.

       1982

Decorative Rasp, Weaved Roots

If I am not a race
Then what am I
If we are not Aboriginals
Then what persons
I am.   5
If indigenous pictures relate descent
then we are facts
If citizens are short sighted
simplified and unrealistic
then similar aspirations will define us.   10

No overemphasised Killorans
Goona reviews assessments
when we know city and urban convenience you live.
Misconception false beliefs
democratically elected   15
self appointed you are
you are

pulling back his chin
cheekily nice grin
hygiene inspectors appeared   20
self importance glares
but she smiled obvious
hurrying chewing gum while being exploited
black employee, award rate soon embarassed your hate.

The bloody paper goggly eyed me   25
loud mouth white bastard
fuzzy fuzzy sly-groggers
we strip distress.
Yell, suddenly
amused that it's Anzac Day   30
buggered people dumbfounded
realised the stupid idiots would shift the mongrels who
informed.
Ridiculous but fucken mouth dropped
the chilling bay stinks   35
laughs in disgust
refilling with conversation
immediate headache croaked
sailing with oil lamp
to get the flagon we need.   40

Plenty flour, plenty beef
Big hassle
Cause instinctively we know we lucky lucky
exaggerated the worry
pinched death   45
dripping dust
lifted the damage halfway around
dragged tossed ripped
lost balance on the rocks
flew through the air.   50
The roadway crowd gathered
bringing sunlight

moaning
nourished crazy
as our belly smuggled the argument   55
poured the ingredients down
one time.

Journeyed away the 'troublemaker'
naturally
headbands of forums spitfired alternatives   60
listening
influenced swayed under the weather friends
primitive slips
they broke the filthy camera crew
whose landing fields were suspicious   65
asked and told questions
we whistled
knowing who cared anyhow ...

Couples contemplating
followed another bunch   70
of friggen portable rubbish public
jumped up propaganda
goddamned watching paradise
fair dinkum mates
think them sick scratched pissed patients   75
inmates of time.
Unloading a barrage of bitterness.
Tolerant 'old cobber' printed frame
printed til he got some great shots
not an entire obscene one.   80

Premier naming dams
excellent resort
signatures began to sign
interviews filmed the common kind.
Jail agents even.   85
The predicament now is bushwalking
with tears
is rumbling across waters
is the deepest de-camped poets
vained twisted and breathtaking   90
goodbye.
Happiness sundances Australian crawl.
That's what suicide say
that's what hate gave
that's what humans live   95
but index 1984
we are at the door

at the door
at the door.
Arise deep spirits.   100
                                                       1982

Ecology

I am a frill necked lizard
        roaming, providing
I am refuge by king brown taipan
        highly delightful sea bird
                catches the flint of my star skin colour.   5
I.
Am we pelicans of woodland brolga
        traditional yamming
yes roots, nuts
        differ to geese, hawks, quails   10
                that number plentiful.

Still I am dugong,
        kangaroo, cockatoo and grasshopper too.
Yes I am a termite, better still
        butterflies are my beetles, wasps friends   15
You are natures crocodile
        even pythons are not inadequate, nor geckoes.
We are goannas
        after salt water got grounded.

I am death   20
        harmless.
You are tropic cycles
        swamps got bad affinity
                says who.

Now a dingo arrives   25
        that diet attractive a woof woof
later bush tucker
        need a barramundi.

Later I am digging sticks
        then I am seeds winnowed for damper   30
I am club, woomera,
        an agile well-balanced bandicoot
flying fox and an ABORIGINAL
        our systems woven from an eco-system
so don't send us to pollution   35
        we are just trying to picture
                this life without frustration.

                                                       1982

For I Come—Death in Custody

I
in a jail.
Even a murri wouldn't know
if him free.
The land is not free.   5
Dreamtime is not free.
No money needed.
See that scarred hand at work
that's cutting away
to freedom   10
Freedom.
Jail not for me
but a lot of my people in jail
White jail are cruel
Set up the family, stay away   15
come to see your murri
look big and grown
in learning, of our gods teaching.
What they give you in here?
Away from the corroboree   20
In the fuckin' jails
Murri get out, so we can fight
like the red man has done
Lord them a come.
My brother die there   25
in white custody
And I hate the way the screws patch up
and cover up.
He died at white hands
it was there, in their stinkin' jails   30
up you might blacks
Him not free
For when white man came
it's been like a jail
with a wife and a family   35
black man can stay in jail
like it's home.
Fuck, they hung us all.

For Brother D.L.

1990

Kath Walker

We are coming, even going
I was born in 1957
the year after I became a realist
I am a full blooded black Aussie
we want racialism   5
you got ostracism
black ascendance
Charter of Rights, she said
Hey, now they got dependents
exploitation is being done here   10
Self-reliance, not compliance
most will say, resign
circumscribe the enemy, not befriend
they will give oversight and
human segregationary rights.   15
No choice. No colour conscious.
Give us bigots who are not biased
Give us prevention, not ambition
Status, not condescension.
Give us Lord Christ and confidence   20
all we do is fellowship bureaucratic protection.
Give me settlements, camped in missions
Prohibition
from old, young time.
Thank you. Education makes us equals   25
Opportunities are disheartening
we defend white over-lordship
rebuff the independence
my laws ain't no cold choice.
Native, old salvation seller   30
we are the conquerors to take over
not Christ
So our land in law
must rank out aliens
in our banished race   35
though you baptised by
Just black …

                                                    1990

Dulpai—Ila Ngari Kim Mo-Man

Moppy, Aborigine, Gumbal Gumbal was he
Aborigines King Billy was him; lived
loved him people

around Tampa lands.
Lowood ancient copper blacks   5
never alive in them town camps.
Nature shared our environments
with physical effects
men, black was aware of that bush secret.
Then interwoven, fictional settlers   10
came upon their homes.
Tents went up. Gunga. Mia-mia.
Burned away. Torn, blown
Taken tribal implements, damaged.
Warlike colonies half-hearted   15
a magnificent death
on honest young Aborigines.
Race at Kilcoy, a bloody massacre.
Peace to a flower
gave more feeding to fires   20
of our escaping leaders.
High-pitched wails echoed
among a reddish-brown caraboo
named the great 'MOPPY'
Low voice, yet spoken aloud.   25
Ten clans, sounds confident
to your old fight
for even 1995 in future, lied Moy
boy and man will laugh mockingly.
Surprise them at morning rise   30
make useful every member of our tribe

Moppy,
Our ceremonies made sure that the children's
tribal nation, would and will
grow to prosper.   35
Dared, afraid, trembled.
Mr Moy Moy thought to make you
their prey after dark.
Moppy went to his people
gleaming eyes ready   40
to cold ray an evil whispered violent
flickering sign.
Moppy declared defiantly:
Elders we noisily here a startled voice
crashing solidly through this   45
civilised families drifted apart.
These were and are wrong, almost impossible

furious revenge came over the muttering.
Moppy 'savage', claimed a white woman.
Well about this forgetting time   50
meeting sat at ground level
and Aborigines talked
how to avoid directly these horse, cattle people
who stay:

Moppy stood on a rock   55
and finished his speaking in front of
over 600 Murri blackies.
Kind Billy Tampa, let his axes be taken
and they antagonise him
visible, plain, quickly people of this day   60
and age, are guilty
cos them hold opposite direction
in-out our history.
Angry Moppy must and still du du in safety
confided in all Murri here   65
So we stood, walked, corroboreed, war
painted in honour
to divert awful living at present '90.

Moppy, my Aborigines sang happy
and gladly   70
at Moppy's swift actions.
Lead us … lead us …
Even with your magical spells.
We all strict to your commandments.
Except, except the empty stomachs.   75
of the boasted, with the loud voices
and waka, no support.
Previous fighter Moppy.
I'm yours,
young, even old, to follow: 80

Over previous 500 years we might turn back
our times, forward times.
Moppy, Moppy … poets wise we am?
Don't balk balk the hero. Inda
Youdu, you you build our cultures.   85

Looking up at Moppy's reflection, father.
Moppy thundered myself to repeat a clearer respect
irrespective …

The great strengthened Pemolroy pride
longer Murri calls, in feelings our same   90
'no shame'.
He show our world he cared
He's ancient, dilli blames the pain
Seize our brothers lame
Gross injustices, victimised miss the richer   95
and in waiting together
he futures a good education
pleasant for us Aborigines.
Tell it like it is
It's us who's on south laws   100
them are shadows to lifeless burries:

Up here blatant accidents
are made
to hand out lost wealth.
Now Mr Pemolroy   105
Australians scared us to death
not to fight.
Now control forefathers washed fears
We have no fear
we are clean   110
are we to inflame our truth:
My people over Australia ...
Perth, Darwin, Cairns, Bamaga, Broken Bay Cove
and Port Phillip Bay
over Murray Bridge and into Oodnadatta ...   115
Your Aborigines are not forbidden to think quickly
of your citizens.
Since trade arrival, they herded us
natives in thought, movements
so we think as them   120
and listen like systems of
controversy:

Well Moppy, Yagan, had respect.
Has private spiritual properties
If had learn a school option   125
Aborigines will find many Aussies
are 'dogs' within a potential 'dobbers' class
Governed like it was right
in your own neighbourhood.
Australia tribespeople are messengers   130
to arrange the visits

once on exchange
Our battle of sick men intruding
on small children's sounds, are mentally
wanderous   135
to hurt their camp feast.

Between Aborigines borders your ordeal
in screaming, robbing, discussing difficult
worked by a frenzy barrage of angry killing
of our beliefs.   140
When will eager poor fights erupt
our lightning bolts to the nam, Moppy
Furtively buried greeting threats:

Why waste the clenching fists
wild, sisters, flare a white insult   145
at last tempers striving companions
desperate clouds dust wattle
over and around those combatants
choking, fought insults
Moppy, Johnny Campbell …   150
Kagariu.
Clash of waddies or spears are helpless
to obscure,
this gashed groaning lost male.
Who have the half-dazed blacks roaming bush.   155
Now Aborigines only commence assault
cos those evil white or half whites
scratch and lash their minds
unbelieving
belief relaxing in homes: 160

Disobeyed.
The gods are what picked faith
will not hideaway.
In the next few moons
carried by our happiest challenge   165
love, are we willing to toughen coolamen.
Then a blurted shudder one gita morning.
Said Dundalli, attack
all through that long summer
so stagger their skilled mistakes.   170
So here are those instinctive moves
in migrant picking on an Aboriginal family.
And instead meat by mighty hunter

full-grown tricks me, your people
have to face: 175

    Unusually they crawled near their rich houses
asking beard or smoke—waterfire strangely
was curiously given.
That's true. When any black man goes to their fence
openly, wanting to speak face to face   180
to indifference that's been dropped …
them hide
their doubters sweetest decisions
just so they won't give up stolen love.
And our leaders will sing out   185
them is frightened of humans
one full to hear out.
This is the protest, not rested even
not honest, given of friendship
these days and nights   190
Oh great fighters in our region
to reach, jump on them from behind, cos trouble
are always overseas.
Forces sneak ageless, called careless
are what gubba man caution.   195
Wanta beware, for guns we can use
Not just whispered words:

    And some may chuckle
But we blackfella recognise them
at probably aroused times   200
timid, taught to live assailants.
Fire-blackened Lionel
I regained my senses
to secret the Murri world.
Submissively them shout terrible injustice   205
Where's the justice?

Duramula came to change
unbeliever to Aborigines present life.
Duramula is the voice bringer
Rhythm sticks we may hit   210
Rhythming a wavering power
won't give death
to those who have betrayed our leaders:

Changer of life
Punjel can change, boy into man   215

girl into woman
Boomed out an answer
now old women, louder and deeper
in the reality world.
Call them from their homes 220
And when they hear my voice
they must obey … Ngunda …
Me … Nulli … me …
Sender, bring him back to life
as they must return to camp 225
Singer you are now living.
Emerging my tribe once more
Clinging to my brother-mate
at homeland, Jagera
Moppy … 230
Wintu …
Gifted I am from Punjel, Duramula
While there is a sun married to the moon
We are to give a raised initiation
Tell Moppy and Lionel, poet Fo 235
Are them sell-out to express emotions unveiled
Punjel, mina lo run Da
Biamie.
For everything that You have given to me
I in return give back to you 240
Moppy.

1990

Alcheringa

We learnt to love you in that
historical jail
and think of your glorious bravery
where intimate sunshine came
over the transparency mountain 5
we saw your black face smile
with whispers in the winter
we hear your black revolutionary
words (kill miggloo, kill darkie)
We are remaining at the fruits 10
of your vines.
Your firm liberating mind
sicks in our spirits
like a lengthening shadow
over all day light falls 15
Your jailed dance is freed

in our bodies and souls
We are breezing a wind of
continuous international
struggles.   20
We are receiving your high
delivered message
our duty is to free your
suppression. Our duty is
to strike the hatred on a hot   25
even cold night
Your love comes out under the land and up to our
hearts 'you swear, your violence'
But we feel your happier laughs
and rejoys at your release   30
You revolt in thunder
we resolute your pain
The flag we hold is on the
walls held in historical jails
We learnt now black man   35
you are not the jail
Cos we felt the death of many
people in history's goals
The historical future jail are
to be given liberation   40
                                                            2004

BRUCE PASCOE
b 1947

Bruce Pascoe, a member of the Wathaurong Aboriginal Co-operative of southern Victoria, has combined writing fiction and non-fiction with a career as a successful publisher. He has also worked as a farmer, fisherman, barman, lecturer, Aboriginal language researcher and as a labourer on archaeological sites.

From 1982 to 1998 Pascoe edited and published *Australian Short Stories*, an influential quarterly journal of short fiction by new and established writers. He has edited educational texts on Wathaurong history and language, and is a highly regarded speaker on Aboriginal culture and social justice. Pascoe has continued to edit and publish anthologies and translations of Australian stories, and has authored detective fiction, children's books and historical and autobiographical works, including *The Great Australian Novel* (1984), *Night Animals* (1986), *Ruby-Eyed Coucal* (1996), *Shark* (1999), *Nightjar* (2000), *Earth* (2001), *Ocean* (2002) and *Convincing Ground: Learning to fall in love with your country* (2007).

The Slaughters of the Bulumwaal Butcher

Bodies had always been found. Dogs, kangaroos, sometimes even cattle and horses had been found, dreadfully mutilated, the heads torn completely from the bodies.

This was Nargun country, and the Aborigines said that these slaughters had been occurring far back in black memory and were attributed to the Nargun, the stone beast which on some still, frosty nights roamed through the hills looking for food.

The white population claimed that an escaped panther from a travelling circus was the culprit; others thought that a Yowie was responsible. Old Clive Glossop, the post splitter, reckoned he had seen a huge hairy beast massacre a big kangaroo in his paddock. The pile of Ruby port bottles outside his shack was enough evidence for most people to discredit this story.

It's true that old Mrs Muir disappeared without trace ten years ago, leaving the kettle on the stove and the radio tuned to 'Evening Concert', and it's also true that Murphy's huge Friesian cow gave birth to an extraordinarily ugly hairy calf; but all of these things were classified by most people as those mysterious affairs that occur, but which have perfectly simple scientific explanations. Mrs Muir could have fallen down a mine shaft, and Murphy's cow probably just had a freak calf. And Glossop—well, everybody knew about Clive Glossop.

But this was a bit different. Since the start of winter over twenty sheep had been killed. Their heads were torn from their bodies, and the guts and feet found strewn in their clotted blood. The manner of the deaths was similar to the mutilations of the kangaroos and dogs. Perc Hopkins, the Aboriginal rouseabout from the saw mill, saw one of the sheep and began grumbling about Narguns and pointed up into the hills where a huge granite tor stood out in the open pasture. That was the Nargun, Perc claimed, and any night he might wake up and come looking for tucker.

Although Perc immediately took his first holiday in thirty years and went to visit his cousins on the Murray, the whites still talked about some logical explanation, like an escaped panther or a Tasmanian Tiger. Clive Glossop insisted on his Yowie story, but he was given two bottles of Ruby port and sent home.

The massacre of sheep continued during the winter, and over the Sunday roast Les Patterson told his wife it was about time something was done. Les, a shire councillor and football club president, went to the pub on the following night and there he met Clarrie Watson, Dan Murphy and Tom Mullins, sheep farmers all. Little Phonce Wallace-Pimble, the chemist and Bulumwaal councillor, was also there, and so a meeting was held, and they determined that they would find the sheep killer and put a stop to this nonsense about Yowies, panthers and Narguns. The council had always held the responsibility for quelling civic imagination.

A week later this same group of solid citizens stood around the latest scene of massacre and counted the heads and remains of eleven sheep. Les pointed out the tyre marks in the mud a hundred yards down the track. Ten days later they stood looking down at the remains of more sheep scattered in the frosty grass.

Phonce Wallace-Pimble was short of breath in the crispness of the morning, and his face was wreathed in vapour as he ventured that this carnage might be the work of wild dogs and dingoes.

Les Patterson looked down at the little chemist and smoke seemed to snort from his nostrils as he declared such talk to be nonsense. Later he told Tom

Mullins that he couldn't expect anything more sensible from a town man who didn't have the good sense to wear decent boots when walking around in frosty paddocks.

Les didn't miss the tyre tracks in the soft soil near the paddock gate, and later that day stood behind Jack Slattery's truck and recognized the same tread. Les rubbed his chin and went to the hotel. He leant on the bar as the others spouted their theories over foaming pots. Narguns, panthers, and Yowies were favoured possibilities, but wild dogs were, as always, clear favourites. Some farmers would have blamed wombats, koalas and corellas if they hadn't been vegetarians.

As the slaughters continued, the more bizarre and frightening theories gained credence. Herb Nash, the local alcoholic and wit, was scared of nothing, but suggested it could be the work of Mrs Kestrel, the local school mistress and witch. This became a popular theory among children: bloody sheep feet began to appear on the teacher's table, and mysterious bleatings would issue from a class of students who appeared to be working harder than they ever had before.

The story of the ram being let loose in the school house seemed a great joke and, in the hotel that night, the story went through many stages of elaboration, including wild exaggerations of the various delights and frights experienced by either the ram or Mrs Kestrel. That the school mistress's bloomers had been rent by the ram's horns could not be doubted because Les Patterson had seen them himself when he went to retrieve his stud ram. As a councillor his word could not be doubted and when he said he would kill the kid who kidnapped his ram, that was not doubted either, and several kids immediately went down with apparently incurable cases of flu, dysentery and fits.

It didn't seem quite so funny the next morning when the cleaner found Mrs Kestrel hanging from the school bell with a note addressed to her sister propped on the desk where all her papers and books had been carefully packed away. She had chalked a 'No School Today' notice on the board and left enough spelling and maths to last two weeks. It was considered by many rather unfortunate in retrospect that the words 'you, yew and ewe' had been included. Among the books she had corrected the night before, police found that a student, beside the poem 'Baa baa, black sheep', had chosen to illustrate it with a picture of a witch and a huge cauldron of dismembered sheep. Mrs Kestrel had begun to write the usual good work legend but had apparently stopped on seeing the illustration accompanying the poem. Neighbours who had heard a desultory clanging of the bell had thought the wind was responsible and had continued to watch Brian Naylor's version of the news.

Les was worried by other things. The death of the schoolteacher was the result of an unfortunate town prank, although he had harboured suspicions about the school mistress since he himself had been a child at the school. Mrs Kestrel had kept him in on one occasion and blasted him with tongue and cane, and he never forgot her piercing eyes and wicked laugh and the way her neck and face flushed with excitement as she beat and harangued her victim.

But Les knew she had not been responsible for the sheep. He also knew Jack Slattery, and Jack was a close friend, a solid citizen and a fellow member of the Chamber of Commerce. Times were becoming hard for graziers, and the whole district was suffering a prolonged recession. The export of stud rams had made an impact on traditional markets for Australian lamb, and many farmers, including Les, were mortgaged several times over.

Les decided that a visit to Jack Slattery was vital. Jack was curious when Les ignored his wife, the good Edith Slattery, and asked for a private talk. Jack was a genial man and thought that Les had found an excuse for the two of them to share a few beers and discuss the latest intrigues in the process of syphoning money away from the pre-school and elderly citizens' funds in order to seal certain access roads to rural properties.

Jack hurried to get cans and chips so that they could get down to tintacks. Les looked uncomfortable and finally said, 'Ar, look, Jack, it's about these sheep.' Jack began pouring beer into glasses with manic concentration.

'What sheep?' he said, apparently uninterested.

'Now come on, Jack, we've been mates for a long time. You know bloody well what sheep.' Jack was short, tubby, red-faced, bristly about nose and ears, but glassily clean shaven elsewhere. Les, lean and weathered with pale grey, penetrating eyes, regarded his friend with impatient discomfort. He was used to the dumb predictability of sheep, dogs and councillors, and this sophistry was making it difficult for him to find a comfortable position in his chair.

'Look, Jack, don't play possum with me. There's been over thirty sheep killed recently, and I've seen your tyre treads at the scene of every—well, every—slaughter.' The word was hard for Les to say, and he took a deep draught of beer.

The local butcher looked carefully at his angular friend, and his mind tried to assess the possibility of subterfuge, but then he relaxed and smiled. He was as concerned as a rabbit when it is cornered by a kangaroo dog. Under such circumstances intelligence is of no use; it is a contest between the relative power of jaws and flesh. Les, Jack decided, definitely had the canines. It was time for whippet and rabbit to make a deal.

Jack explained the expense of bringing meat from Bairnsdale, the poor economic climate of the town, his own financial difficulties due to an unfortunate gamble in gold investment and how he had decided to procure cheap meat for his butchery.

'We've always been good mates, Les,' he said, and on a sudden inspiration his pouch of brains tossed up an idea. 'Now, look, we could organize this properly. You farmer blokes are getting nothing for your sheep at the markets, and I can't compete with the big butchers, so why don't we keep the old panther scare going. We could—' He searched for details. 'We could form a syndicate of farmers and butcher our own sheep, leave the heads in the paddock and make a decent profit for a change. All we'd have to do would be to keep it quiet.' Jack and Les looked at each other.

The following evening a small group of farmers—Tom Mullins, Dan Murphy, Les Patterson, Clarrie Watson, Jack Slattery the butcher, and inevitably, despite Les's distaste for the man, Phonce Wallace-Pimble the chemist—talked over the scheme at a quiet table in the pub. A darts competition kept the other patrons engaged, and as the barman called for blokes to get their last drinks and get out, the syndicate shook hands.

The slaughters continued. The financial prospects of a few farmers improved, the butcher flourished, and the syndicate muddied the waters by shredding their sheep dogs' winter coats and fixing tufts of dog hair into the barbed-wire fences wherever a slaughter had taken place.

The wild-dog theory gained immediate credence, and syndicate members pointed at various reprobate town dogs, which were at once put to death. Les, Jack and Phonce got the council to put up vermin notices calling for the death of wild dogs, the government was approached by the shire to begin trapping dingoes, and funds were poured in by the local farmer-elected politician. Most of the money went to finish road works out to the farms of syndicate members and to provide a new awning for the chemist and butcher shops.

The dog trapper visited his traps for a fortnight without trapping or even seeing a wild dog, but the Lands Department forgot they had sent him there, and the computer kept on paying him. It seemed like a fair thing to him so he stayed on, bought a house, married the baker's daughter, failed to catch dogs, but succeeded in supporting the bar of the hotel.

The slaughters went on. Disgruntled sheep dogs had tufts of fur torn from their bodies so that it could be applied to barbed wire but, in general, rural life continued. Even the fortunes of the local footy sides picked up, and the Bulumwaal Blues registered their first win in three seasons. The butcher supplied free lamb chops to celebrate their victory.

One morning Jack Slattery and Clarrie Watson were just loading the last carcasses into the butcher's van when they saw old Clive Glossop hurrying into the bush towards his hut in the hills. Jack and Clarrie were holding the warm carcass of one of Clarrie's wethers between them, and they looked at each other. Old Clive had certainly seen them, but would anyone believe him? They quickly covered up the evidence of the slaughter and didn't even knot dog fur into the barbed wire.

That night in the hotel the syndicate met and digested the news that Jack and Clarrie brought to the meeting. The bar was rowdy and still incoherently celebrating the one consecutive win of the local footy team. Clarrie and Les were selectors for the team, and it was assumed that they were planning an assault on the Tabberaberra Tigers.

The syndicate could reach no decision. Their scheme was financially rewarding at a time when farmers around the continent were leaving their farms. And yet, one word from Clive Glossop, despite his reputation as an alcoholic, could cause a scandal, especially among the farmers in more desperate financial plight who had not been invited to join the Bulumwaal butchers' syndicate.

It was tentatively decided to buy off Clive with a side of lamb each month, a case of Ruby port and a generous contract for fence posts. Some of the syndicate members felt that the very inclusion of such vast quantities of Ruby port would make Clive an untrustworthy member of the party. They decided to meet the next night to discuss the matter further and in the meantime slaughters would temporarily cease.

The next night the syndicate stood silently at the bar ready to begin their meeting after a couple of quick pots to clear the head. Les put his glass down and was just about to begin when Phonce Wallace-Pimble burst in through the doors, hair dishevelled, tie askew, and eyes wild. The dart spectators stared at the little chemist, who was covering his face with tiny pink hands. The pub fell silent. The darts player stood with dart poised to throw. The barman poured beer all over his hand. The syndicate members were frozen, some in the act of finishing off the last drops of beer. Jack had a hand in his pocket ready for his shout, and Les's hand was placed on the bar in the manner of a chairman impatient to begin. All looked towards Phonce.

'It's Clive,' the chemist said, and passed an arm across his eyes. 'He's dead, he's dead, the dogs must have got him! His—his head's been torn off, and his body's gone except for the legs—' The barman came around the bar and pressed a stiff brandy into the chemist's quivering hand. Phonce drank quickly and went on. 'He'd been sick for a few days, and I ordered some medicine from Melbourne, and when I took it out to him, there he was—with this.' Phonce held up a port bottle and only Les noticed the peculiar brownish stain on the under side of Phonce's sleeve.

The syndicate members looked from one to the other, searching for the eyes of the one who had found the solution to their problem. Les looked at Phonce, and Phonce looked back. Les moved to the chemist's side and took the bottle from him and carefully lowered Phonce's upraised arm.

'Well, it looks like the dogs, all right,' said Les, and immediately the bar was full of conjectures, predictions and proposals, and more local dogs came under the scrutiny of the bar-room investigations. 'I betcha it's the bookie's Pekinese,' said a rugged gambler. Other eyes cast about the bar for dogs. The publican's black labrador, which had slept in a corner of the pub every night for fifteen years, suddenly woke up and found thirty men staring at him; he yelped once, dashed for the door, and was never seen again.

The council redoubled its efforts to raise government funds to deal with the menace, the Lands Department discovered that it still had a dog trapper in the area and immediately gave him the sack. The computer continued to pay for him for five years.

Worst of all, the sheep slaughters were repeated regularly, and on these nights many people had seen the ghost of old Clive Glossop roaming the paddocks screaming in a voice that echoed far across the moonlit paddocks, 'Butchers! butchers, butchers!'

The menace that threatened the flocks by night became known as the Bulumwaal Butcher and speculation on the form of the dread beast was both varied and bizarre. The local council had no answer to the problem, and people learned to live with the ravages of local livestock. And besides, the footy team won another game and the chemist turned on a pie night. Not such a bad bloke after all—for a chemist.

1986

IDA WEST
1919–2003

Ida West was born on an Aboriginal reserve on Cape Barren Island. In the 1920s the family moved to Killiecrankie, Flinders Island. She married Marcus Sydney West, had one daughter and two sons, and divorced in 1960.

West spent much of her life as a tireless advocate for the Tasmanian Aboriginal community's rights to land and cultural self-determination. In 1987 West published her autobiography *Pride Against Prejudice: Reminiscences of a Tasmanian Aborigine.* Her many years of struggle finally resulted in the Wybalenna Aboriginal Community's acquisition of land title on Flinders Island on 18 April 1999. She was named Tasmanian of the Century by the *Mercury* and NAIDOC National Female Aboriginal Elder of the Year (2002) and NAIDOC Elder of the Year (2003).

From *Pride Against Prejudice*
Chapter 2: The Middle Years

BROTHER-IN-LAW AND BILLY SAMUEL

My brother-in-law, Andy, was bringing a heifer over from Pine Scrub one day. He was riding a horse and he took a short cut from Tanners Bay to Killiecrankie. He was going around the bushes, but the heifer was going through the bushes. Andy was going to give it up when he saw another man on a horse. The horse belonged to Charlie Jones and was being ridden bareback by Billy Samuel. The horse was called Tunny. Mr Billy Samuel, an Aborigine from Queensland, was a boxer. The heifer was going through the bushes, so Billy Samuel went through the bushes too. Billy Samuel was an expert in the bush, and they got the heifer to Killiecrankie.

Billy Samuel used to be at the Quoin with us doing some work. He would put on a clean shirt each evening and go over to another man and his wife and little girl to listen to the boxing on the wireless. The champion, Mr Samuel, would bob his head and put his fist out during the fighting. The little girl was looking at him and she said to him, 'Why don't you go home and wash your hands and face?' He told me, 'That's the best line ever put over me.' He said he had been called 'old smoke' or a 'big thunder cloud', but he reckoned that was the best. The little girl's father was going to hit her and Billy told him, 'You have never explained to her about coloured people.' So he did that and they were friends then, Mr Samuel and the little girl.

Mr Samuel told me that up in Queensland they saw white people rounding their cows and calves, and branding them. The Aboriginal people saw this, and the Aboriginal children had the branding irons in a fire ready to start branding their little brothers and sisters. I think that they did do one! There's a lot that should have been learnt years ago.

He also told me about his Uncle, Gerry Jerome, when he won his first fight, they asked him what he wanted in money. Instead of saying so much money, he said he wanted a new horse, saddle and bridle. That was what he wanted.

ABORIGINES SWIMMING

I was on Killiecrankie Beach with Aunty Sarah Beeton and her children, and Billy Samuel was on the beach somewhere as well. Billy, a full-blood Aborigine, was staying with us and he was a champion boxer in his day. Dad liked him very much. I was sitting with Aunt Sarah when I looked towards the bay and saw three small boys, they seemed to be sitting on the water, but they were moving. I said to Aunt Sarah, 'Look at your boys.' The reason they looked like they were sitting on the water was because they were sitting on Billy's back. Billy was like a whale. He put his head up, blew out his nose and would then go under a little way. The boys were having a wonderful time. Billy was a very good swimmer, he and his brothers had taught themselves to swim, he said.

FLOODS AT KILLIECRANKIE

Girlie and Tim lived in a hut near a swamp and we lived in a tent not far away. Aunty Sarah Beeton, Elvin and Les had a tent in the scrub towards the beach at Killiecrankie. We were all snaring for kangaroo and wallaby. Wallaby snares were called footies because we caught them by the foot, and the ones for roos were neckies as they were caught by the neck. The rain came—it rained and rained and the swamp filled up. Markie and I were in bed. We were roused up because the tent was leaking and water was coming in underneath. We got up, dressed, put knee boots on and went over to Girlie and Tim's hut thinking that they would be dry. When we were nearly there Markie said, 'The water is nearly up to the hut.' We had a lantern and we knocked at the door noticing the water coming through the door, Girlie said, 'Come in'. We told her that we were flooded out and that the water was coming through their door. Tim and Girlie had been in bed asleep. We lit the lamp and they couldn't believe that the water was coming through the door. They opened their eyes when the two, unused, jerry pots came floating out from under the bed and across the floor! They got dressed and then we talked it over, we had to go over to Aunty Sarah and the boys' tent. We started through the bush to Aunty Sarah when we heard someone cooee-ing. It was raining very hard. We listened. It was coming from up the track, cooee, cooee, again. We found Aunty Sarah with a blanket around her shoulders wet through. She had got off the track and was trembling all over. We took her back to her tent. Aunty Sarah's tent was dry so we didn't know why she left it. It was up a little hill and she had a big fire going outside. We put dry clothes on her and the men built up the fire. We stayed there all night.

It was a flood all right.

ELDERLY GENTLEMEN

Mr Frank Boyes left Robertdale and built a hut in the bush at North East River. He was a great age. He would cut wood and pile it up for when he got old. He used to talk to himself. Mr Jack Gardner, who kept the store at

Lughrata, would bring food up to him, and another man, Mr Wattie Archer, who lived alongside for a while. This man was brother to Mr Archer on Cape Barren Island and he died before Mr Boyes. They lived like hermits, but you were always sure of a cup of tea when you called there. The Robinsons from Five-Mile used to take a short cut from Five-Mile to see these elderly gentlemen. Frank and George Boyes were well educated. Mr Frank was the best. He had a wireless and would argue with the men on the wireless and tell them that they were wrong.

We were going down the road, Mum and I. Our wireless was broken at the old home so we had to go down to Esma's to hear the serial, 'It Walks by Night'. There were gum-tree roots all over the road. It was a dark night and I had my hand around Mum's arm. The torch wasn't very good because the batteries were nearly out. I said to her, 'Jump.' She said, 'What are you jumping for?' I said, 'There's an extra gum root on the road.' I said, 'I think it's a snake. At certain times they travel of a night.' So we jumped and we turned around to have a look. When we put the torch on it, it was moving. We kind of knew how many gum roots there were on the road—so there was always these stories.

COOKING

Mutton-birds can be cooked several different ways. We used to make a brown stew in the old iron pots. There is grilled mutton-birds, fried mutton-birds, baked mutton-birds with onions and stuffing, curried mutton-birds with rice, sea pie, and salted birds.

For smoked mutton-birds we used to thread the birds on a stick and put them over a drum and keep the fire in the drum for four to six weeks.

We made kangaroo tail soup and brawn. We would dip the kangaroo tails in hot water and scrape the skin off.

We had coupons to buy meat, sugar, tea, butter and clothes. We made our own soap out of dripping and we used mutton-bird oil for rubbing our chests for flu. Garlic in your shoes was a remedy for whooping cough. We would boil the buzzies from the vine of the bush and bottle. We ate grass tree bread which is the meat of the tree—white in colour and sweet in taste. We loved it.

All my people cooked fruit cakes with mutton-bird fat dripping. The women were good cooks.

They used to cook bread, damper and johnny cake in bakers [camp ovens]. Uncle Bun Beeton used to make his damson jam in the baker. Uncle Bun used to have an orchard at Pine Scrub which had peaches, damson, grapes and a vegetable garden. On my school holidays I used to stay with Johnny Maynard, his wife Nellie and their children, Hazel, Phillip, and Ruby. They lived on top of the hill at Pine Scrub. They had a cow which was the best I have seen for producing cream. They would boil the milk and skim the cream off it. Nellie used to make butter, but it was just about butter before we started. We used to take it to the salt water to wash it. When we cooked our crayfish we put them straight into boiling water—all Aboriginal people do it that way.

One of the prettiest sights I ever saw in my life was in about 1937, on my first trip out to Babel Island. As I was going past Cat Island I saw it smothered with lovely white gannets. It was a picture. The last time I was out at Babel there were only a few there. It's a shame seeing these lovely white birds disappearing but it was a sight to see when the island was full of them.

1987

ERIC WILLMOT
b. 1936

Scholar, award-winning engineer, administrator and author, Willmot was born on Cribb Island, near Brisbane. In boyhood he moved from school to school in Queensland and NT. After primary school he became a drover and horse breaker, completing his education after a rodeo accident at eighteen left him unable to ride. He graduated from the University of Newcastle in 1968 with a science degree, then taught mathematics before gaining a master's degree in educational planning.

Willmot has worked throughout the world as an educator and administrator. He has been Director-General of Education in South Australia, and head of AIATSIS. His advocacy for a national Aboriginal media network assisted in the creation of the Broadcasting for Remote Aboriginal Communities Scheme and satellite services for Aboriginal communities. He has published scholarly work and historical fiction, notably *Pemulwuy: The rainbow warrior* (1987). Willmot's inaugural David Unaipon lecture at the University of South Australia in 1988 was published as 'Dilemma of Mind' (1991).

From *Pemulwuy*
Chapter 44: A War of Worlds

Pemulwuy followed Wilson's advice carefully. His forces spent the spring and early summer of 1800 terrorising the settlers—and more importantly their families. The Eora would wait patiently until all or at least some of the adult males were away from the homesteads, then attack it. These raids were aimed strictly at inspiring terror: spears through thatching and windows, firing sheds, stealing supplies, and all done with much noise and fuss. The attacks usually lasted less than an hour, and then the Eora were gone.

This was hardly what Pemulwuy would have called war, but it destroyed the cunning and dangerous wheat protection squads. They became too afraid to leave their families. Pemulwuy did not set fire to the wheat in 1800. He was poised for the summer of 1801, the year of Governor King.

Pemulwuy had Wilson write out for him a message to the new governor. It was written on a piece of canvas with charcoal and hung from a tree on the outskirts of Sydney. It read:

GOVERNOR KING

ALL ENGLISH GO BACK TO SYDNEY

PEMULWUY

The response to Pemulwuy's offer was very simple and quickly delivered. Pemulwuy must surrender himself to the authorities in Parramatta where King and the New South Wales judiciary would then consider his future with some leniency.

Pemulwuy's reply was equally swift. He set fire to virtually all of the country west of Toongabbie. This was again part of the strategy of terror. Pemulwuy had found that the threat of a bushfire sent the protection squads home. Burning wheat on its own brought them onto the offensive.

The skies above Sydney remained black and grey with the smoke from the burning of the New South Wales forests. The huge fuel burden from the last summer and winter now kindled a wall of fire that swept down on Parramatta. The Eora people had been warned well in advance. Not only did they move from the path of the fire; they placed themselves in suitable positions to hunt the fleeing fauna. The British settlers, on the other hand, had no way of dealing with these horrific fires. They seemed so well placed that all suspected they had been deliberately lit. When Pemulwuy's warriors started appearing from the flames and smoke, setting fire to everything that had not burned, they were sure.

The Eora rode the flames like surf, assisting them to jump the firebreaks, lighting them anew when they went out.

While Awabakal and Weuong burnt out Toongabbie and Castle Hill, Pemulwuy set fire to Prospect Hill. By April the whole Parramatta district was a black, bleak mess of charcoal. The wheat and maize crops were virtually a total loss. Looting and minor raids picked the bones of the corpse of this latest British adventure.

Late in April the fires started to move down the north side of the harbour towards Lane Cove, but they were stopped by rain. The summer offensive ended.

The British were in complete disarray. The grain crops had failed, and they were now burdened by refugee settlers. Their old enemy of eleven years had unleashed a weapon against which they had no defence. The dreams of these adventurers lay in the ashes of New South Wales.

A meeting in Sydney of senior officers of the New South Wales Corps had almost ended in a riot. Lieutenant Marshall had finally cracked, physically attacking Abbott and Macarthur and calling them rogues and scoundrels.

King stepped in.

'We have a colony facing its gravest threat and you fight among one another like unruly children!' he scolded.

He gave the Rum Corps an ultimatum:

'Drive the natives from the Parramatta region or abandon all the inland settlements.'

This did, indeed, send the Corps scurrying back to their posts. Not only had King threatened their own holdings, but he had now given them a direct order to take the land from the Eora. The age of the peacemakers, Phillip and Hunter, was finally over.

Under this new policy, the approach of the New South Wales Corps was simple: take a large force, attack all known Eora campsites, and kill everybody found there.

Wilson argued bitterly with Pemulwuy.

'They are using the same method against you,' he insisted. 'Your advantage is that your people are mobile. You must continue to attack their houses.'

Pemulwuy reluctantly agreed. He pursued a desperate war of attrition.

No-one will ever know how many people were killed in New South Wales in that winter of 1801. Both societies were devastated, and when the green grass grew in the blackened valleys of New South Wales in September, there were few British or Eora families to welcome it. If Pemulwuy had not been alive the Eora nation would have given up in that spring of 1801.

Pemulwuy's power among his people remained undiminished, but the Eora, like the Tharawal, had lost the heart to fight on. The spring brought with it an epidemic of influenza, which swept through the weakened Eora groups like Pemulwuy's summer fires. This particular epidemic also hit the settler families hard and weakened their resolve to return to their burnt and wasted farms. The pressure from British society to return was, however, very great. If one family failed to return, another would quickly step into their shoes. This fierce competitive spirit among the Europeans was something that the Eora could not even imagine, and certainly did not possess.

The bushrangers were in high spirits. They saw their ally Pemulwuy as achieving a brilliant victory over the British.

'One more summer,' Thrush said to Pemulwuy, 'and we will have them in the sea.' Pemulwuy smiled, but most of his face showed no emotion whatsoever. Pemulwuy was very concerned at the ability the Rum Corps and their police had shown in locating Eora camps that winter.

'I must leave for a while,' he said. 'Special business.'

In mid-September Pemulwuy left his group and walked to his secret place. A dreaming site of his father's.

The site was not very imposing. It lay on the side of a hill in a sandstone outcrop. This site had been continuously maintained by Pemulwuy's paternal line for thousands of years. Pemulwuy entered a small, shallow cave. Its walls had been marked by men so distant and mysterious in their antiquity that the question of what the marks were never crossed Pemulwuy's mind.

Pemulwuy touched the rock walls with his fingertips, closed his eyes and sang a soft, melodious chant. The cave slowly filled with the song, which deepened in timbre. The song floated down to the face of the rise and fulfilled its meaning and purpose.

Its meaning was the land: as it had always been. Its purpose was renewal: renewal of the spiritual communion of the Eora people and this land their source.

When he had done with the site Pemulwuy climbed to the hilltop and sat with his chin on his knees. He looked across this countryside as he had with his father. He could see nothing but the forest, but he had a vision of open space and farms. He struck his head to put the vision away, but it persisted. He cried out:

'What is it I must do?'

The voices of the land swept up the slope in answer; there was an urgency in them. They gave him warnings, but had no special form; no words on which to form action, only sadness.

1987

GLENYSE WARD
b. 1949

Born in Perth, at the age of one Glenyse Ward was removed from her parents by the Native Welfare Department and placed in the St John of God's orphanage, Rivervale, WA. She was later sent to St Francis Xavier Native Mission in Wandering Brook.

When her mission education ceased she was put to domestic work, first at the mission and in 1964 as a servant to a wealthy white family. A year later she left for Busselton, where she was employed as a domestic in the Busselton Hospital kitchen. In 1987 she began publishing autobiographical fiction, winning the Federation of Australian Writers' Patricia Weickhardt Award to an Aboriginal Writer in 1992.

From *Wandering Girl*
Running Whenever She Needed Me

Just as I was about to be attacked by a mob of vicious turkeys, I awoke to the sound of high pitched ringing. Jolted out of my terrible nightmare, I reached out, grabbed the clock to turn the alarm off, then lit up the old burner. I pulled my towel off the edge of my bed, to wipe the sweat off my face. My heart was still beating fast and my legs felt as if they had been running all night!

I lay back to let my nerves settle down and to come back to reality with myself. I lay there thinking about what sort of a day I was going to have. I felt real happy that they were going out again. It would give me an opportunity to go down and have a yarn with old Bill. I'd get him to come up and have a cup of tea with me. I might even ask him to help me cut some wood, because the thought of all that chopping made me feel weak. I just wished I knew what time her sons were going out. As soon as they left, I'd head straight down to the orchard.

I thought I'd better hurry up and get started on my jobs. Suddenly, I remembered that she wanted breakfast early. Now that I had shaken that horrible nightmare out of my system, I got myself dressed. Thinking, 'It's too cold for a shower,' I decided I'd have one later when everyone had left the farm.

I could use her shower room. It was so much nicer and warmer, as her toilet and shower room were in her bedroom. I remembered her powder smelt lovely. I liked the lavender one. I'd put some of that on me after my shower.

As soon as I was dressed I went to my own wash-house and freshened up my face and combed my hair. Back at my room, I just chucked my toiletries on the bed and slammed the door. Then I grabbed the old burner and broom, intending to start down from the orchard and work my way up to the front, then finish off my chores at the shoe rack. I had to polish their shoes and make sure they were spotless before they left for town.

So I made my way down to the bottom end of the driveway and started sweeping up all the leaves and dust. The wind was blowing hard, and I began to get a bit frustrated. I was fighting a losing battle—the more leaves I swept together the more the wind would blow them all over the place.

I thought, 'I'll just sweep from side to side. Too bad if the wind blows the leaves back again.' So I hurried up and made a quick job of it. I put the lantern and broom back where they belonged, then went to the shoe rack to start polishing the shoes.

When I finally finished the shoes I didn't feel like going all the way down to the paddock to pick her oranges. So I went into my room and got two out of my fruit bowl, which I had picked from the orchard a week before. They were a bit soft, but she wouldn't know. At least, there'd be a lot of juice in them. In the kitchen, I took a glass from the cabinet and squeezed the week-old oranges.

Um they were juicy too! I poured the rich juice into the glass and filled it up. I had a taste to see if the juice was sweet. It tasted alright to me, so I tidied my mess up, put a clean doyley over the glass, then set about getting breakfast.

When I put the bacon and eggs on I didn't forget myself. If she told me off I'd just say that I was making some for her sons too, playing dumb to the fact that she had already explained to me about the boys—besides, I couldn't help the way I was, just a shadow in this mansion. I went into the dining room to set the table up and make sure everything was laid out correctly, then went back into the kitchen. I glanced at the clock. It was about ten minutes to seven. I put the kettle on.

She called out to me from the dining room that she and Mr Bigelow were ready for their breakfast, but as I was setting up the trolley, she came in to drink her orange juice. The perfume she had on her was very strong, a sickly sort of smell. I caught a good whiff of it as she passed me. Her rouge and makeup always fascinated me. She often looked like she was ready for the circus.

I was just about to take the trolley in when she sort of tugged at the sleeve of my dress and told me that she'd wheel it in. She moved me out of the way abruptly and told me to bring in the bacon, eggs and toast when she rang the bell. 'Don't worry about making coffee. Just put the boiling water in a jug and bring it in with you when I am ready for the main breakfast.'

She went into the dining room with the trolley and shut the door behind her, leaving me standing there empty-handed. I thought that I'd better have my cereal, so I got my old tin plate out, filled it up with weeties, poured milk and sugar over them, then began. She rang the bell.

I dropped the spoon, quickly hopped up, got the plates of bacon and eggs, took them into the dining room, placed them on their individual places, then stood back to see if there was anything else she wanted before I went back into the kitchen.

As I stood there I got a fit of the sniffles and took out my old rag, which I had tucked in my sleeve jumper, and blew into it in a most profound manner, making the most peculiar noise.

She stood up in a very angry mood and told me to leave the room at once. What I had done was very rude—to blow my nose in front of decent citizens like her and her husband. If I happened to do it again she was going to report me to the priest at the mission. This was one thing she would not tolerate, especially from her servant. I shook as I made my way out to the kitchen.

Every time she scolded me I felt like I was dirt; but as I explained before, I sort of overlooked the situation. I could see the funny side of things. I was a person that nothing could ever get down for long. I was a happy go lucky girl!

Sometimes when she scolded me, I thought she was quite comical, but I never dared laugh in front of her. It was always at the back of her, or when she was out of my sight.

Even when the nuns scolded me at the mission, I could always see the funny side, especially when my mates were around me. We used to think it was a big joke to be slapped and told off. I mean we wouldn't laugh straight away, but only afterwards when we caught up with one another in the dining room or kitchen. We'd look at one another, and that was it! We'd have a good old laugh.

How I wished my mates were with me. Next time I went to town, I'd get some writing paper and write some letters. It seemed ages since I'd heard from anyone. My only contact with the mission had been about two weeks previously, when she mentioned that the priest from the mission wrote to ask her how I was progressing. 'Great news,' I thought. I could imagine the reply back from her, probably a real thriller!

Suddenly, I heard her yoohooing out for me. I put my thoughts to one side, and ran into the dining room to see what she wanted.

Over the months that I had been here, through her manner of expectation and through fear of being scolded, I had developed a habit of running whenever she needed me. So I ran in to see what she wanted.

She just told me she was on her way out and my last instructions were not to touch the phone, and also her bedroom needed doing. She told me I was to cook tea for them and have everything ready for them when they pulled up. She told me where I would find a leg of silverside. I was to boil that up and they would have it with cauliflower, pumpkin and mashed potatoes.

So off she went with Mr Bigelow to her car. I waited back in the dining room till I saw the car go down the driveway and head in the direction of town. I thought to myself that I'd clear all the dishes away and make sure the dining room was tidy and clean for her sons.

I wished they would hurry up and have their breakfast and go, as I felt uncomfortable knowing that they were around. I couldn't relax. I wanted to eat my bacon and eggs in peace, have my shower and then escape down to the orchard.

1987

SALLY MORGAN
b. 1951

Sally Morgan's *My Place* (1987) is one of the most successful Australian autobiographies ever published. Morgan grew up in Perth and, after her father's death, she and her four siblings were raised by her mother and grandmother. Having been told that she had an Indian background, she discovered at the age of fifteen that she was of Aboriginal descent, from the Palku (or Bailgu) people of the Pilbara. This discovery culminated in the writing of *My Place*, which incorporates the life stories of her mother, grandmother, and her grandmother's brother. *My Place* was an immediate bestseller (it has sold more than half a million copies), receiving numerous awards and extensive critical attention, including some criticism for its depiction of Aboriginal identity. It was later adapted into a four-book collection for younger readers. Morgan subsequently gained an international reputation as an artist, and has written and illustrated children's books. Works include *Wanamurraganya: The story of Jack McPhee* (1989), *The Flying Emu and other Australian Stories* (1992) and *The Art of Sally Morgan* (1996).

In 1997 Morgan was appointed director of the University of Western Australia Centre for Indigenous Art and History.

From *My Place*
Chapter 24: *Where There's a Will*

[...] A few days later, I rang Aunty Judy. I explained that I was writing a book about Nan and Arthur and I thought she might be able to help me. We agreed that I would come down for lunch and she said she could tell me who Nan's father was. I was surprised. I had expected to encounter opposition. Perhaps I wanted to encounter opposition, it fired my sense of injustice. I felt really excited after our talk on the telephone. Would I really discover who my great grandfather was? If I was lucky, I might even find out about my grandfather as well. I was so filled with optimism I leapt up and down three times and gave God the thumbs up sign.

My day for lunch at Aunty Judy's dawned, and was too beautiful a day for me to fail. Mum had agreed to drop me in Cottesloe where Judy was now living, and mind the children while we had our talk.

'Can't I come, Mum?' Amber wailed as we pulled up out the front of Judy's house.

'Sorry, Amber,' I replied, 'this is private.' I leapt from the car, all vim and vigour. 'Wish me luck, Mum.'

During lunch, we chatted about diet, health foods and the impurities in most brands of ice-cream, then Aunty Judy said, 'You know, I think I have some old photos of your mother you might be interested in. I'll have to dig them out.'

'Oh great! I'd really appreciate that.'

'I'll tell you what I know about the station, but it's not a lot. You know, a relative of ours published a book a while ago and they got all their facts wrong, so you better make sure you get yours right.'

'That's why I'm here. I don't want to print anything that's not true.'

After lunch, we retired to the more comfortable chairs in the lounge-room.

'Now, dear,' Aunty Judy said, 'what would you like to know?'

'Well, first of all, I'd like to know who Nan's father was and also a bit about what her life was like when she was at Ivanhoe.'

'Well, that's no problem. My mother told me that Nan's father was a mystery man. He was a chap they called Maltese Sam and he used to be cook on Corunna Downs. He was supposed to have come from a wealthy Maltese family, I think he could have been the younger son, a ne'er-do-well. My mother said that he always used to tell them that, one day, he was going back to Malta to claim his inheritance. The trouble was he was a drinker. He'd save money for the trip and then he'd go on a binge and have to start all over again. He used to talk to my father, Howden, a lot. He was proud Nanna was his little girl.'

'Did he ever come and visit Nan when she was at Ivanhoe?'

'Yes, I think he did, once. But he was drunk, apparently, and wanted to take Nanna away with him. Nan was frightened, she didn't want to go, so my mother said to him, you go back to Malta and put things right. When you've claimed your inheritance, you can have Daisy. We never saw him again. I don't know what happened to him. Nan didn't want to go with him, we were her family by then.'

'Did you meet Maltese Sam?'

'Oh, goodness, no. I was only a child. My mother told me the story.'

'How old was Nan when she came down to Perth?'

'About fifteen or sixteen.'

'And what were her duties at Ivanhoe.'

'She looked after us children.'

'Aunty Judy, do you know who Mum's father is?'

'Your mother knows who her father is.'

'No, she doesn't. She wants to know and Nan won't tell her.'

'I'm sure I told your mother at one time who her father was.'

'She doesn't know and she'd really like to. It's very important to her.'

'Well, I'm not sure I should tell you. You never know about these things.'

'Mum wanted me to ask you.'

Aunty Judy paused and looked at me silently for a few seconds. Then she said slowly, 'All right, everybody knows who her father was, it was Jack Grime. Everyone always said that Gladdie's the image of him.'

'Jack Grime? And Mum takes after him, does she?'

'Like two peas in a pod.'

'Who was Jack Grime?'

'He was an Englishman, an engineer, very, very clever. He lived with us at Ivanhoe, he was a friend of my father's. He was very fond of your mother. When she was working as a florist, he'd call in and see her. We could always tell when he'd been to see Gladdie, he'd have a certain look on his face. He'd say, "I've been to see Gladdie", and we'd just nod.'

'Did he ever marry and have other children?'

'No. He was a very handsome man, but he never married and, as far as I know, there were no other children. He spent the rest of his life living in Sydney, he was about eighty-six when he died.'

'Eighty-six? Well, that couldn't have been that long ago, then? If he was so fond of Mum, you'd think he'd have left her something in his will. Not necessarily money, just a token to say he owned her. After all, she was his only child.'

'No, there was nothing. He wasn't a wealthy man, there was no money to leave. You know Roberta?'

'Yes, Mum's been out to dinner with her a few times.'

'Well, she's the daughter of Jack's brother, Robert. She's Gladdie's first cousin.'

'Mum doesn't know that, does Roberta?'

'Yes, she knows. She asked me a year ago whether she should say something to your mother, but I said it'd be better to leave it.'

'Perhaps Mum could talk to her.'

'Yes, she could.'

'Can you tell me anything about Nan's mother?'

'Not a lot. Her name was Annie, she was a magnificent-looking woman. She was a good dressmaker, my father taught her how to sew. She could design anything.'

Our conversation continued for another half an hour or so. I kept thinking, had Mum lied? Did she really know who her father was? Was she really against me digging up the past, just like Nan? I had one last question.

'Aunty Judy, I was talking to Arthur, Nan's brother, the other day and he said that his father was the same as yours, Alfred Howden Drake-Brockman. Isn't it possible he could have been Nan's as well.'

'No. That's not what everyone said. I've told you what I know; who Nan's father is. I'm certain Arthur's father wasn't Howden, I don't know who his father was.'

'Arthur also told me about his half-brother Albert. He said Howden was his father, too.'

'Well, he went by the name of Brockman so I suppose it might be possible, but certainly not the other two.'

'Well, thanks a lot, Aunty Judy, I suppose I'd better be going, Mum will be here any minute. She's picking me up.'

'You know who you should talk to, don't you? Mum-mum. She's still alive and better than she's been for a long time.' Mum-mum was a pet name for Aunty Judy's mother, Alice.

'She must be in her nineties by now', I said. 'Do you think she'd mind talking to me?'

'No, I don't think so, but you'd have to go interstate, she's in a nursing home in Wollongong. You could probably stay with June.' June was Judy's younger sister, Nan had been her nursemaid, too.

'I'll think about it, Aunty Judy. Thanks a lot.'

'That's all right, dear.'

I walked out to the front gate and, just as I opened it, Mum pulled up in the car.

'How did you go?' she said eagerly.

'All right,' I replied. 'Mum, are you sure you don't know who your father is? You've lied about things before.' It was a stupid thing to say, Mum was immediately on the defensive.

'Of course I don't know who my father is, Sally. Didn't you find out, after all?' She was disappointed. I felt ashamed of myself for doubting her.

'No Mum, I found out. It was Jack Grime, and Roberta is your first cousin.'

'Oh God, I can't believe it!' She was stunned.

'Can you remember anything about him, Mum? You're supposed to look a lot like him.'

'No, I can't remember much, except he used to wear a big gold watch that chimed. I thought it was magical.'

'Judy said he used to visit you when you were working as a florist, can you recall any times when he did?'

'Well yes, he popped in now and then, but then a lot of people did. I was a friendly sort of girl. Sometimes, I would go and have lunch with him at Ivanhoe, that was after Nan had left there. To think I was lunching with my own father!'

An overwhelming sadness struck me. My mother was fifty-five years of age and she'd only just discovered who her father was. It didn't seem fair.

'Mum, are you going to say anything to Nan?'

'Not now, maybe later, after I've had time to think things over. Don't you say anything, will you?'

'No, I won't. Does she know I've been to see Judy?'

'Yes, she knew you were going. She's been in a bad mood all week. Did you find out anything else?'

'Judy says Nan's father was a bloke called Maltese Sam. That he came from a wealthy family and wanted to take Nan away with him.'

'Maltese Sam? What an unusual name. I've never heard anyone talk about him. Arthur's coming tomorrow night, I'll ask him what he thinks. Of course, you know who he says is Nan's father, don't you?'

'Yeah, I know. Judy doesn't agree with him.'

The following evening, Mum and I sat chatting to Arthur. After we'd finished tea, I said, 'I visited Judith Drake-Brockman the other day, Arthur.'

'What did you do that for?'

'Oh, I thought she might be able to tell me something about Corunna Downs and something about Nan.'

'You wanna know about Corunna, you come to me. I knew all the people there.'

'I know you did.' I paused. 'Can I ask you a question?'

'You ask what you like.'

'Judy told me Nan's father was a chap by the name of Maltese Sam, have you ever heard of him?'

'She said WHAT?'

Arthur was a bit hard of hearing sometimes, so I repeated my question.

'Don't you listen to her,' he said when I'd asked again. 'She never lived on the station, how would she know?'

'Well, she got the story from her mother, Alice, who got the story from her husband, Howden, who said that Annie had confided in him.'

Arthur threw back his head and laughed. Then he thumped his fist on the arm of his chair and said, 'Now you listen to me, Daisy's father is the same as mine. Daisy is my only full sister. Albert, he's our half-brother, his father was Howden, too, but by a different woman.'

'So you reckoned he fathered the both of you.'

'By jove he did! Are you gunna take the word of white people against your own flesh and blood? I got no papers to prove what I'm sayin'. Nobody cared how many blackfellas were born in those days, nor how many died. I know because my mother, Annie, told me. She said Daisy and I belonged to one another. Don't you go takin' the word of white people against mine.'

Arthur had us both nearly completely convinced, except for one thing, he avoided our eyes. Mum and I knew it wasn't a good sign, there was something he wasn't telling us. So I said again, 'You're sure about this, Arthur?'

'Too right! Now, about this Maltese Sam, don't forget Alice was Howden's second wife and they had the Victorian way of thinking in those days. Before there were white women, our father owned us, we went by his name, but later, after he married his first wife, Nell, he changed our names. I'll tell you about that one day. He didn't want to own us no more. They were real fuddy-duddies in those days. No white man wants to have black kids runnin' round the place with his name. And Howden's mother and father, they were real religious types, I bet they didn't know about no black kids that belonged to them.'

We all laughed then. Arthur was like Mum, it wasn't often he failed to see the funny side of things.

When we'd all finally calmed down, he said, 'You know, if only you could get Daisy to talk. She could tell you so much. I know she's got her secrets, but there are things she could tell you without tellin' those.'

'She won't talk, Arthur,' I sighed. 'You know a lot about Nan, can't you tell us?'

He was silent for a moment, thoughtful. Then he said, 'I'd like to. I really would, but it'd be breakin' a trust. Some things 'bout her I can't tell. It wouldn't be right. She could tell you everything you want to know. You see, Howden was a lonely man. I know, one night at Ivanhoe, we both got drunk together and he told me all his troubles. He used to go down to Daisy's room at night and talk to her. I can't say no more. You'll have to ask her.'

'But Arthur, what if she won't tell us?'

'Then I can't, either. There's some things Daisy's got to tell herself, or not at all. I can't say no more.'

After he left, Mum and I sat analysing everything for ages. We were very confused, we knew that the small pieces of information we now possessed weren't the complete truth.

'Sally,' Mum said, breaking into my thoughts, 'do you remember when Arthur first started visiting us and he said Albert was his full brother?'

'Yeah, but that was before he knew us well.'

'Yes, but remember how he almost whispered when he told us the truth about Albert? He didn't want to hurt the feelings of any of Albert's family and he loved him so much I suppose he thought it didn't matter.'

'Yeah, I know. You think there might be more to Nan's parentage.'

'It's possible.'

'There's another possibility. Howden may have been her father, but there could be something else, some secret he wants to keep, that is somehow tied in with all of this. Perhaps that's why he didn't look us in the eye.'

'Yes, that's possible, too. And I can't see why he wouldn't tell us the truth, because he knows how much it means to us. I don't think we'll ever know the full story. I think we're going to have to be satisfied with guesses.'

'It makes me feel so sad to think no one wants to own our family.'

'I know, Mum, but look at it this way, just on a logical basis, it's possible he was her father. We know he was sleeping with Annie, and Arthur said that even after he married his first wife, he was still sleeping with Annie, so he could have sired her.'

'Yes, it's possible.'

'Well, that's all we can go on then, possibilities. Now Judy said Jack Grime was your father, but maybe he wasn't. He was living at Ivanhoe at the time you were born, but that doesn't necessarily mean he fathered you, does it?'

'Oh God, Sally,' Mum laughed, 'let's not get in any deeper. I've had enough for one night.'

1987

PAT TORRES
b. 1956

Born in Broome, WA, Pat Torres is a writer, artist, illustrator, community worker, health worker, educator and Aboriginal administrator. Since 1987 she has published autobiographical works, stories for children, poetry and critical writing, and is involved in recording Aboriginal oral history in the Kimberley.

Gurrwayi Gurrwayi, The Rain Bird

Gurrwayi Gurrwayi
It's the Rain bird call,
Don't hurt him or kill him,
Or the rain will always fall.

Gurrwayi Gurrwayi
Gawinaman jina gambini bandalmada.
Malu minabilga gamba bandalmada.
Galiya yiljalgun wula widu jayida.

1987

Wangkaja, The Mangrove Crab

Wangkaja, the mangrove crab,
His meat is so good to eat.
Hiding under the muddy sand,
Look out it's under your feet.

Mabu warli wangkaja miliya.
Ingadin jimbin jabarlbarl burrgadja ingan niminy.
Niwalgun juyu wangkaja ingan
jabarlbarl ingan walabunda juyu.

1987

RUBY LANGFORD GINIBI
b. 1934

Born at Box Ridge Mission, Coraki, NSW, Dr Ruby Langford Ginibi is an elder of
the Bundjalung Nation. She grew up in Bonalbo and attended high school in Casino.
At fifteen she moved to Sydney where she qualified as a clothing machinist. For many
years she lived and camped in the bush around Coonabarabran, fencing, lopping and
ringbarking trees, pegging kangaroo skins and working in clothing factories.

Following her first book, *Don't Take Your Love to Town*, published in 1988, she has
produced many award-winning works of autobiography, and published poetry and
critical pieces on Aboriginal writing and politics. Her books include *Real Deadly* (1992),
My Bundjalung People (1994), *Haunted by the Past* (1999) and *All My Mob* (2007). Ginibi
is also a respected lecturer and speaker, having taught Aboriginal history, culture and
politics at universities and colleges.

Her tribal name, Ginibi ('black swan'), was given to her in 1990 by her aunt,
Eileen Morgan, a tribal elder of Box Ridge Mission. The mother of nine children and
many grandchildren and great-grandchildren, Ginibi was NAIDOC National Female
Aboriginal Elder of the Year in 2007. In 2005 she was awarded the NSW Premier's
Literary Awards' Special Award and in 2006 won the Australia Council for the Arts
Writers' Emeritus Award.

From *Don't Take Your Love to Town*
Chapter 10: Corroboree/Phaedra

[…] When we first moved into Ann Street, Surry Hills, we survived on my
endowment and any casual work Lance could get, but it only covered food. I
took the kids to The Smith Family to get outfitted and with eight of them we
took up two fitting rooms. They got to know us well and we'd go home loaded
up with brown paper parcels and cardboard boxes of tinned food. One morning
they approached me at home and asked if they could take photos of the kids
for their Christmas appeal. Somewhere in their files is a picture of me with a
beehive hairstyle sitting on the front step of Ann Street nursing Pauline, who
was two, and Ellen (four) sitting beside us.

Lance was working on the Water Board and I got a job around the corner
at Silknit House making trousers for Reuben F. Scarf. I asked my cousin and
his wife to stay and they saw the kids off to Cleveland Street School each day.
Things were looking up. We bought a Ford Mainline ute and went to Paddys
each Saturday for food, then we took the kids swimming at Coogee.

Nerida and her new man Booker Trindle turned up. Booker was a mate of
Lance's from the days after Lance's mother had died and he was on the road.
They'd worked together in the bush. I remembered Booker from the Clifton
one night where Lance had introduced him as his brother. I shook his hand.

He was very handsome and dressed in a suit. I was taken in but they were only conning me up. Now Booker and Neddy were living in Redfern.

Our favourite Koori watering hole was the Rockers. Its real name was the Macquarie, it was down in Woolloomooloo on the docks. They had big jazz bands and we got dolled up and went down sometimes to listen to the bands and have a few beers.

Lance and Booker wouldn't let Neddy and me go down there by ourselves, that was where the sailors drank and they were frightened they might lose us two good-looking sorts. We decided to give them a piece of their own medicine.

We sneaked down there one night and we were having a great time when who should walk through the doors of the pub but Lance and his sidekick Booker. 'There you are, you two,' they said, and, 'We've been looking for you everywhere.' We said we'd only just gotten there, which was a lie, we'd been there for a couple of hours and we were having a great time, but they frogmarched us out and told us to get home.

We said, 'We'll get a taxi,' and they said, "Start walkin".' Big men, and they made us walk all the way to Surry Hills. Blokes were driving past and whistling at us, and they'd tell them to piss off, and say to us, "Keep walkin".' I thought we'd never make it and we were buggered when we did get home. Well we never did that again, I mean sneak away by ourselves, it was a lesson well-learned for Neddy and me.

Not that they could put anything over us two, we were too cunning. They'd have to wake up early to catch us out.

'Look here,' Neddy said one day, 'there's a photo of you and the kids in the paper.' She handed me a copy of the *Mirror* and there we were, smiling for the Smithos.

Booker came in late that night, hair and clothes everywhere, he must've been on a binge for a week. Lance grabbed him by the arm. 'What the hell are you doin'? Look at you, why don't you look after yourself,' he said. 'Use my razor, come on, get in here and have a bath, here's a clean shirt, come on Booker, straighten yourself up.' The times Booker came in and didn't take any notice of Lance, Lance thumped him. They were like that, like brothers.

The kids were going to Sunday School round the corner in Commonwealth Street. The place was run by Central City Mission and was also a soup kitchen for the needy. They gave the kids bread and pies and cakes to bring home when we had no food. The Brown Sisters came to our rescue, they were called Our Lady of the Poor and wore brown habits.

I'd heard about the Aboriginal Progressive Association and I decided to go to the meetings. Charlie Perkins was there, and the Bostocks, Eadie and Lester, also Bertie Groves, Charlie and Peggy Leon, Joyce Mercy, Ray Peckham, Helen Hambly, Allan Woods and Isobel McAllum whose father was Bill Ferguson, a member of the Aborigines' Protection Board. We elected Charlie Perkins spokesman—he was still at university—and we met at the Pan Hellenic Club rooms in Elizabeth Street. Charlie organised that because he played soccer for the club. I was elected editor for our newspaper *Churringa* (meaning message stick). Ever since school and the long stories I'd wanted to do some writing, so I was happy.

It was about 1964 when we formed our first Sydney APA. We heard some dancers were coming down from Mornington Island to perform a corroboree at the Elizabethan Theatre in Newtown. At the next meeting we decided to apply for concessions. I'd never seen a corroboree or been in a big theatre before. Our seats were upstairs overlooking the stage.

When the lights went out we could see the glow of a fire on centre stage, with bodies huddled around it, and we could hear a didgeridoo in the background and clapping sticks and then the chanting. In a while the whole stage was aglow with the light from the fire, and the corroboree began.

A narrator talked over a microphone, explaining the action as the dancers performed. After each performance we clapped and clapped. Something inside me understood everything that was going on. I had tears in my eyes and I could feel the others in the group were entranced like me.

One story in particular made me sad. It was about a tribal family—man, woman and child. It told how another man came and took the woman away, and left the baby to die. The father searched and hunted until he found the man and speared him. His wife threw herself over a cliff and died. The final scene showed the father burying his child, and it was the most moving part of the corroboree. It showed him digging the earth up with his hands and placing the bark-covered body into the ground, and, as he was covering it with earth he'd smite himself across the chest and wail for the loss of his child and cover more soil over the body then smite himself again and this went on until he had it completely covered. I was crying by then.

Afterwards, we asked permission to visit them backstage. It was strange because they were dressed in khaki overalls and they were so tall, big rangy warriors all over six feet. Only one of them could speak English, a bit pidgin and they were wary as they looked at us, until the one who could speak explained that we were part of them, and then they gave us big toothy grins and we were shaking hands all round. I can remember almost every detail from that night.

I went to a meeting of the APA on National Aborigines' Day in Martin Place. The Governor General and several other dignitaries (black and white) were going to speak. I wore a fur stole over my dress. I put my stilettos on and did my hair up. At Martin Place I met up with the others and found a seat. The Police Band sat behind us. A man on the dais was singing in the lingo and I listened closer. It was Bundjalung language, words and sounds I hadn't heard for a long time. It was an eerie feeling in amongst the skyscrapers.

I looked harder and I recognised the singer, it was Uncle Jim Morgan. When the singing stopped a hand tapped me on the shoulder and a voice said, 'Hello Mrs Campbell.' Someone from the time I was with Gordon, I thought, turning around. Coona. It was Max Gruggan, the policeman who used to pull Gordon out of the pub and send him home to Charlie Harvey's property. 'I didn't hardly recognise you, all done up,' he said. We swapped notes—he'd transferred to

Penrith in the meantime. I couldn't concentrate much because I was thinking about Uncle Jim Morgan and the singing.

In a while I went and found Uncle Jim. I hadn't seen him since I was at school in Bonalbo and he was glad to see me too, like meeting someone from your own town in another country. He had to go soon after and so I put word out about him.

Some time later my cousin Margaret in Wollongong sent me two paper clippings—one about Grandfather Sam and one about Uncle Jim. JAMES MORGAN LIVED IN TWO WORLDS, it said. He had collapsed and died shortly before he was to address a large crowd in Casino for National Aborigines' Day. 'A full-blood Aborigine, Mr Morgan was known as "the last of the Dyrabba tribe".' Dyrabba? That was the name of our street in Bonalbo. 'He was born on the site of Casino racecourse … He was a fluent speaker of Bunjalong [spelt that way] and had a working knowledge of the twelve dialects in the Bunjalong area which extends from Ipswich to Grafton … He was also an expert on folklore of this area. He made many recordings for the Richmond River Historical Society …'

This meant I could find out some more about my history. I decided to write to the RRHS for the tapes.

His funeral was to be held at the chapel at Box Ridge, he was to be buried at Coraki cemetery. Home ground.

1988

BURNUM BURNUM
1936–1997

Born at Wallaga Lake, NSW, Burnum Burnum was an activist, rugby player, actor, author, dreamer and respected Aboriginal elder. Removed from his parents at the age of three months and named Harry Penrith, he spent his early years in children's homes, where he was raised to believe he was white. In the 1960s, he searched for his Aboriginal identity, joined the struggle for Aboriginal rights, and took the name of his great-grandfather, meaning 'Great Warrior'. He attended the University of Tasmania and became an active member of the Aboriginal community, helping to organise the 1972 Aboriginal Tent Embassy in Canberra. On Australia Day 1988 he famously declared Aboriginal possession of England, raising the Aboriginal flag on the English coast at Dover.

The Burnum Burnum Declaration

I, Burnum Burnum, being a nobleman of ancient Australia do hereby take possession of England on behalf of the Aboriginal People.

In claiming this colonial outpost, we wish no harm to you natives, but assure you that we are here to bring you good manners, refinement and an opportunity to make a Koompartoo—'a fresh start'.

Henceforth, an Aboriginal face shall appear on your coins and stamps to signify our sovereignty over this domain.

For the more advanced, we bring the complex language of the Pitjantjajara; we will teach you how to have a spiritual relationship with the Earth and show you how to get bush tucker.

We do not intend to souvenir, pickle and preserve the heads of 2000 of your people, nor to publicly display the skeletal remains of your Royal Highness, as was done to our Queen Truganinni for 80 years. Neither do we intend to poison your water holes, lace your flour with strychnine or introduce you to highly toxic drugs.

Based on our 50,000 year heritage, we acknowledge the need to preserve the Caucasian race as of interest to antiquity, although we may be inclined to conduct experiments by measuring the size of your skulls for levels of intelligence. We pledge not to sterilize your women, nor to separate your children from their families.

We give an absolute undertaking that you shall not be placed onto the mentality of government handouts for the next five generations but you will enjoy the full benefits of Aboriginal equality.

At the end of two hundred years, we will make a Treaty to validate occupation by peaceful means and not by conquest.

Finally, we solemnly promise not to make a quarry of England and export your valuable minerals back to the old country Australia, and we vow never to destroy three-quarters of your trees, but to encourage Earth Repair Action to unite people, communities, religions and nations in a common, productive, peaceful purpose.

1988

ERROL WEST
1947–2001

Born in Tasmania of the Pairrebeene clan, Errol West (Japanangka) is best known for his strong advocacy in national and international forums of Aboriginal education. West worked closely with Aboriginal communities and chaired numerous committees that funded Aboriginal education, teacher employment and policy development. He also made a significant contribution to Aboriginal scholarship through his work at various universities.

'Sitting, wondering, do I have a place here?'

Sitting, wondering, do I have a place here?
The breast of Mother Earth bore me, yet long I host a shell of
emptiness, a human husk winnowed in the draught of history,
    my
essence ground on the mill of white determination.   5

I fight though mortally wounded, life blood and spirit ebbing away
in the backwater of despair, caused by long-winded politicians'
promises and administration's cumbersome gait;
another realisation of my hopelessness produces; another promise,
implementation of a band-aid gimmick, you had better hurry   10
    it's
getting late, red tape, budgets, strategies,
Rape!

Return me to my beloved land, let me be me, don't you understand?
All I want is a private dying in the arms of my Mother earth,   15
    she
too is suffering; as a mother must when her children are ripped
away from her love, and the safety of her arms, no more to be cradled,
tenderly caressed by her heavenly smoldering essence.

1988

GALARRWUY YUNUPINGU
b. 1948

A member of the Gumatj clan of the Yolngu people, Galarrwuy Yunupingu was born at Melville Bay near Yirrkala, NT. He first attended the mission school at Yirrkala and for two years studied at the Methodist Bible College, Brisbane. In the early 1960s he joined his father Mungurrawuy, a Gumatj clan leader, in the struggle for Aboriginal land rights and the Yirrkala protest against bauxite mining, helping to create the Yirrkala Bark Petition in 1963 and bringing Aboriginal land rights to national attention. In 1975 he joined the Northern Land Council of which he was chairman from 1977 to 2004 and in 2001 was elected as co-chair of the Aboriginal Development Consultative Forum in Darwin. A senior ceremonial leader of his people, he was Australian of the Year in 1978 and named an Australian Living National Treasure in 1998. Barunga is located in the Northern Territory. Wenten Rubuntja, an artist and activist who died in 2005, was Chairperson of the Central Land Council when he co-presented the following petition to Prime Minister Bob Hawke.

Barunga Statement

We the indigenous owners and occupiers of Australia call on the Australian Government and people to recognise our rights:

- to self determination and self management including the freedom to pursue our own economic, social, religious and cultural development;
- to permanent control and enjoyment of our ancestral lands;
- to compensation for the loss of use of our lands, there having been no extinction of original title;
- to protection of and control of access to our sacred sites, sacred objects, artefacts, designs, knowledge and works of art;
- to the return of the remains of our ancestors for burial in accordance with our traditions;
- to respect for promotion of our Aboriginal identity, including the cultural, linguistic, religious and historical aspects, including the right to be educated in our own languages, and in our own culture and history;
- in accordance with the Universal Declaration of Human Rights, the International Covenant on Economic, Social and Cultural Rights, the International Covenant on Civil and Political Rights, and the International Convention on the Elimination of all forms of Racial Discrimination, rights to life, liberty, security of person, food, clothing, housing, medical care, education and employment opportunities, necessary social services and other basic rights.

We call on the Commonwealth to pass laws providing:

- a national elected Aboriginal and Islander organisation to oversee Aboriginal and Islander affairs;
- a national system of land rights;
- a police and justice system which recognises our customary laws and frees us from discrimination and any activity which may threaten our identity or security, interfere with our freedom of expression or association, or otherwise prevent our full enjoyment and exercise of universally-recognised human rights and fundamental freedoms.

We call on the Australian Government to support Aborigines in the development of an International Declaration of Principles for Indigenous Rights, leading to an International Covenant.

And we call on the Commonwealth Parliament to negotiate with us a Treaty or Compact recognising our prior ownership, continued occupation and sovereignty and affirming our human rights and freedoms.

1988

BILL NEIDJIE
c. 1913–2002

Bill Neidjie was born at Alawanydjawany on the East Alligator River in Arnhem Land, NT. Prior to the Second World War, Neidjie had a variety of jobs for which he was paid in tea, sugar, meat, flour and tobacco. After the 1942 bombing of Darwin, he assisted affected Aboriginal people. Around this time he was initiated in a Ubarr ceremony at Paw Paw Beach. For nearly 30 years Neidjie worked on a lugger along the north coast of WA. In 1979 he returned home to his Bunitj clan land, becoming a claimant in the Alligator Rivers Stage II land claim.

He was an author of 'Indjuwanydjuwa: A report on Bunitj clan sites in the Alligator Rivers region' (1982), which helped the Bunitj people of the Gagadju language group gain title to their land. Neidjie was instrumental in the decision to lease the traditional lands to the Commonwealth of Australia so it could be managed as a resource for all Australians. He became a senior elder of Kadaku National Park and was a keen conservationist throughout his life. On his death the Gagadju tongue died with him. He died near Kakadu, the park named after his language. He is the author of two works, *Australia's Kakadu Man* (1985) and *Story about Feeling* (1989).

Ahh ... Bush-Honey There!

You cannot see.
I cannot see but you feel it.
I feel it.
E can feeling.
I feeling.   5

Spirit longside with you.
You sit ... e sit. Telling you.
You think ...
   'I want to go over there.'

E tell im you ... before!   10
Anything you want to look ...
   'Ahh ... go tree.'

But e say ...
   'Hey! You go look that tree.
   Something e got there.'   15

You look ... well you look straight away.
You might look snake, you might look bush-honey.
E telling you to have a look ...
   'Look up!'
   'Ahh ... bush-honey there.'   20

Alright, you say ...
   'I go somewhere else. I go look painting.'

All that painting, small mark ...
they put cross, cross and over again.
White, yellow and little bit charcoal, little bit red clay ...   25
that's the one all small meaning there.
They put it meaning.
They painting fish ... little mark they make im, you know.
That's the one same as this you look newspaper.
Big mob you read it all that story,   30
e telling you all that meaning.
All that painting now, small,
e tell im you that story.

That meaning that you look ... you feel im now.
You might say ...   35
   'Hey! That painting good one!
   I take im more picture.'

That spirit e telling you ...
   'Go on ... you look.'

Taking picture.   40

Well all that meaning there.
E say mother, granny, grandpa, grass, fire, bird, tree.
All that small thing, little thing,
all that mark they make it, when you go sleep
you dream ...   45
going through your feeling.
You might sleep. Well you feel ...
   'Hey, I bin dream good dream!'

White paint might be big hawk ... before.
Yellow clay where sunset ... e tell im you that secret.   50
  You got to put im on yellow clay
because all that dream, all that story is there.
  You got to put charcoal
because e got 'business' there, what we call Dhuwa.
Yellow clay ... Yirridtja.   55
Well all that piece, piece they paint im, all that story
secret, grandpa, granny, back, chest, head ...
e coming through your feeling.
That painting you say ...
    'That lovely painting.'   60

Finger prints ...
E put finger prints because hand e put it.
Where you grab it thing, you know.
Fruit or cutting it anykind ... with your fingers!
They put it finger prints.   65
They said ...
    'They can look.'

Some foot prints ...
That's the one they feel it.
They used to feel it turtle there   70
or might be water–python, snake.
They feel ...
    'Hey! Snake!'

That way all that painting they left it behind,
dead ... on the rock.   75

No matter who is.
E can feel it way I feel it in my feeling.
You'll be same too.
You listen my story and you will feel im
because spirit e'll be with you.   80
You cannot see but e'll be with you and e'll be with me.
This story just listen careful.

Spirit must stay with us. E longside us.
E can feel it spirit e's there.
That way all that dreaming they left ... to see.   85

        1989

BOB RANDALL
b. 1934

Bob Randall is a singer, songwriter, teacher and activist. He is from the Yankunytjatjara people and is a traditional owner of the Uluru lands, NT. His mother, Tanguawa, worked as a housemaid at Angus Downs cattle station for Randall's father, station owner Bill Liddle. Randall and his mother lived away from the main house with their extended family and he had little contact with his Scottish father. Randall was taken from his mother at the age of seven. He spent time in an Alice Springs institution for children, Croker Island Reservation, and in Sydney.

Randall married, completed a welfare residential worker's course, moved to Darwin and began finding his family while establishing a career as an Aboriginal educator.

In 1970, Randall helped establish the Adelaide Community College for Aboriginal people and lectured at the college on Aboriginal cultures. Randall has also established Aboriginal and Torres Strait Islander centres at other universities. Many consider his song 'Brown Skin Baby' an anthem of the stolen generation.

Brown Skin Baby

Yaaawee, yaahaawawee,
My brown skin baby they take 'im away.

As a young preacher I used to ride
my quiet pony round the countryside.
In a native camp I'll never forget   5
a young black mother her cheeks all wet.

Yaaawee, yaahaawawee,
My brown skin baby they take 'im away.

Between her sobs I heard her say,
'Police bin take-im my baby away.   10
From white man boss that baby I have,
why he let them take baby away?'

Yaaawee, yaahaawawee,
My brown skin baby they take 'im away.

To a children's home a baby came,   15
With new clothes on, and a new name.
Day and night he would always say,
'Mummy, Mummy, why they take me away?'

Yaaawee, yaahaawawee,
My brown skin baby they take 'im away.   20

The child grew up and had to go
From a mission home that he loved so.

To find his mother he tried in vain.
Upon this earth they never met again.

Yaaawee, yaahaawawee,   25
My brown skin baby they take 'im away.

                                                                          1990

SAM WATSON
b. 1952

Sam Watson is a poet, activist, lecturer, playwright and storyteller of the Birri-Gubba (from his grandfather) and Munaldjali (from his grandmother) nations and lives in Brisbane. His political activism began as a student in the 1960s over the White Australia policy. He went on to play support roles in the 1967 referendum campaign, the Gurindji land rights struggle and other campaigns for Indigenous equality and justice. He studied law and arts at the University of Queensland in the early 1970s. Watson pioneered programs in law, medicine and housing, focusing on Indigenous communities, and was a co-founder of the Brisbane chapter of the Black Panther Party of Australia. His novel *The Kadaitcha Sung* was published in 1990. Watson co-produced the film *Black Man Down* (1995), and made his playwriting debut in 2007 with *The Mack*, written in association with the Brisbane-based Kooemba Jdarra theatre company. Watson is the father of the poet Samuel Wagan Watson (qv).

From *The Kadaitcha Sung*

When time was still young the gods created substance from the firmament. They made the land and the waters, and then they made life. The land and the waters would serve to reflect the void, and life would bow down and worship the gods, as the gods needed to be worshipped. They brought forth fowl for the air, fish for the oceans and beasts for the land. Men and women were created to have dominion over all; they would live upon the land. The men and women must worship the gods and keep the laws of the gods, and they must ensure that the natural order of all things was kept. One god, a greater being, made his camp on the rich veldts and in the lush valleys of the South Land. He was called Biamee and he loved all life. In time he came to love the tribes of man above all others, for they revered him and his laws. For many aeons the land and the people basked in Biamee's beneficence, and all was well. But there came the time when Biamee longed for his camp among the stars and he made plans to return there. But the tribes became fearful. The world was still a savage place.

So the great one made a veil of mists that hung upon the South Land and hid it from all. Then Biamee called an ancient clan of sorcerers from the heavens to stand in his place. They were known as the Kadaitcha and they were powerful. Then came the day that the tribes farewelled Biamee as he ascended from his most sacred altar, in the vast red rock that sat upon the heart of the land.

The tribes welcomed the Kadaitcha into their midst and the ancient ones took the shape of men, so that they could live within the camps and not cause fear. The chief of the Kadaitcha clan was called Kobbina. He made his camp beneath the red rock that held Biamee's altar and then he looked for a wife. A handmaiden at the court of the moon spirit was fair and she had no man, so she became Kobbina's woman. Her name was Meeyola and she gave the chief twin sons, named Koobara and Booka.

There came the time when Biamee and his fellow gods needed the wisdom of Kobbina in their council, so they called for the chief to join them for all eternity among the stars. Kobbina's heart swelled with pride, but then his spirit became heavy, for now he would have to choose which of his sons would follow him as the Turrwan, or high man. The law was such that only the oldest son could follow, but Meeyola loved them both and would not reveal which of the babies was first born. Kobbina must make the decision and he cast his eye upon the young men. Koobara was tall and fair, and even though he was only a novice his wisdom was great and his patience legend. On the other hand Booka was squat and ugly, possessed of a violence that was fearful to behold. But Biamee's patience grew thin and the chief had to decide, so Kobbina called to his hosts to gather at his camp at the next full moon.

At that sit-down Kobbina walked to his sons and laid his hand upon Koobara, but Booka's rage exploded into a terrible cataclysm of bloodletting. He smote his father and killed him; Booka's followers leaped to his side and fell upon Koobara and his sub-priests. Meeyola fell with a mortal wound and blood ran in a terrible flood. From on high Biamee saw all, and with a heavy heart he began to descend from the astral plane so he could take a direct hand in the dispute. The conflict raged until Koobara's forces sensed the coming of Biamee, which gave them new strength. The evil Booka left a rearguard and fled the battlefield; he had to stop Biamee.

Beneath the red rock was a vast cavern and within the bowels of that cavern was a stone platform that held the Rings of Bora, nine sacred circles of stones that were Biamee's only doorway into the world of men. Booka attacked the altar with a desperate fear, for unless he closed the Ring, Biamee would return and banish Booka to the eternal pits.

The altar was guarded by the four sisters of the winds, who were no match for the violence of Booka and his band. Booka secured the cavern and then he strode through the Rings of Bora and removed the key to the circle, the egg-shaped Kundri stone, the heart of the Rainbow Serpent. The Rings were locked and Biamee was denied his garden. From on high the god swore eternal vengeance, but he was powerless and Booka mocked him. The renegade then raped and blinded the four sisters, to signify his ultimate rejection of Biamee and his laws. By the time Koobara arrived, Booka was gone and the Kundri stone had been stolen. He tended to the four female spirits and then he tried to commune with Biamee, but it was useless. The mortal plane was now isolated and godless.

Booka waged a long and terrible campaign against his brother, and great was the devastation and loss of life. The evil one caused the mists to lift from the land and other mortals saw its wealth and abundance; they came in their hordes and they slaughtered the helpless tribes with a monstrous lust. These new tribes came from all corners of the outside world and from all the families of man, but they did not know Biamee and they did not know of his laws. The fair-skinned ones laid waste to the garden and the chosen people.

Denied his birthright by his own tribe, Booka joined with the new settlers so he would secure position within their order. The unholy alliance was awesome and the tribes were decimated; they lost their lands and they were herded into compounds like animals. Koobara and his sub-priests were overwhelmed until finally Biamee was able to re-establish a fragile link with them. The god told them of an ancient spell that would imprison Booka within a magic wall and would give them time to recover. Koobara sang the proper songs and danced the proper dances: he called to the proper gods and at the right time the spell was invoked. Booka was confined to a thin strip of coastal land that housed a new village called Brisbane, and there he stayed while Koobara regathered the tribes and strengthened their defences against the invaders.

As time passed the violence lessened and the tribes that survived began to rebuild. They started to adapt to life under the new masters and Koobara was pleased. He had secured most of the sacred sites, and now that the people were safe, he could make preparations to wrest the Kundri stone from Booka.

Booka raged within his gaol, but he could do nothing until, sensing that his brother had grown careless and vulnerable, he plotted for his death. From afar, he murdered Koobara and became the last of the Kadaitcha clan. Such had been the scale of the killings that none other remained to deny him.

But Koobara's son had been born of a white woman, and Biamee promised his people that the Kadaitcha child would deliver them.

1990

GRAEME DIXON
b. 1955

Graeme Dixon, whose mother is Noongar from Katanning and whose father is an English migrant orphan, grew up at the now infamous Fairbridge Farm School in NSW. At the age of sixteen, Dixon was sent to Fremantle Prison where he spent most of the next nine years, and it was there that he began writing. His poetry collection *Holocaust Island* (1990) was the inaugural winner of the David Unaipon Award in 1989. He is also the author of *Holocaust Revisited: Killing time* (2003).

Six Feet of Land Rights

If we never succeed in reclaiming our country
doomed to live life paying rent to the gentry
It would be a good thing if after our death day
for that six feet of earth we didn't have to pay
It would ease the pressure, on those of our kind   5
Poor, mourning, sad people, left living behind
It would make the last day easier to face
if that financial burden was lifted

from our poverty-ridden race
Then when the reaper comes   10
to switch off our lights
our souls may rest in peace, knowing
at last! Six feet of land rights.

1990

Holocaust Island

Nestled in the Indian Ocean
Like a jewel in her crown
The worshippers of Babel come
To relax and turn to brown
To recuperate from woe and toil   5
and leave their problems far behind
To practise ancient rituals
The habits of their kind

But what they refuse to realise
Is that in this little Isle   10
are skeletons in their cupboards
of deeds most foul and vile
Far beneath this Island's surface
In many an unmarked place
lie the remnants of forgotten ones   15
Kia, members of my race.

1990

ARCHIE ROACH
b 1955

The award-winning singer-songwriter Archie Roach was born at Mooroopna, south-west Victoria. In 1956 he and his family were moved to Framlingham Mission (near Warrnambool), after which Roach was removed from his family, placed in an orphanage and eventually fostered to a family that nurtured his interest in music. As a young man, Roach left his foster family and spent many years living on the streets as an alcoholic, attempting to find his family. Roach met up with Ruby Hunter, his lifelong partner, and together they have made a home for their children, continuing to make music. Based in Melbourne, their band The Altogethers was noticed by singer-songwriter Paul Kelly, who supported Roach's musical career and who co-produced his first album, *Charcoal Lane* (1990). Roach's 'Took the Children Away' became an iconic song of the stolen generation. Roach has released three further albums, and he features on the soundtrack to Rolf de Heer's film *The Tracker* (2002). In 2000 Roach filmed *Land of the Little Kings*, about the stolen generation, and worked with the Bangarra Dance Theatre on the production *Skin*.

Took the Children Away

This story's right, this story's true
I would not tell lies to you
Like the promises they did not keep

And how they fenced us in like sheep
Said to us come take our hand   5
Sent us off to mission land
Taught us to read, to write and pray
Then they took the children away.

Took the children away
The children away   10
Snatched from their mother's breast
Said it was for the best
Took them away

The welfare and the policeman
Said you've got to understand   15
We'll give to them what you can't give
Teach them how to really live
Teach them how to live they said
Humiliated them instead
Taught them that and taught them this   20
And others taught them prejudice

You took the children away
The Children away
Breaking their mother's heart
Tearing us all apart   25
Took them away

One dark day on Framlingham
Came and didn't give a damn
My mother cried go get their dad
He came running fighting mad   30
Mother's tears were falling down
Dad shaped up, he stood his ground
He said you touch my kids and you fight me
And they took us from our family

Took us away   35
They took us away
Snatched from our mother's breast
Said this is for the best
Took us away

Told us what to do and say   40
Told us all the white man's ways
Then they split us up again

And gave us gifts to ease the pain
Sent us off to foster homes

As we grew up we felt alone   45
Cause we were acting white
Yet feeling black
One sweet day all the children came back
The children came back
The children came back   50
Back where their hearts grow strong
Back where they all belong
The children came back
Said the children came back
The children came back   55
Back where they understand
Back to their mother's land
The children came back

Back to their mother
Back to their father   60
Back to their sister
Back to their brother
Back to their people
Back to their land

All the children came back   65
The children came back
The children came back
Yes, I came back

                                                          1990

JIMMY CHI
b. 1948

Jimmy Chi was born in Broome, WA, of a Chinese-Japanese-Anglo father and a
Scottish-Bardi Aboriginal mother. After a serious car accident when he was 21, Chi
began writing contemporary music, forming the band Kuckles and collaborating with
the Pigram Brothers.

Chi's musicals *Bran Nue Dae* (*1990*/1991) and *Corrugation Road* (*1996*/unpublished)
have won numerous awards and are recognised as significant contributions to the
development of contemporary Aboriginal theatre. Their success was also instrumental
in the formation of the Black Swan Theatre in Nedlands, WA, as well as launching the
careers of many Aboriginal actors. He received the 1991 Human Rights Award for
Literature and Other Writing.

From *Bran Nue Dae*
Act 2, Song 'Bran Nue Dae'

TADPOLE: [*Recitative*:] This fella song all about the Aboriginal people, coloured people, black people longa Australia. Us people want our land back, we want 'em rights, we want 'em fair deal, all same longa white man. Now this fella longa Canberra, he bin talkin' about a Bran Nue Dae—us people bin waiting for dijwun for 200 years now. Don' know how much longer we gotta wait, and boy it's makin' me slack.

> [*Sings*:] Here I live in this tin shack
> Nothing here worth coming back
> To drunken fights and awful sights
> People drunk most every night.
>
> CHORUS:
> On the way to a Bran Nue Dae
> Everybody everybody say
> On the way to a Bran Nue Dae
> Everybody everybody say.

TADPOLE: [*Recitative*:] Other day I bin longa to social security, I bin ask longa job—they bin say, 'Hey, what's your work experience?' I bin tell 'em, 'I got nothing.' They say, 'How come?' I say, "Cause I can't find a job.'

> TADPOLE: We've nothing old, and nothing new
>   want us all to be like you,
>   We've no future we have no past
>   Hope the sun will shine at last.
>
> CHORUS:
> On the way to a Bran Nue Dae
> Everybody everybody say
> On the way to a Bran Nue Dae
> Everybody everybody say.

1991

MANDAWUY YUNUPINGU
b. 1956

A Yolngu man of the Gumatj clan, Yunupingu was born at Yirrkala in Arnhem Land, NT. His father was a signatory to the 1963 Yirrkala Bark Petition, and he was raised in a politically active environment. He gained his teaching certificate in 1977, started teaching at the Yirrkala Community School, and was the first Yolngu person to earn a university degree, graduating with a Bachelor of Arts (Education) from Deakin University in 1988. He was assistant principal of the Yirrkala Community School from 1989 and its principal from 1990; he became a leader in the 'both-ways' curriculum, teaching both Yolngu and European cultures. While teaching, Yunupingu also wrote songs and in 1985 he co-founded the music band Yothu Yindi (Yolngu for 'child and mother') with his nephew Witiyana Marika. Yothu Yindi's second album *Tribal Voice* (1991) was extremely successful, its hit single 'Treaty' (co-written by the band with Paul Kelly and Midnight Oil's Peter Garrett) topping the charts as a focal point for popular awareness of Aboriginal social justice. On 26 January 1993, Yunupingu was named Australian of the Year by the National Australia Day Council. He continues to make music and is a significant contributor to Aboriginal cultural and political life.

Treaty

Well I heard it on the radio
And I saw it on the television
Back in 1988, all those talking politicians
Words are easy, words are cheap
Much cheaper than our priceless land   5
But promises can disappear
Just like writing in the sand

Treaty yeah treaty now treaty yeah treaty now

Nhima djatpangarri nhima walangwalang
Nhe djatpayatpa nhima gaya' nhe marrtjini yakarray   10
Nhe djatpa nhe walang
Gumurr-djararrk Gutjuk

This land was never given up
This land was never bought and sold
The planting of the Union Jack   15
Never changed our law at all
Now two rivers run their course
Separated for so long
I'm dreaming of a brighter day
When the waters will be one   20

Treaty yeah treaty now treaty yeah treaty now

Nhima gayakaya nhe gaya' nhe
Nhe gaya' nhe marrtjini walangwalang nhe ya
Nhima djatpa nhe walang
Gumurr-djararrk yawirriny'   25

Nhe gaya' nhe marrtjini gaya' nhe marrtjini
Gayakaya nhe gaya' nhe marrtjini walangwalang
Nhima djatpa nhe walang
Gumurr-djararrk nhe yå

Promises disappear—priceless land—destiny   30
Well I heard it on the radio
And I saw it on the television

But promises can be broken
Just like writing in the sand

Treaty yeah treaty now treaty yeah treaty now   35
Treaty yeah treaty now treaty yeah treaty now
Treaty yeah treaty ma treaty yeah treaty ma
Treaty yeah treaty ma treaty yeah treaty ma

1991

JIMMY PIKE
c. 1940–2002

Walmajarri man Jimmy Pike was born and grew up in the Great Sandy Desert, WA.
A former stockman on Kimberley cattle stations, Pike was imprisoned for murder in 1981.
While in prison he took up painting and met the writer Pat Lowe. Born in England in 1941,
Lowe migrated to Australia in 1972. In the late 1970s she worked as a clinical psychologist
at Fremantle Prison. She moved to Broome in 1979. After Pike's release from prison in
1988, Pike and Lowe went to live at Kurlku, near Fitzroy Crossing. In the early 1990s they
returned to Broome and Pike's career as an artist began to flourish. In 1999 he became the
first Australian artist to have his work displayed in the China National Art Gallery, Beijing.
Pike and Lowe collaborated on a number of children's books, including *Jilji: Life in the Great
Sandy Desert* (1990), *Yinti: Desert child* (1992), *Desert Dog* (1997), *Jimmy and Pat Meet the Queen*
(1997), *Desert Cowboy* (2000) and *Jimmy and Pat Go to China* (2006). Lowe is also the co-
author of *Two Sisters: The story of Ngarta and Jukuna* (2004), a book about Pike's nieces.

From *Yinti*
Ranyjipirra!

One early morning, Yinti had a drink of water, picked up his spear, and set off
on his own. After walking for a while, he found the fresh tracks of a cat, and
started to follow them. This was hot-weather time, and Yinti walked fast, while
the morning was still cool enough. The tracks led him all the way to a foxhole.

Yinti looked in at the entrance to the hole, and he saw a cat, sleeping. He
looked in the other entrance and there, to his surprise, was another cat. Both
cats woke up suddenly, and they rushed out of the hole and took off running
before Yinti had time to aim his spear.

Yinti started off after one of the two cats. It was a big male. He followed it
for a long, long way. The sun was high now and the day was hot. Yinti's mouth
was getting dry from lack of water.

After a long time the cat's tracks led Yinti right up to a bandicoot's hole. By
the time he got there, the cat had already run down inside it. Now, a bandicoot
digs a deep hole, with lots of twists and turns. That's what makes it such a difficult
animal to catch. A hunter can spend half the day trying to dig it out, and all the
time he is digging from the top, the bandicoot is busily digging itself deeper still.

Yinti knew he would not be able to dig the cat out of the bandicoot's hole.
He was already tired and hot and very thirsty. All he could do was turn round
and head back to the waterhole.

The journey back to camp took much longer than the journey out. Yinti set off walking, but before he got far he had to stop to rest. He lay down under a tree and closed his eyes, trying not to think about his dry throat. As soon as he closed his eyes, he could hear a strange noise: 'Toom, toom, toom, toom!' Ranyjipirra!

Yinti's eyes popped wide open. He looked round, but could see nothing. All he could hear was that fearful noise: 'Toom, toom, toom, toom!' He jumped up, and started off again across the hot sand.

Before long, Yinti had to have another rest. He lay down again, in the shade of a turtujarti tree, and started to go to sleep. But no sooner had he closed his eyes than the noise began again: 'Toom, toom, toom, toom!' The ranyjipirra was following him!

Yinti knew about ranyjipirra. His mother had often warned him to be careful when he went out alone, in case a ranyjipirra got him. And now here was one of them, coming up behind him. What if it jumped on him and grabbed him while he slept?

Really frightened now, Yinti jumped up and went on walking. Every time he stopped to rest, the same thing happened: 'Toom, toom, toom, toom!'

At long last, Yinti could see the sandhill where his family had their camp. He was so tired and thirsty he could hardly walk. He just managed to climb the last few steps up to the tree where his brother Kana and Mana his niece were already sitting. By their side was the big makura of water Yinti's mother had filled and left for them.

Yinti was perishing for a drink of water. He fell down on the sand, and put his mouth to the coolamon. He sucked up some water, and swilled it round his mouth, then spat it out again.

He drank and swallowed a few small mouthfuls. Thirsty as he was, Yinti knew that if he drank a lot of water all at once after hunting on a hot day, he would make himself sick. So he drank slowly, a little at a time. Then he lay down, eyes closed, in the shade of the tree, his arms flung out on the sand. His voice was so hoarse he couldn't speak.

Kana and Mana could see that Yinti was exhausted. Instead of asking him questions about his day's hunting, they sat quietly beside him. The two youngsters filled up their mouths with water, bent over Yinti, and sprayed the water over his body to cool him down. The sound of the ranyjipirra had gone, and Yinti fell into a deep sleep.

1992

PHILIP McLAREN
b. 1943

Philip McLaren's family comes from the Warrumbungle Mountains area, NSW, and he is a descendant of the Kamilaroi people. He has worked as a television producer, director, designer, illustrator, architect, sculptor, lifeguard and copywriter. He has been a creative director in television, advertising and film production companies, both in Australia and overseas. After this varied career, McLaren focused on writing and was one of the first

Aboriginal authors to publish in the crime-writing genre. His books include *Sweet Water ... Stolen Land* (1993), *Scream Black Murder* (1995), *Lightning Mine* (1999) and *There'll Be New Dreams* (2001).

From *Sweet Water ... Stolen Land*
Chapter 1

The raw, tumultuous outback lay open.

The horse sensed the storm ahead. His nostrils flared and he tossed his head as he sniffed the wind. There was a sudden drop in temperature—it had been a very warm day. Red dust was carried high on the wind as it swirled, gaining in velocity as it moved south across the open plains. Dark clouds rolled over the spectacular Warrumbungle Mountains towards Gudrun and Karl Maresch as they rounded a bend and headed directly into the strong wind. The rain came soon after. The wind drove the cool rain onto the faces of the newcomers. Huge icy raindrops that usually preceded hail fell in walls of water, soaking deep into the dry red loam.

Karl steered the horse and sulky off the wide stock trail to shelter behind an outcrop of sandstone boulders. He took an oilskin sheet from under the seat and pulled it over them both in a makeshift tent as they moved to sit on the floor of the buggy.

Lightning flashed all around. A mighty thunderclap directly overhead caused Gudrun to tense her grip on Karl's arm. He was of true stoic German character. He knew Gudrun feared electrical storms yet he could not find it in himself to comfort her.

They had been to Gunnedah. It was an unusual trip for them to make because the Coonabarabran township was much closer. But Karl had decided they should see Gunnedah in the summer. It was 1869, an exciting time in Australia. The newly settled land declared its challenge to the adventurous.

Coonabarabran, along with almost every plains community in Australia, had already planned its future based on agriculture: wool, wheat and cash crops for the tables of Europe. A certain Lewis Gordon first proposed a town plan survey for Coonabarabran in 1859 although the area had been opened up by a Government sponsored expedition in 1817.

'The storm's moving quickly,' Karl said quietly in German. 'It will blow over soon.' He was wrong; the lightning became more frequent, the rain heavier.

Gudrun was often bemused by the fact that she now lived in Australia. She had never seriously considered living abroad, although when she was in her early teens occasionally she thought it might be exciting to live in London for a time—she spoke English very well. Then she met Karl Maresch and was totally swept off her feet. He was so confident. He had strong, unwavering opinions about the world that he couched in well developed philosophical and theological argument. To a young woman growing up on a farm on the outskirts of Munich, he was every inch the intellectual. He had read the lesson frequently at her church and took charge of a Bible class that she attended during the week. She had always admired him, even when she was a little girl. Gudrun was nineteen and Karl thirty-five when they married four years ago. The simple ceremony was conducted by his father, also a Lutheran pastor, in the tiny church at Grafing, south of Munich.

Lightning flashed and thunder followed immediately. Now the storm's centre was directly overhead. In another bright flash Gudrun suddenly saw an Aboriginal family sitting opposite them. They were huddled together, sheltering under an overhanging rock about thirty yards away across a small clearing.

The Aboriginal family—a man, his wife and two children—were looking at the white-skinned Europeans under their makeshift shelter on the horse buggy.

Ginny and Wollumbuy were married under Aboriginal law. Both their families still followed the old ways. At first it was said they could not marry, but later a way was found so that they could conform to complicated kinship laws. Wollumbuy first saw Ginny when he came to visit her clan several summers ago at Gunnedah, where she was born and raised. His own large family had walked more than one hundred and fifty miles over the mountains from their camp on the coast near the newly-built town of Coffs Harbour. It was a very long walk of the kind families used to make. Wollumbuy sang Ginny his love songs and she heard them in her sleep. He danced a magic, erotic love dance for her around the campfire and she awoke feeling stirred and excited. Their two children came quickly, answering the hope and tradition of Kamilaroi marriages.

Now Ginny took her youngest to her breast. He needed comfort from the storm. The wind blew in on them and Wollumbuy grimaced as another thunderclap shattered the air. He grabbed at the stone talisman Ginny's mother had made for him as a wedding gift which he always had hanging from his belt. He held it firmly.

They had come from Gunnedah to set up camp at the foot of Old Belougerie, a massive sacred rock spire that rose vertically from the foot of the mountains, towering high above the well-treed peaks. His people knew that the good spirits protected all people living within sight of the rock so that they lived long and happy lives.

Ginny suspected that some day Wollumbuy would want to take her back to his father's country, to stay at his home at Moonee beach camp. She thought it would be exciting to live near Belougerie, even for a short while. Large Aboriginal camps were seen less now than ever before. The Kamilaroi people had been forced off their ancestral lands onto hastily established missions. The whites were building fences everywhere. They had no regard for wild life, no understanding or feeling for the land. All hunting would soon be ruined. They had already cleared far too many plants and trees. Her three favourite bunyah-bunyah nut trees were destroyed last year to make way for more grazing land for sheep and other animals whose cloven hooves destroyed the delicate topsoil and laid bare the earth.

White people actually wanted to *own* the land! She wondered secretly if some day they would claim ownership of the sky, the stars, the clouds, the rain, the rivers and the ocean. She suspected that if they could find a way to do it, they would.

'There, I think it's stopped,' Karl said, almost in a whisper. The rain had eased but it certainly had not stopped. As he pulled the oilskin back, small pools of water that had collected on it ran down his arms under the sleeves of his jacket. He cursed, wiped the water away and took up the reins. He called to the horse as he sat upright on the leather upholstered seat. They were on their way again. The Neuberg Lutheran mission was only a couple of hours away. It was thirty miles from Coonabarabran and fifty-five miles from Gunnedah, built at the foot of Baraba Mountain on the eastern side of the Warrumbungle Range. Lutherans made ideal missionaries. They were well received by almost all international governments because of their basic belief that the State ought to be above the church.

Ninety years ago, Australia was built by convict labour. The government of Mother England transported convicts to aid the colonisation of the large South Land. The number of convicts needed for the planned settlements seemed to override more important criteria for transportation, such as skills, age or marital status. Fleets of convict slaves sailed south. The wretched human cargo knew little about the colonies, except for terrifying rumours of black savages and strange animals that aided Satan's work in a new-fashioned hell.

The Australian Government was still benefiting from the gold rush of the previous decade, which brought with it a huge influx of free immigrants. Whole towns sprang up overnight as the plains west of Sydney offered up their riches. Now plans of bigger proportions were being hatched; anything seemed possible. But the problem that always caused delay was the scarcity of labour. Back in England, the idea that transportation was a beneficial and morally sound way to rehabilitate prisoners had nowadays to be demonstrated to the government.

The colony of South Australia was founded in 1834 by free settlers. They were wealthy Nonconformists dissatisfied with government rule in England; they banded together to form the South Australian Colonisation Committee. One of its members, George Fife Angas, emigrated to South Australia in 1848. He put forward his high-flown reasons for a new settlement:

> My great object was in the first instance to provide a place of refuge for pious Dissenters of Great Britain who could in their new home discharge their consciences before God in civil and religious duties without any disabilities. Then to provide a place where the children of pious farmers might have farms in which to settle and provide bread for their families; and lastly that I may be the humble instrument of laying the foundation of a good system of education and religious instruction for the poorer settlers.

Angas advanced the princely sum of eight thousand pounds to entice persecuted Prussian Lutherans into establishing missions to 'enable Aborigines to come to where they might worship God and at the same time bind them to the missions as tenant farmers for a mandatory thirty years'. As well as destroying large segments of Aboriginal culture for ever, Angas had put in place his perfectly legal method of solving the rising costs of labour: the enslavement of Australia's Aboriginal people. Yet slavery was something he had publicly opposed forty years earlier in England. Obviously, when it came to his private business dealings a different set of principles applied.

Filled with righteousness and armed with faith, the Lutherans ventured to outback Australia to convert the Aboriginal people—to tell them, with absolute conviction, that forty thousand years of Aboriginal Dreaming was wrong. They passed on the word of the Lord and set about redeeming the heathen Australians through education, Christian principles and ethics, and tenant farming.

1993

KEV CARMODY
b. 1946

Kev Carmody grew up on a cattle station in the Darling Downs area of south-eastern Queensland. When he was ten, he was taken from his parents and sent to a Christian school, which he has described as 'little more than an orphanage'. A travelling singer-songwriter based in southern Queensland, Carmody regularly tours Australian jails, where he plays to the Aboriginal inmates. His music employs a ranges of styles, including country, folk and rock'n'roll. He collaborated with singer-songwriter Paul Kelly (b. 1955) on the musical *One Night the Moon* (2001). Their 1992 song 'From Little Things Big Things Grow', about the Gurindji strike and Vincent Lingiari (qv), an Aboriginal rights activist who led the Wave Hill walk-off, has become an anthem for Indigenous rights and other grassroots movements for social change.

From Little Things Big Things Grow

Gather round people, I'll tell you a story
An eight year long story of power and pride
British Lord Vestey[1] and Vincent Lingiari
Were opposite men on opposite sides

Vestey was fat with money and muscle   5
Beef was his business, broad was his door
Vincent was lean and spoke very little
He had no bank balance, hard dirt was his floor

From little things big things grow
From little things big things grow   10

Gurindji[2] were working for nothing but rations
Where once they had gathered the wealth of the land
Daily the pressure got tighter and tighter
Gurindji decided they must make a stand

---

1   Lord Vestey of the British Pastoral Company Vestey's, which owned Wave Hill Cattle Station.
2   Gurindji: the Aboriginal people in the Kalkaringi (Wave Hill) region.

They picked up their swags and started off walking   15
At Wattie Creek they sat themselves down
Now it don't sound like much but it sure got tongues talking
Back at the homestead and then in the town

From little things big things grow
From little things big things grow   20

Vestey man said 'I'll double your wages
Seven quid a week you'll have in your hand'
Vincent said 'Uh-uh we're not talking about wages
We're sitting right here 'til we get our land'
Then Vestey man roared and Vestey man thundered   25
'You don't stand the chance of a cinder in snow'
Vince said 'If we fall others are rising'

From little things big things grow
From little things big things grow

Then Vincent Lingiari boarded an aeroplane   30
Landed in Sydney, big city of lights
And daily he went round softly speaking his story
To all kinds of people from all walks of life

And Vincent sat down with big politicians
'This affair' they told him 'it's a matter of state   35
Let us sort it out, your people are hungry'
Vincent said 'No thanks, we know how to wait'

From little things big things grow
From little things big things grow

Then Vincent Lingiari returned in an aeroplane   40
Back to his country once more to sit down
And he told his people 'Let the stars keep on turning
We have friends in the south, in the cities and towns'

Eight years went by, eight long years of waiting
'Til one day a tall stranger appeared in the land   45
And he came with lawyers and he came with great ceremony
And through Vincent's fingers poured a handful of sand

From little things big things grow
From little things big things grow

That was the story of Vincent Lingiari   50
But this is the story of something much more
How power and privilege cannot move a people
Who know were they stand and stand in the law

From little things big things grow
From little things big things grow   55
                                                          1993

PATRICK DODSON
b. 1948

Born in Broome, WA, Patrick Dodson is of Yawuru descent. He and his younger brother Mick (qv) were made wards of the state in 1960 after the death of their father. They were sent to Monivale College in Hamilton, Victoria, on scholarships to finish their education. Patrick became a seminarian and was ordained in 1975 as the first Indigenous Catholic priest. In this challenging role he sought to balance and blend Catholicism and Aboriginal spiritual belief. After many years of confrontation with the ecclesiastical hierarchy he left the priesthood in 1981.

Since then he has been an Aboriginal rights activist, and a civil member of a number of official commissions concerned with Aboriginal affairs. He is a former director of the Central Land Council and of the Kimberley Land Council. In 1989 Dodson was appointed a commissioner for Aboriginal Deaths in Custody and was chairman of the Council for Aboriginal Reconciliation (1991–97).

Welcome Speech to Conference on the Position of Indigenous People in National Constitutions

[…] A century ago our Constitution was drafted in the spirit of *terra nullius*. Land was divided, power was shared, structures were established, on the illusion of vacant possession. When Aboriginal people showed up which they inevitably did they had to be subjugated, incarcerated or eradicated: to keep the myth of *terra nullius* alive.

The High Court decision on native title shatters this illusion and Aboriginal and Torres Strait Islander people have survived to make their contribution to the shape of the nation's political and legal future.

The nation has now woken from two centuries of sleep to become aware that Aboriginal and Torres Strait Islander people were owners of the land and were managers of the country long before the Union Jack was raised and rum drunk, here or elsewhere. While it may seem to be a new dawn for Australia's indigenous people, it has been a rude awakening for others. A moment of truth has arrived. The deeds of the past and present require those who have benefited most to take the steps towards those who have suffered most in the last 204 years. They must reconcile themselves with a new reality and then find the path of restitution that will lead to reconciliation.

No longer can Aboriginal property rights be ignored. No longer can indigenous customary laws and traditions be disregarded. The decision brings the wider Australian community closer to a true reconciliation on honest, negotiated terms with Aboriginal and Torres Strait Islander Australians.

A century after the original constitutional debate we have an opportunity to remake our Constitution to recognise and accommodate the prior ownership of the continent by Aboriginal and Torres Strait Islander people. But in this new debate there is a danger of history repeating itself. There is a danger of Aboriginal and Torres Strait Islander rights to land and cultural identity being ignored in the rush to establish a republic with minimal change to the Constitution. There is a danger of new arrangements to share power being developed without seeing and somehow meeting the Aboriginal and Torres Strait Islander peoples' yearning to escape the powerlessness of exclusion and dispossession. There is a danger of a new Constitution being drafted that tries to capture the spirit of a modern Australia, but that denies the spirit of indigenous Australia.

Terra nullius may be gone but the old habits of constitutional drafters die hard. The silences and omissions of the past echo loudly in the present. [...]

1993

MARCIA LANGTON
b. 1951

A leading Aboriginal scholar and a descendant of the Yiman people, Marcia Langton grew up in Queensland and spent many years working as an activist with local and overseas social justice organisations. During the 1980s she trained in anthropology at the Australian National University, and from the 1990s she has researched and taught in a range of disciplines, including gender and identity studies, Aboriginal land rights, resource management and Aboriginal creative expression. Langton's films include: *Jardiwampa: A Warlpiri fire* and *Blood Brothers*. She was professor of Aboriginal and Torres Strait Islander Studies at Charles Darwin University before being appointed Foundation Professor of Australian Indigenous Studies at the University of Melbourne.

From 'Well, I Heard It on the Radio and I Saw It on the Television ...'
Section 3: Decentering the 'Race' Issue

THE RETURN OF JEDDA

[Charles] Chauvel's *Jedda* (1955) expresses all those ambiguous emotions, fears and false theories which revolve in Western thought around the spectre of the 'primitive'. It rewrites Australian history so that the black rebel against white colonial rule is a rebel against the laws of his own society. Marbuk, a 'wild' Aboriginal man, is condemned to death, not by the white coloniser, but by his own elders. It is Chauvel's inversion of truth on the black/white frontier, as if none of the brutality, murder and land clearances occurred.

The witchcraft or sorcery of Marbuk lures away Jedda, the young Aboriginal woman, from the civilising influence of the homestead couple who have adopted her and provided her with decent clothes, food and education (symbolised by Humphrey McQueen's piano[1]). As Jedda plays the piano, 'tribal chants' rise up and take control of her Aboriginal mind buried deep within her

---

1 In a famous essay in *The New Britannia* (1970), historian Humphrey McQueen described the piano as 'the inevitable accompaniment of colonial hopes and despairs'.

new, constructed, made over, civilised one. She follows Marbuk into the bush where he performs a magical rite, to which she has no resistance. She pays for her 'instinctive, native weakness' with her life when she is dragged over a cliff by Marbuk who is fleeing from Joe, the good 'half-caste boy'.

In *Night Cries, A Rural Tragedy* (1990), [Tracey] Moffatt brings Jedda (played by myself) back to life as if forty years have passed. Jedda is now caring for her adoptive mother who is ancient and waiting to die. None of the male characters have survived and the homestead is a ruin.

Moffatt's 'feminine gaze' reconstructs the relationship between Jedda and her adoptive mother as one between women as independent beings, but perhaps they are not whole. The characters are imagined beings, ghostlike, merely guides to what the audience might invent, just as Chauvel's *Jedda* was. *Night Cries* can be read as an autobiographical exploration of Moffatt's relationship with her own foster mother. The film asks questions about the role of 'mother' in adoptive mother/daughter relationships.

The lives and experiences of Jedda and her adoptive mother in Moffatt's reconstruction of them are not mediated by men, not by Jedda's adoptive white father nor by Marbuk, the handsome black outlaw/seducer, nor by Joe, the sensible, civilised half-caste ringer to whom Jedda should have been *attracted* and become married.

All the men are disappeared.

What Moffatt was trying to *correct* in the text of *Jedda* is the Western fascination with the 'primitive'.

Moffatt's inversion of colonial history is to play out the worst fantasies of those who took Aboriginal children from their natural parents to assimilate and 'civilise' them. Perhaps the worst nightmare of the adoptive parents is to end life with the black adoptive child as the only family, the only one who cares. Moffatt's construction of that nightmare is subversive because the style and materiality of the homestead set is so reminiscent of Aboriginal poverty.

Chauvel's once privileged homestead now resembles the inside of a humpy. Moffatt takes us from the homestead—an exhibition of the wealth extracted from the slave labour of the Aboriginal men and women on the Australian pastoral station—to the poverty represented in her sets. The middle-aged Aboriginal woman on the now deserted station feeds the dying white mother canned food, and all the excesses of the historical/economic moment of the Australian cattle station are collapsed.

But what about the black men disposed of by Moffatt? Their absence deserves some attention because of what they signify some forty years after the making of *Jedda*. Moffatt's inversion forces the audience to look not at the desire of Chauvel's *Jedda* but at death, and at the consequences of Western imagination of the 'primitive', as we wait in the deteriorating homestead with a middle-aged Aboriginal woman and her dying mother.

Today, *Jedda* is sickening and, at the same time, laughable in its racism. (Indeed, some people might have seen it then as racist.) It was a big, although not very successful feature movie, and has become since an icon of Australian film.

What response did the audience of the 1950s have to this film? Our speculations might begin with the possible colonial/gender reactions. There is the implicit impossibility of white men being threatened by Marbuk, precisely because he inevitably dies as a result of his breach of Aboriginal law. He is eliminated. So inexorably will his 'race' die out because of the asserted inherent Darwinian weakness of Aborigines, morally and genetically, according to Australian eugenicist theory.

Could there have been a secret identification with Jedda among the white women in the cinema audience? Might they have been captivated and fascinated by the story of Marbuk's sorcery and seduction (silently subverting in the heat of the dark cinema the repressive patriarchy which they had to endure); a seduction so much more exciting and dangerous than the Rock Hudson type of seduction in the Hollywood romance?

Tarzan of the Apes, also known as the Earl of Greystokes, may have had a similar attraction. But Marbuk is 'genuinely' 'wild' and so much more mysterious and *unknowable*. Chauvel really did exceed, however subtly for the times, the pinnacle of primitive sexual licentiousness as Tarzan represented it then [...]

Tarzan can go on for hundreds of episodes because he is the coloniser, if somewhat mystified in his pseudo-primitive costume. Indeed, Tarzan and Jane marry, presumably in a High Church of England ceremony, and social relations are normalised even if the monkeys are still living in the bedroom in the trees.

But Marbuk and his paramour, the poor seduced Jedda, must die. It is precisely because of Marbuk's lust that Chauvel destroys him. His is the lust of a 'real primitive'. He is an outlaw. He refuses to submit to civilization.

As fictive male characters, Tarzan, Marbuk and Joe are imagined models of 'race' and gender. The difference between them as models of men is their place in colonial mythology and in the power relations which they represent. They have their equivalents in the anthropomorphised models of colonialism.

Tarzan's equivalent is Babar the Elephant orphaned by a white hunter. On finding civilisation after a short walk from the jungle, he is clothed in a delightful green suit and is educated in Paris, all at the expense of the rich old woman who finds him wandering the streets of the city.

Joe is the emasculated native and black buffoon of a thousand movies. Marbuk's equivalent is King Kong.

BLACK LIKE MI

Each representation of Aboriginal people is a reconstruction, an imagined experience, a tale told with signifiers, grammatical and morphological elements, mythologies.

The *Black Like Mi* series (1992) is a photographic essay by Destiny Deacon on representations of black women using images of black dolls and covers from books such as *Venus Half Caste*. It was shown at the Boomalli Co-operative. Deacon, a tutor in English Literature at Melbourne University, identifies the resonances of early melodramatic representations of native women in films and literature of the 1940s and 1950s through the medium of photography.

Previously, Moffatt had reinvented the half-caste siren in the photographic essay, *Something More* (1989).

Deacon explains to us in the two photographs, *Dark times with Otis and Alias 1* and *2*, that the 'black velvet' perception of the lascivious white male gaze on Aboriginal woman is a mediated sexual experience. These two photographs in particular, but also the series as a whole, reverse the pornographic experience—the signification of the 'black velvet' image.

There is a song about 'black velvet' from the Australian pastoral frontier which expresses the colonial lust of drovers demanding a fuck after a hard day's work. The term has passed into 'redneckspeak', and the subliminal power of the concept also ricochets around most of the sexual images of Aboriginal women.

Deacon has a black female doll, dressed in red, black and yellow, who lies in bed next to a black male doll. She is reading to him from the novel, *Venus Half Caste*. In the next scene, she has rolled over on her side and is reading to herself from the book, doubtless having a little black doll fantasy about 'inter-racial sex'.

'Ha, ha ha, I wonder how little black dolls do it?' she forces us to ask. We black girls have a special experience with little black dolls because they are a very recent, modern artefact in Australia. When we were growing up there were only golliwogs. Then Black Americans demanded in the 1970s that the toy market produce beautiful, well-dressed black dolls, formed in plastic to appear life-like, just like the white dolls. So we came to them late in life.

I remember my first experience in my thirties, standing gazing at a black doll. Everywhere around were these white dolls, loaded with cultural meaning: Barbie, with her gorgeous wardrobe, an appendaged boyfriend, the ultimate toy boy, with a lot of style; Cindy, with a pretty pink gingham check dress and white shoes and socks, who walked and talked. But only little white girls could look into the eyes of these post-oedipal mirrors and find that wonderland of self-imagination.

Imagine the power we black girls derived from, at last, having that experience with a black doll. Deacon gazes through the mirror of the little black doll. Hers is also the feminine gaze. As she looks at the black dolls, boy and girl, in bed, she erases the possibility of white men seeing this sexual scene that she has created. She denies white male voyeurism. She denies the aural, sexual and colonialist conquest. At the same time, in a sideways glance, she places the white male within her view, the white male who imagined the 'black velvet' and who, as a subject/object of Deacon's representation, is denied a peep at the doll.

She makes impotent the white male fantasy of 'black velvet'.

1993

RITA HUGGINS and JACKIE HUGGINS
1921–1996   b. 1956

Rita Huggins (née Holt) was born at Carnarvon Gorge, Queensland. The Holt family was forcibly removed from their traditional Bidjaraher country in the late 1920s, and were taken to what was then known as Barambah Mission (known today as the Cherbourg Aboriginal Reserve). From that time Rita worked for herself, her family and her people, and was an active member of the One People of Australia League. Thousands attended her funeral, a testimony to her standing in the Aboriginal community and beyond.

Her daughter Jackie Huggins, born in Ayr, Queensland, is an author, historian and activist dedicated to reconciliation, social justice, literacy and women's issues within Indigenous communities. Jackie has been involved in many organisations at local, state and national levels, ranging from reconciliation and Aboriginal welfare forums to appointments on editorial and performing arts boards. She co-wrote the auto/biography *Auntie Rita* with her mother. A collection of her political writings, *Sister Girl: The writings of Aboriginal activist and historian Jackie Huggins*, was published in 1998.

From *Auntie Rita*
Chapter 1: Don't Cry, Gunduburries

I was only a small child when we were taken from my born country. I only remember a little of those times there but my memories are very precious to me. Most of my life has been spent away from my country but before I tell you any more of my story I want to tell you what I remember about the land I come from. It will always be home, the place I belong to.

My born country is the land of the Bidjara–Pitjara people, and is known now as Carnarvon Gorge, 600 kilometres northwest of Brisbane. This was also the land of the Kairi, Nuri, Karingbal, Longabulla, Jiman and Wadja people. Our people lived in this land since time began. In our land are waterfalls, waterholes and creeks where we swam and where the older people fished. Our mob always seemed cool, even on the hottest days, because the country was like an oasis. There were huge king ferns. I believe they have been described as living fossils because their form has not changed for thousands of years.

We were never left with empty bellies. The men hunted kangaroos, goannas, lizards, snakes and porcupines with spears and boomerangs. The women gathered berries, grubs, wild plums, honey and waterlilies, and yams and other roots with their digging sticks. Children stayed with the women when the men hunted so that they wouldn't be close to the hunt and frighten away the animals. The creeks gave us lots of food, too—yellow belly and jew, perch and eel.

My mother would use leaves from trees to make soap for washing our bodies with, and unfortunately for us kids there was no excuse not to take a bogey. I remember goanna fat being used for cuts and scratches as well as being a soothing ointment for aches and pains. Eucalyptus leaves were used for coughs, and the bark of certain trees for rashes and open wounds. Witchetty grubs helped babies' teething, and we used charcoal for cleaning teeth.

There were huge cliffs and rocks, riddled with caves where many of my people's paintings were. Most caves and rock faces showed my people's stencilled hands, weapons and tools, and there were engravings here, too. Fertility symbols and the giant serpent tell us of the spiritual significance of the place. This place is old. My people and their art were here long before the whiteman came.

The caves were cool places in summer and warm places in winter, and offered shelter when the days were windy or when there was rain. They offered a safe place for the women bringing new life into the world. As had happened for my mother and her mother before her, going back generation after generation, I was born in the sanctuary of one of those caves. My mother would tell us how my grandmother would wash my mother's newborn babies in the nearby creek, place them in a cooliman and carry them back to suckle on my exhausted mother's breast.

We lived in humpies, or gunyahs, that the men built from tree branches, bark and leaves. Gum resin held them together. We would sleep inside the gunyahs, us children arguing for the warm place closest to Mama, a place usually kept for the youngest children. More gunyahs would be built as they were needed in this serene valley that had nurtured my people since time began.

My mother, Rose, had a Bidjara–Pitjara mother known as Lucy Conway from the Maranoa River and a white father who was never married to her mother. I never knew who her father was. I don't know much about the contact my mother had with whites. She had a whiteman's name, but she also had a tribal name, Gylma, and she spoke language and knew the old ways. My father, Albert Holt, was the son of a Yuri woman known as Maggie Bundle and a whiteman, the owner of Wealwandangie Station. My father was named after that man. My grandmother may have been working at the homestead. Dadda was brought up on the station, away from his mother's people. When he grew older he wanted to be with Aboriginal people, and started visiting the camps. He saw my mother there and wanted to marry her. After that, he stayed in the camp with her, and then the children started coming.

One winter's night, troopers came riding on horseback through our camp. My father went to see what was happening, and my mother stayed with her children to try to stop us from being so frightened. One trooper I remember clearly. Perhaps he was sorry for what he was doing, because he gave me some fruit—a banana, something as unknown to me as the whiteman who offered it. My mother saw, and cried out to me, 'Barjun! Barjun!'

Dadda and some of the older men were shouting angrily at the officials. We were being taken away from our lands. We didn't know why, nor imagined what place we would be taken to. I saw the distressed look on my parents' faces and knew something was terribly wrong. We never had time to gather up any belongings. Our camp was turned into a scattered mess—the fire embers still burning.

What was to appear next out of the bush took us all by surprise and we nearly turned white with fright. It was a huge cage with four round things on it which, when moved by the man in the cabin in front, made a deafening sound, shifting the ground and flattening the grass, stones and twigs beneath it. We had never seen a cattle truck before. A strong smell surrounded us as we entered the truck and we saw brown stains on the wooden floor.

They packed us in like cattle with hardly any room to move. The troopers threw a few blankets over us (we thought they were strange animal skins). There weren't enough blankets for all of us, and so the older people gave them to us younger ones while they went without. The night was cold and colder still on the back of the open truck.

It took the whole night across rough dirt tracks to reach our first destination of Woorabinda Aboriginal Settlement. Woori was a dry and dusty place compared to the home we were forced to leave. My memory of the place at that time is not clear but I do remember seeing some gunyahs and some people there watching us. The people were not smiling—just like us. Although curious to see us, the people did not come too far outside their gunyahs but watched from a safe distance as our older people were unloaded by the troopers.

I will never forget how they huddled, frightened, cold and crying in their blankets. Some of our old relations were wrenched from our arms and lives that day and it is for them that I shed my tears. One old lady broke away from the others and screamed, 'Don't take my gunduburries! Don't take my gunduburries!' as the truck moved off, taking us away from her. After running a small distance she was stopped and held by the officials who wanted to keep 'wild bush Blacks' on these reserves.

My father's ashen face told the story and we were never to see our old people again. Dadda could never bring himself to speak about it. Our tribe was torn away—finished. Perhaps the hurt and pain always remained for him. It was understandable then why he would hate and rebel against the authorities for the rest of his days after what they did to our people.

The old people from both Cherbourg and Woorabinda always told the story that the 'full bloods' were sent to Woorabinda and the fairer-skinned to Cherbourg. Both my parents were considered 'half-castes' because they both had white fathers. I had always wondered why our people were split up and found out sometime in my twenties that the government people thought that those of us who looked whiter would more easily assimilate than the darker ones, but this was not so. Sometimes it was vice versa. But skin never mattered to us. It was how we felt about being Aboriginal that counted. It was when I was in my twenties, too, that I was given a certificate which specified my 'breed'. 'Cross out description not required', it said. 'Full blood, half caste, quadroon.'

The truck went on, travelling for two terrible days, going further south. As if in a funeral procession, we were loud in our silence. We were all in mourning. I can't remember what we had to eat or drink, or where we stopped on the journey, but by the time we reached our destination we were numb with cold, tiredness and hunger. And this new country was so different from our country—flat, no hills and valleys, arid and cleared of trees.

It was Barambah Reserve (renamed Cherbourg in 1932) that we'd been brought to, just outside Murgon on the Barambah River. Here we were separated from each other into rough houses—buildings that seemed so strange to me then, with their walls so straight. Each family was fenced off from the others into their own two little rooms where you ate and slept. The houses were little cells, all next to each other in rows. A prison. No wonder that, along with 'mission', 'reserve', 'settlement', 'Muddy Flats' and 'Guna Valley', Cherbourg has been named 'prison' and 'concentration camp' by Aboriginal people. The place in fact had its own gaol. A prison in a prison. There were white and Aboriginal areas. Government authorities and teachers stayed away from us, and their areas were off-limits to all Aboriginal people.

One of the Aboriginal living areas was called top camp, and it was dotted with gunyahs. It was here that Annie Evans lived with her large family. She was the first person to greet us when we arrived, and gave us food. Her generosity was never forgotten by my parents or by myself. Her daughter Barbara was my age and we became best friends and stayed that way all our lives.

No one had the right to remove us from our traditional lands and to do what they did to us. We were once the proud custodians of our land and now our way of life became controlled by insensitive people who knew nothing about us but thought they knew everything. They even chose how and where we could live. We had to stay in one place now while the whiteman could roam free.

We took a trip back to my born country in 1986. It was the first time I had been back since that night we were taken over sixty years before. Tourism has taken its toll in the area, but the place still has its wild beauty. I felt the call of my people billowing through the trees and welcoming me home again. I saw the smiling faces of my elders, the embers of the campfire, heard the women singing. In my heart was such a deep happiness because I knew I was home again. 'Rita Huggins was born somewhere out there,' I said over and over again in my mind.

Returning to my mother's born country as she refers to it complemented my own sense of identity and belonging, and my pride in this. It was important that together we make this trip as she had been insisting for quite some time, pining for her homelands. We shared a special furthering of our mother–daughter bond during this time, although we argued incessantly about nothing as usual or, as she calls it, 'fighting with our tongues'. I began to gain an insight into and understanding of her obvious attachment and relationship to her country and how our people had cared for this place way before the Royal Geographic Society and park rangers ever clapped eyes on it. The way my mother moved around, kissed the earth and said her prayers will have a lasting effect on my soul and memory because she was paying homage and respect to her ancestors who had passed on long ago but whose presence we could both intensely feel.

The land of my mother and my maternal grandmother is my land, too. It will be passed down to my children and successive generations, spiritually, in the manner that has been carried on for thousands of years. Fate dictates that nothing will ever change this. As Rita's daughter, I not only share the celebration and the pain of her experience but also the land from which we were created.

Like most Aboriginal people, it is my deeply held belief that we came from this land, hence the term 'the land is my mother'. The land is our birthing place, our cradle; it offers us connection with the creatures, the trees, the mountains and the rivers, and all living things. There are no stories of migration in our dreamtime stories. Our creation stories link us intrinsically to the earth. We are born of the earth and when we die our body and spirit go back there. This is why land is so important to us, no matter where and when we were born.

The removal of Aboriginal people from their lands has gone on since the arrival of the whiteman, and it still goes on. Alienation from traditional lands has just taken different forms at different times. Reserves like Cherbourg and Woorabinda onto which my mother's people were placed were set up under the Queensland Aborigines Protection and Restriction of the Sale of Opium Act *of 1897. The decades that followed the introduction of the Act were a period of acute isolation and control of Aboriginal people. Aboriginals were deliberately and systematically cut off from their traditional ways of life and made to conform to, and become dependent on, European ways. The reserves refused Aboriginals the rights to their own languages, ceremonies, religious beliefs and marriage laws, and in their place was put a culture of control and surveillance. Every action and association was monitored; employment—including any wages—was managed by the reserves' superintendents; personal relations were intervened in. Punishment, including days and nights in the gaol, sometimes in solitary confinement, was meted out with imperialist assurance.*

Reserves were supposedly established for the care and protection of Aboriginal people, and there is a double irony in that. Not only were Aboriginals subjected to humiliating treatment in the reserves, but if they needed protection it was from whites. In the decades preceding the introduction of the Act, bloody massacres had taken place in Carnarvon Gorge, and all across the country. The massacres were ritualised violence, intended to demonstrate white superiority and power. The poisoning of flour and waterholes may be common knowledge; burying Blackfellas alive in sand, tying them to trees for use in shooting practice, is less so. Who were the barbarians?

The history of violence on the frontier has only been partially addressed. More orthodox historians have tended to downplay the extent of the violences committed against Aboriginal people, and revisionist historians, such as Ray Evans and Gordon Reid, who have attempted to reconstruct the massacres around my family's area, are marginalised.

In 1857, the Jiman of the Carnarvon Gorge area, reacting against the rape of Jiman women, the dispossession of hunting grounds, and the destruction of sacred sites, killed the whites present at the Fraser homestead at the Hornet Bank Station. In revenge, whites conducted the six-month 'little war' over a vast area unrelated to the Gorge, shooting down men, women and children as they ran. No measures were taken to stop this slaughter.

The killings went on long after, and all over Australia. Aboriginal people were nearly wiped out and it is a wonder that we are alive to tell the story. Because our beginnings as Black and white Australians were steeped in bloodshed and murder, and Black survival depended on such flimsy pieces of fate, it makes it almost impossible for us to pick up the pieces, forget about it and make up.

1994

JESSIE LENNON
c. 1925—2000

A Maṯuṯjara woman born in the station country of outback SA, Jessie Lennon is daughter of Nylatu and Kutin (Rosie Austin), and younger sister of Molly. Through her mother she has links with Tjalyiri or Tallaringa, north-west of Coober Pedy. She attended the mission school at Ooldea. When she met Joe Lennon at Coober Pedy, their families would not allow them to live together because they were too young.

Later, Joe found her again and they were married. Lennon had six children and many grandchildren and great-grandchildren. *And I Always Been Moving! The early life of Jessie Lennon* was published in 1995 and *I'm the One That Know This Country! The story of Jessie Lennon and Coober Pedy* in 2000.

From *And I Always Been Moving!*

Wilgena, I born Wilgena, I grewed up there:
mother had me there—baby.
Carried me round there—grow me up.
Big sister, Molly born there too—*Angkal*, her *Anangu*—
Aboriginal name, again.   5

After that we came to Kingoonya.
Mum married to my stepfather, Willie Austin's father.
We stopped there, Kingoonya.
Looked after me there.

We always go where they want.   10
'We'll go back to Wilgena working, shearing sheep.'
We'll go back to the place where I was born.

Old people used to camp there—at Lake Pirinya—Lake Phillipson.
Kanku—wurlies—nice *kanku* they made there. Shady.

Lake Pirinya full of water.   15
Yes, *malu*—kangaroo—there every day, all hanging up on the tree.
They killed them, cook 'em, they cut 'em up and hang 'em out.
They eat that part there.

Emu, they sometimes come—*kallaya*.
One time I saw, Old People say,   20
'Don't you fellas make too much noise!'
They wait for emu too—a lot of sweet tucker they want.
Kalaya come to the water and 'BANG!'
Kill two or three—so a big lot of people, you know, can eat.

                                                                   1995

ROMAINE MORETON
b. 1969

A writer, film-maker and performance poet, Romaine Moreton is from the Goenpul people of Stradbroke Island, Queensland, and the Bundjalung people of northern NSW. Her family worked as seasonal farming labourers, later settling in the country town of Bodalla, NSW. In August 2002 Moreton toured Australia with African-American acapella band, Sweet

Honey in the Rock, performing her signature spoken words before a sell-out crowd at the Sydney Opera House. Moreton's work responds to the environment and explores issues of identity. Two of her short films were shown at the Cannes Film Festival in 1999 and she appeared in an ABC documentary about her work, *A Walk With Words*, in 2001. She has published *The Callused Stick of Wanting* (1996) and *Post Me to the Prime Minister* (2004).

Genocide is Never Justified

And the past was open to gross misinterpretation.

Why do the sons and daughters of the raped and murdered
deserve any more or any less than those who have prospered
from the atrocities of heritage?
And why do the sons and daughters refuse to reap   5
what was sown
from bloodied soils?
And why does history ignore their existence?

This land, *terra nullius* was never barren and
unoccupied!   10

This land was never void of human life!

Instead
thriving with the knowledge of tens of thousands of years.

Everywhere I look!
Ghosts!   15

Vacant, colourless faces stare back

Sans culture
sans the belief of deserving of equality,

Who was here first is not the question
anymore   20

It is what you have done since you arrived,
the actions you refuse to admit to,
the genocide you say you never committed!

Then why are my people so few
when they were once so many?   25
Why is the skin so fair when once as black as the land?

Colonised Rape.

Why are you so rich, by secular standards
and we now so poor, by secular standards
The remnants of a culture though,   30
still

> *Rich*
> In
> *Spirit*
> and   35
> *Soul*

                    1995

Don't Let It Make You Over

if you were doin' time
like a fine wine, brother
you would make a beautiful
bouquet

if you were doin' time   5
like a fine wine, sister
you would make a beautiful
bouquet

when they rounded
us up   10
took our land
put the shackles
on our hand
stayin' free has been
a burden ever since   15

the cultural claustrophobia
of a hard prison cell
occupies my blood
choruses through my veins

makes me fear   20
my choices

'cos freedom
can be lost
to impoverished voices

do not take freedom   25
for granted
for she is a very fickle lover

she will leave you in a
heart
beat   30

'cos for now
she is married
to colonisation

a cruel and murderous
spouse   35

if you were doin' time
like a fine wine, brother
you would make a beautiful
bouquet

if you were doin' time   40
like a fine wine, sister
you would make a beautiful
bouquet

the greatest prospect of the constabulary
is that one begins to patrol   45
one's self

brother you have
been
     patrolled
     controlled   50
     enrolled
in the state's
design

they want you to step back
from the black   55
not cut you any slack
before they send ya back
for a colonist crime

please my brother
do not go where freedom does not   60
reside

please, my sister
I don't want to see you
go back inside

you're not alone, brother   65
you're not alone
when they lock the door to your cell

you're not alone, sister
you're not alone
I am here as well   70

we want you
to be free

we need you
to be free

if you're gonna be   75
the best
that you can be

let's take the shackles off our minds
let's pretend we're doing time
in the Dreaming   80

let's pretend we're down
on our knees scheming
redemption

if you were doin' time
like a fine wine, brother   85
you would make a beautiful
bouquet

if you were doin' time
like a fine wine, sister
you would make a beautiful   90
bouquet

prison is as hard as lightning
and
as
heavy   95
as
the
boulder
which has rested upon your shoulder

while freedom feels softer than cream   100
freedom must
be softer than cream

take a chance, brother
let yourself fall in love with
possibility   105

take a chance, sister
let yourself fall in love with
prosperity
it's a fact

it ain't easy bein' black   110
this kinda livin' is all political
this kinda living
can be all up hill

but there is
a way back   115

I like to ascend
with hope in my heart

I like to wake
with freedom on my breath

I like to float to the top like cream   120

and never give up on
the Dreaming

never give up on
the Dreaming

if you were doin' time   125
like a fine wine, brother
you would make a beautiful
bouquet

if you were doin' time
like a fine wine, sister
you would make a beautiful   130
bouquet

it's in your gait

the bearing of all that weight
which has relaxed itself   135
upon your recall

let it
fall

let it
fall   140

let
it fall

move it over, brother
move it over

move it over, sister   145
move it over

don't let it make
you over

do not let it take
you over   150

'cos
if you were doin' time
like a fine wine, brother
you would make a beautiful
bouquet   155

but you're not wine,
brother
and doin' time ain't fine,
sister

you will be over, brother   160
before you've just begun

you will be over, sister
more times than one

we all need you to be free
if there is any chance   165
of prosperity

do not accept
the illegality
of blackness

'cos you can be softer   170
than cream

yes
let's pretend we're down on our knees in
the Dreaming

we will not pretend   175
about scheming

redemption

'cos
while you're behind bars
brother   180

my heart is in chains
sister

do not refrain
brother

do not maintain   185
sister

this spiritual bondage

your shackles do not belong
to you

your shackles   190
do not
belong
to you

if you were doin' time
like a fine wine, brother
you would make a beautiful   195
bouquet

if you were doin' time
like a fine wine, sister
you would make a beautiful   200
bouquet

2004

I Shall Surprise You By My Will

I will make oppression work for me
with a turn and with a twist
be camouflaged within stated ignorance
then rise

I surprise you by my will 5

I will make oppression work for me
with a turn and with a twist
I shall sit cross-legged like a trap door
then rise

I surprise you by my will 10

I will let you pass me over
believe me stupid and ill informed
then once you believe me gone or controlled
will rise

and surprise you by my will 15

I shall spring upon you words familiar
then watch you regather as they drop about
like precious tears thick with fear
hear you scream and shout

then I shall watch convictions break away 20
and crumple like paper bags
and then as beauty I shall rise

and surprise you by my will

it is only when you believe me gone
shall I rise 25
from this place where I
wait
cross-legged
wait
to surprise you by my will 30

in the alleys, in the clubs, in the parliaments
in courts of law, parking cars, driving buses,
and generally watching you
watching me

as you pass me by 35

I shall wait cross-legged
wait
to surprise you by my will

for I shall stumble from houses of education
and I shall stumble from institutions of reform   40
I shall stumble over rocks, over men, over women, over children
and surprise you by my will

I shall stumble over poverty, over policies, and over prejudice,
weary and torn
I stumble   45
then bleary and worn I shall rise
from this place where I wait cross-legged
wait

to surprise you by my will
for the mountains we crossed   50
they were easy
and the rivers we swam
they were easier still
and even then
as I attempted to outrun inhumanity   55
I surprised you by my will

I have witnessed the falling of many
heard them cry and hear them still
even with grief inside me growing
I command my spirit to rise   60
and surprise you by my will

and for all people
we are here and we are many
and we shall surprise you by our will

we will rise from this place where you expect   65
to keep us down

and we shall surprise you by our will

for the bullets we dodged
they were difficult
and this ideological warfare   70
more difficult still

but even now
as we challenge inhumanity

we shall rise
and surprise you by our will

75
2004

HERB WHARTON
b. 1936

Born in Yumba, an Aboriginal camp in the south-western Queensland town of Cunnamulla, Wharton worked as a stockman, drover and labourer before taking up writing around the age of 50. His first novel, *Unbranded* (1992), is based on his experiences as a stockman in the Australian outback. Since then he has published several collections of prose and poetry, and a young adult novel. He is popular around the world for his storytelling. His works include *Yumba Days* (1991), *Where Ya' Been, Mate?* (1996), *Imba (Listen): Tell you a story* (2003) and *Kings with Empty Pockets* (2003).

Boat People—Big Trial

From high up on the crumbling ochre-red ridge, the dark men looked down on the wet glistening mudflats of the mangrove swamps as the tidal waters receded. Farther along, a crocodile slithered and slid across the mud bank, disturbed by voices from a boat that drifted across the flats towards the watching men. The frantic hand waving and gesturing from the people in the boat looked comical to the Aborigines. It seemed as though the boat mob had only just realised they were stranded high and dry, miles inland, as the king tide rapidly receded into the now shallow tidal channel.

From the ridge, the dark men observed about ten people on the deck of the small boat, all talking excitedly as they waved. 'Bloody boat people' the Aborigines thought. As they looked down they could not make out any of the words spoken by the boat mob—and in any case they would not have been able to understand their lingo. Looking up, the boat mob pointed towards the Aborigines, dark shapes against the reddish hill and cloudless blue sky.

One Aborigine standing at the edge of the rocky outcrop gave a small, regal wave as a friendly gesture. This brought renewed waving and louder talk from the boat, 'Looks like the silly bastards are stranded high and dry until the next king tide,' the Aborigine remarked.

'Bloody boat people,' muttered another Murri, one of the elders of the group. 'What shall we do with them? For hundreds of years they've been coming here. At first they used to come then sail away again. Now they come to stay. For over two hundred years they've come here, taken our land, killed our people and disrupted our laws.'

All the Aborigines knew the stories handed down from father to son—of murder, rape and mayhem and the theft of their tribal land.

Cursing all boat people once again, the old man was for leaving these new arrivals to their fate. But another Aborigine said: 'We can't judge these boat people by others of the past. That's like judging people by the colour of their skin.'

The old man repeated in powerful lingo what he thought of boat mobs, whatever the colour of their skins, but the younger man argued: 'We can't just walk away and leave them stranded.'

Soon the Aborigines were deep in an earnest discussion about what they should do, while the old man shook his head. 'Only bad omens come in boats,' he muttered.

By now, the boat people had begun to wade ashore, stumbling knee-deep in mud towards the hill top where the heated discussion still raged. Finally justice prevailed, and soon the Aborigines were heading down the ridge towards them.

The Murris had prepared themselves for hunting as their ancestors had done for tens of thousands of years. They carried spears and boomerangs and their bodies were marked in red and white. Only the headbands they wore—red, black and yellow, the colours of their national flag—belonged to the present day.

This was no ordinary Aboriginal mob straight out of the Dreamtime, even though this is how they would have appeared to the descendants of that first great wave of boat people who landed two centuries ago. As they headed towards the boat people, who were now stepping out of the soft slimy mud onto high ground, one Aborigine was heard to remark: 'At least these fellas aren't wearing leg irons.'

'No guns either,' said one of his companions. These boat people evidently belonged to some small peaceful tribe.

Amongst the Aboriginal 'savages' were two trained lawyers, as well as office workers and school teachers, besides the tribal elders, who knew and cared nothing about the laws and legends, history and religion of the White man, brought to their land a mere two hundred years ago. The lawyers, office workers and school teachers had gathered together to learn from the elders about their own culture and their own laws, which dated back one hundred thousand years or more. They were learning of other ways besides adaptation to ensure the survival of their tribe. Out here they had discovered the greatest school of all. For a week now they had been on pilgrimage through their tribal homeland, renewing their affinity with the land and the laws and legends of the Dreamtime.

Led by one who appeared to be their leader, the boat mob approached the now silent band of Blacks. Here was a mob of real wild Blacks, the leader thought to himself, just as they had so often been portrayed by White Australia. The leader of the boat mob could speak English, but he doubted whether these Black savages would understand him. And he was quite sure they would not understand his own lingo. So he began to speak in pidgin English, gesturing wildly with his arms all the time.

'We boat people,' he said. He pointed to himself, then to the boat, and gestured towards the distant horizon. 'We look for asylum—we refugees.'

His words came out like bullets from a machine-gun, thought one of the Aborigines, who had served in the Vietnam War. He and the rest of his tribe remained silent, their faces expressionless.

'We lost, we boat people seeking refuge,' the leader went on. But he thought that no matter what he said it would all be meaningless to these ignorant Stone-Age Blacks. 'We want to go see your big fella boss,' he said despairingly. Then he fell silent as the Aborigines gathered around in a circle and began talking in their own lingo. The boat people watched them fearfully. Maybe they would be speared and eaten, they thought. The Blacks talked on, with occasional bursts of laughter.

'These silly bastards want to find refuge—they want to know how to get to the nearest town and police station or government office,' said one of the Aboriginal school teachers. 'They also need fresh water and food—they've probably lived for months on that boat, escaping from their homeland.'

The old tribal elder who had spoken before said that he did not trust people who could leave the place where they had been born, to go to another country. For him, for all of them, their land was their mother, a sacred place. No matter what injustices they had suffered, nothing could ever break that tie with their own land and with the Dreamtime. Yet every one of this boat mob had left his own land.

At last one of the lawyers, who specialised in Aboriginal legal rights, addressed the leader of the boat mob in a cultured English accent. 'You are certainly lost, old chap. Miles from anywhere—two hundred kilometres from the nearest township and about a thousand from the nearest government Immigration office. But I can surely tell you exactly where you are right now.' Looking up at the sun, he recalled the exact place where the tidal stream appeared on the White man's map. 'You are twenty-eight degrees south of the twenty-second parallel. Furthermore, I must inform you that you are standing on the ancient tribal land of the Mungas—and you are trespassing.'

Taken aback, the boat leader gaped at the Aborigine for a moment. Then he began to talk again in his machine-gun voice, his arms still waving wildly as he repeated desperately, over and over: 'We refugee, refugee. Want asylum, big asylum …'

'Oh, I know where they want to go,' said one of the tribal elders who had once visited the city. 'I know that place where all them *womba* people been locked up.'

'Nah, nah, not that asylum,' said another Aborigine. 'They looking for a proper sit-down place. Might be they okay, this mob. No leg irons, no guns. Might be we getting a better class of boat people, old man. What you think?'

1996

DORIS PILKINGTON
b. 1937

Doris Pilkington was born on Balfour Downs Station in the East Pilbara, WA. At a young age she and her sister were removed by authorities from their home and were sent with their mother to Moore River Native Settlement. At eighteen, Pilkington left the mission system as the first of its members to qualify as a nursing aide at the Royal Perth Hospital. After marrying and raising a family, she studied journalism and worked in film and television production.

Her novel *Caprice: A stockman's daughter* (1991) won the David Unaipon Award in 1990. As well as adult fiction, she has written children's fiction, and autobiography, most notably *Follow the Rabbit-Proof Fence* (1996), which was adapted into the internationally acclaimed feature film, *Rabbit-Proof Fence* (2002), directed by Phillip Noyce. *Home to Mother* (2006) is a version of the story written for younger readers.

In 2002 she became co-patron of the state and federal Sorry Day Committee's Journey of Healing.

From *Follow the Rabbit-Proof Fence*
Chapter 5: Jigalong, 1907–1931

[…] In July 1930, the rainy season was exceptionally good. For the Mardu people throughout the Western Desert this was the season for taking long walks in the bush, foraging for bush tucker and feasting on the day's catch. Every Mardu welcomes the glorious warm weather, when the azure skies are even bluer against the grey-green mulga trees and the red dusty earth; grass grows under the small shrubs and between the sandy patches around the rocky ledges and even the spinifex is fresh and green. Alas, like everything that is revived and resurrected by the winter rains their beauty and brilliance is shortlived. They seem to fade and die so quickly.

Molly and Gracie spent a lovely weekend with their families digging for kulgu yams and collecting bunches of yellow flowers from the desert oaks, which they brought home to share with those who stayed behind to take care of the old people and the dogs. They soaked bunches of flowers in a bucket of water to make a sweet, refreshing drink. The other bush foods, such as the girdi girdi, murrandus and bush turkeys, were shared amongst the community. After supper the weary girls curled up in their swags and in no time at all, they were fast asleep.

Early next morning, Molly's step-father Galli rose at dawn and lit the fire. He made a billy of tea and sat under the shade of a large river gum, drinking a mug of warm tea. He glanced over to the sleeping forms of his two wives, and called out, 'Come on, get up.' The women began to stir. Galli then cut a piece of plug tobacco and crushed it in his hand, mixed the pure white ashes of the leaves of the mulga tree into it then put it into his mouth and began to chew the gulja, spitting the juice occasionally. In the old days, the people would collect and chew the leaves of wild or bush tobacco that grew on the cliffs or on rock ledges.

The Mardus preferred the white man's tobacco, plug tobacco, because it was easily available and also it was stronger and lasted longer. They chewed it and spat out the juice, the same way that other races chewed betel leaves.

Maude was Galli's second wife. She and his other wife both belonged to the same group under the kinship system. Both were Garimaras, the spouse category for Galli. Between them they prepared breakfast for the whole family, which included three big dampers cooked in the hot ashes of the fire and the girdi girdi left over from the hunting trip in the bush. They all agreed that it had been a successful and enjoyable day.

Molly and Daisy finished their breakfast and decided to take all their dirty clothes and wash them in the soak further down the river. They returned to the camp looking clean and refreshed and joined the rest of the family in the shade for lunch of tinned corned beef, damper and tea. The family had just finished eating when all the camp dogs began barking, making a terrible din.

'Shut up,' yelled their owners, throwing stones at them. The dogs whinged and skulked away.

Then all eyes turned to the cause of the commotion. A tall, rugged white man stood on the bank above them. He could easily have been mistaken for a pastoralist or a grazier with his tanned complexion except that he was wearing khaki clothing. Fear and anxiety swept over them when they realised that the fateful day they had been dreading had come at last. They always knew that it would only be a matter of time before the government would track them down. When Constable Riggs, Protector of Aborigines, finally spoke his voice was full of authority and purpose. They knew without a doubt that he was the one who took their children in broad daylight—not like the evil spirits who came into their camps in the night.

'I've come to take Molly, Gracie and Daisy, the three half-caste girls, with me to go to school at the Moore River Native Settlement,' he informed the family.

The old man nodded to show that he understood what Riggs was saying. The rest of the family just hung their heads refusing to face the man who was taking their daughters away from them. Silent tears welled in their eyes and trickled down their cheeks.

'Come on, you girls,' he ordered. 'Don't worry about taking anything. We'll pick up what you need later.'

When the two girls stood up, he noticed that the third girl was missing. 'Where's the other one, Daisy?' he asked anxiously.

'She's with her mummy and daddy at Murra Munda Station,' the old man informed him.

'She's not at Murra Munda or at Jimbalbar goldfields. I called into those places before I came here,' said the Constable. 'Hurry up then, I want to get started. We've got a long way to go yet. You girls can ride this horse back to the depot,' he said, handing the reins over to Molly. Riggs was annoyed that he had to go miles out of his way to find these girls.

Molly and Gracie sat silently on the horse, tears streaming down their cheeks as Constable Riggs turned the big bay stallion and led the way back to the depot. A high pitched wail broke out. The cries of agonised mothers and the women, and the deep sobs of grandfathers, uncles and cousins filled the air. Molly and Gracie looked back just once before they disappeared through the river gums. Behind them, those remaining in the camp found strong sharp objects and gashed themselves and inflicted wounds to their heads and bodies as an expression of their sorrow.

The two frightened and miserable girls began to cry, silently at first, then uncontrollably; their grief made worse by the lamentations of their loved ones and the visions of them sitting on the ground in their camp letting their tears mix with the red blood that flowed from the cuts on their heads. This reaction to their children's abduction showed that the family were now in mourning. They were grieving for their abducted children and their relief would come only when the tears ceased to fall, and that will be a long time yet.

At the depot, Molly and Gracie slid down from the horse and followed Constable Riggs to the car.

Mr Hungerford, the Superintendent, stopped them and spoke to Riggs.

'While you are here, there's a native woman with a fractured thigh, in the other natives' camp, the one on the banks of the river. Can you take a look at her, Constable?'

'Yes, I'll examine her,' replied the Constable.

'I'll come with you,' said Hungerford. 'We'll borrow that native boy Tommy's horse and sulky,' he added. 'I'll fix him up with some rations later as payment.'

After Riggs had splinted the woman's leg, he told Hungerford that he would have to take her back with him to the Marble Bar Hospital. 'Lift her gently onto the sulky,' he asked her two brothers who were standing watch nearby.

As Hungerford seated himself beside Constable Riggs he said, 'And by the way, the other woman, Nellie arrived from Watchtower Station while you were collecting Molly and Gracie. You know the one suffering from VD. She needs to go to the hospital too.'

'Alright,' Riggs replied. 'But I still intend to speak to Frank Matthews, the station manager about her and remind him that he has no right to examine or treat any of the natives here. That should be left to us. We are the Protectors of Aborigines in this district.'

Constable Rigg was referring to the Protection Policy Regulation, number 106m:

> Whenever a native falls ill, becomes diseased or sustains an accident and such illness, disease or accident appears to an employer to require medical attention or hospital treatment beyond that which can be efficiently or reasonably given at the place of employment, the employer shall as soon as reasonably possible, send the native to the nearest or most accessible hospital or to the nearest protector and thence to the nearest and most, accessible hospital at the protectors discretion.

The crippled woman, Mimi-Ali, was transferred from the sulky to the car with Molly and Gracie.

'Tommy,' yelled Constable Riggs. 'Take your horse and sulky to Walgun Station and wait for me there,' he ordered.

'Molly and Gracie, you had better sit in front with me, and you Nellie, can sit in the back with Mimi-Ali,' said Riggs as he cranked the car.

Half an hour later he was greeted by Matthews. 'You have a load this time, Constable Riggs,' he said as the officer got out of the car.

'Yes, I know. It can't be helped. I've got the two sick native women. Which reminds me, there is something I must speak to you about.'

The Constable explained the duties of the Protectors of Aborigines in the Nullagine district and cautioned Matthews that he should not take on those responsibilities himself.

'I'd better get moving,' said Constable Riggs. 'I have to search around for Daisy. I'll call in next time I'm on patrol in the district.'

The patrol officer drew up in front of the Walgun Homestead gate and was greeted by Mr and Mrs Cartwright, managers of the station.

'Hello,' said Don Cartwright as he shook hands with the visitor.

'Come inside and have a cuppa tea,' said his wife warmly, pointing towards the door.

'Thank you, but not just yet. I must find the half-caste girl, Daisy,' he said. 'She's somewhere between here and Murra Munda Station, near the soak. I already have the other two, Molly and Gracie in the car with Mimi-Ali from Jigalong and Nellie, the cook from Watchtower Station who are in need of medical attention.'

'But where are you taking those half-caste girls?' asked Mrs Cartwright.

'They're going south to the Moore River Native Settlement, where we hope they will grow up with a better outlook on life than back at their camp,' he answered with great satisfaction.

'I'll leave the car here but first I'll drop the women off at the native workers' camp. I'll take Molly and Gracie with me, though,' he said. 'I don't want them to clear out.'

Constable Riggs drove slowly down to the camp, followed closely by Tommy with his horse and sulky. Soon, he and Tommy were heading across the flats, over the spinifex grass and through the mulga trees in search of Daisy, who was with her family at the camp. Finding her had proved more difficult than the Constable expected. He had searched the Jimbalbar and Murra Munda area on horseback covering 60 kilometres, and a further 30 kilometres in the dry, rough country between Murra Munda and Walgun stations before he finally found her. The search was so tiring that he decided to spend the night at Walgun Station. His passengers stayed at the camp with Gracie's mother Lilly, her grandmother, Frinda, and some other relatives.

At 3.30 in the morning, on 16 July, the Constable noticed that rain was threatening. The roads were bad enough as it was, but when wet they were even more hazardous so he decided to make a start.

'I don't want to be marooned on the road with these natives,' Constable Riggs explained to the Cartwrights.

'We understand,' said Mrs Cartwright, 'we'll see you when you're in the district. Have a safe trip home.'

'Thank you. I'd better get going,' he said. 'The women must have finished their breakfast by now, so I'll go down and pick them up. Thanks again for your hospitality.'

Grace's mother, old Granny Frinda and other relations in the camp began to wail and cry.

'Worrah, Worrah! He take 'em way, my grannies [granddaughters], wailed the old lady, as she bent down with great difficulty and picked up a billy can and brought it down heavily on her head. She and the rest of the women began to wail louder, their hearts now burdened with sadness of the girls' departure and the uncertainty of ever seeing them again. The girls were also weeping. The wailing grew louder as the vehicle that was taking them away headed towards the gate. Each girl felt the pain of being torn from their mothers' and grandmothers' arms.

As the car disappeared down the road, old Granny Frinda lay crumpled on the red dirt calling for her granddaughters and cursing the people responsible for their abduction. In their grief the women asked why their children should be taken from them. Their anguished cries echoed across the flats, carried by the wind. But no one listened to them, no one heard them.

A couple of hours after the three girls had been driven away, Gracie's mother, distraught and angry, was still sitting on the ground rocking back and forth. Maude and her brother-in-law had ridden over in a horse and cart to discuss the distressing news and stayed to comfort and support each other. Some time later, she calmed down enough to hurl a mouth full of abuse at Alf Fields, Gracie's white father, who was standing silently near the galvanised iron tank. She screamed at him in Aboriginal English and Mardu wangku, and beat his chest with her small fists.

'Why didn't you stop them?' she cried out in anger and frustration.

'I couldn't stop them taking my daughter—yes, she is my daughter too,' he said sadly. He was so proud of his beautiful black-haired daughter whom he had named after his idol, English singer Gracie Fields.

He tried to explain to her mother that the patrol officer was a government representative and an officer of the Crown. Had he interfered or tried to stop the man he would have been arrested and put in gaol and charged with obstructing the course of justice. Gracie's mother didn't listen.

'You are a white man too, they will listen to you. Go and talk to them,' she pleaded softly.

'I am sorry but I can't do anything to stop them taking our daughter away from us,' he said finally.

She couldn't accept his excuse or forgive him for just standing by and doing nothing to prevent their daughter from being taken away from them. She packed up and moved to Wiluna.

1996

ALF TAYLOR
b. 1947

Alf Taylor is a poet and short story writer born in Perth. He spent his early years with his family then was taken with his brother, as part of the stolen generation, to the New Norcia Mission. As a young man he worked around Perth and Geraldton as a seasonal farm worker, then joined the armed forces. He and his wife had seven children, only two of whom survived. Taylor is the author of three collections of poetry, and a collection of short stories called *Long Time Now: Stories of the Dreamtime, the here and now* (2001).

The Wool Pickers

When the warm months take effect on the dry land, after the crops have been taken and the grass has been singed by the hot summer sun, that's the reminder of the fully fleeced sheep that perished during the bitterly cold winter. That's when Barney and his nephew Bill go wool picking (with the farmer's permission of course).

'Well,' said Barney to his nephew, 'It's a good day for the wool pickin', unna.'

'Yeah, Unc,' said Bill, looking up at the early morning sun, 'It's gunna get hot later on.'

'What ya reckon, feel like comin' out?' asked Barney.

'Course, you know me Uncle, bugger all else to do, runnin' low on tucker, dole cheque next week. Hell, dunno how we gunna live 'til then,' responded Bill.

'Right,' said the old fella, 'I'll get the ute ready, an' tell Auntie Florrie you an' me goin' out. You tell your yorgah too.'

'Course Unc, gotta tell my yorgah, she growlin' cruel already …'

'Get off your black hole Bill an' do somethin' solid, not wanna muntj alla time,' said Bill mimicking his woman. The old Uncle laughed as he watched his nephew walk away. *When you an' your yorgah fight, even the good Lord ducks for cover,* he thought, laughing to himself, making off to tell his wife Florrie.

Barney and Florrie were in their late sixties, and fifty of those years were together. Through thick and thin, through the days of alcoholic stupor and nights of alcoholic amnesia—and they were still together. Their three children, two boys and a girl, were living in Perth. All had good jobs and most importantly, they had lives of their own.

Barney often cursed himself for not having a clear head when they were growing up. Thankfully they understood now, stating a lack of opportunities for the Nyungah community in a small wheat-belt town.

'Me an' Bill goin' out to see if we can get some wool,' said Barney to his wife Florrie.

'You might gotta go long way out. Nyungahs bin pickin' close here,' she said.

'Boyyah any?' he asked and in the same breath added, 'You know petrol.' Knowing his wife usually had some put away somewhere. Ever since they both gave up the grog, about fifteen years ago, she always had enough till next Pension Day.

'Ready Unc?' asked Bill carrying his waterbag. Seeing Aunty Florrie he added, 'How you bin Aunty Florrie?'

'I bin good since I chuck away that stinken gerbah,' she replied, shaking her head.

'Yeah, you two look solid now,' said Bill. *Since these two gave up the gerbah, they seem so full of life. They looked better than the younger ones still on the gerbah,* he thought.

'Boyyah wa or you gimme, unna?' Bill asked, searching his pockets.

'Take em here,' Florrie said, passing a ten dollar note to Barney.

'How many bags you got Unc?' asked Bill.

''Bout five empty wheat bags,' replied Barney.

'Let's bullyaka then,' suggested Bill.

'You gottem gun?' asked Florrie.

'Yeah, under seat, you make em big damper. Might get yonga,' he said as he and Bill prepared to leave. He started the ute and pulled away from the house, both waving to Florrie.

As they headed north, they could see that the hot summer's sun had already done its damage to the landscape. About five months ago, the land was covered by lush green crops of wheat and a thick carpet of glistening green grass. Seeing the land now, with its lack of rain, even had the sand restless. The sands seemed to move with the strong breeze, although the gentle winds slowly stirring in the summer, were very few and far between. The soil with its great patience, suffered the onslaught of the menacing sun.

Nothing was said between the uncle and nephew. Barney moved along at a steady pace. He didn't want to go too fast in this heat, he was afraid the radiator might boil.

Gotta get it fixed next Pension Day, he thought. *Come next Pension it'll still be the same.* When he was home travelling within his own Shire boundary, he never had to worry, but trips like this it always came to his attention. He cursed himself out aloud.

'Hey, wassa matter Unc?' asked Bill and wondering if his old Uncle had lost his marbles.

'Nothing … um orright, juss diss bloody radiator. Keep meanin' to get him fixed. I don't worry about him, till I go on trips like diss,' he growled.

'How far you reckon we come Unc?' asked Bill.

Keeping his eye on the temperature gauge, 'Might be twenty miles, might be more,' he replied.

'Let's try the first farm we come to Unc,' said Bill, not wanting to be stuck in the middle of nowhere on this hot day. Barney slowed the ute down; it was a left turn towards the farm house. He could see that the sheep were thin as they ran away from the oncoming vehicle. *Rain and feed obviously very scarce out this way too*, thought Barney.

'Reckon he got some dead ones here,' said Bill, noticing the condition of the sheep.

'By gee, that cold weather we had in the winter musta downed a few,' replied Barney.

'Wonder if any Nyungahs been this way?' asked Bill as he slowed the ute down in front of the house, only to be greeted by barking dogs that seemed to come from nowhere.

'Where in the hell these poxy dawgs come from?' called out Barney as he wound his window up. There were about five sheep dogs running around his ute, barking and pissing all over the tyres. One big bastard was standing on his hind legs, his front paws leaning against Barney's door, barking furiously at him.

'Bugger diss!' said Barney, counting the fangs on the mutt's jaw.

'Shoo! Gone! Get!' shouted Bill also winding his window up very quickly.

Barney looked at his nephew and with a smile on his face said, 'Gone, go up to the house an' knock on the front door.'

'You gotta be jokin' Uncle! I'd rather fight ten drunken Nyungahs than wrestle with these poxy dawgs.'

'Ni, Boss comin' now,' said Barney, pointing towards the house.

'Duss him orright,' replied Bill as he watched him come towards the ute.

'Go on, piss off you bastards!' shouted the Boss. The dogs slinked off on his command. Winding the window down Barney said, 'Thanks Boss, I was a bit frightened for awhile.'

'Don't have to worry about them,' said the Boss, 'More likely to lick you to death.'

Duss what you reckon, thought Barney. 'That big bastard lookin' me in the eye, would frighten the shit out of the devil himself. He got more teeth than a crocodile, an' more sharper.'

'Well, what can I do for you?' asked the Boss.

Good, thought Barney, *no Nyungahs been out here.* Getting out of the ute and looking to see if the coast was clear, he asked, 'Wondering if you got any dead wool around the place?'

'Dead wool?' asked the Boss confused.

'You know,' said Barney, 'any sheep died over the winter months.'

'Oh, I understand now,' replied the Boss. 'As a matter of fact I have. That cold snap we had at the end of May and the beginning of June, that really took its toll on the sheep,' as he pointed towards the west paddock. 'There were quite a few that didn't survive.'

'Be orright if we have a look?' asked Barney.

'I suppose it's okay. As long as you shut the gates behind you and try not to frighten the sheep. I hate to see my sheep running around on a day like this,' he said.

'Duss true Boss,' said Barney. 'We be careful orright.'

'Also beware of your exhaust pipe when you travel over the stubble,' said the Boss pointing to the back of the ute. Barney got out and both he and the Boss checked under the ute.

'Your exhaust looks safe. Okay then … and don't forget the gates,' said the Boss.

'We won't,' said Barney.

'By the way,' said the Boss, walking away and laughing, 'I guess you blokes wouldn't have won that four million in last night's Lotto draw!'

What datt yortj talkin' 'bout, thought Barney, 'Four million dollars. I wouldn't be here pickin' your dead wool, would I?' Shaking his head and getting into the ute.

'Choo, you solid Unc,' said Bill with the dollar signs in his eyes.

'Yeah,' said Barney. 'As soon as he said, what can I do for you, I knew Nyungahs never been here.'

They had to go through three gates before hitting their jackpot. Barney drove carefully through the paddocks, keeping away from the high stubble. Barney himself also climbed out with Bill to shut the gates.

'Here, look Unc!' shouted Bill, pointing. There before their very eyes, dead sheep were everywhere. The winter had been cruel to these sheep, which had yet to be shorn. Barney and Bill quickly and happily ripped the wool from the dead carcasses. These dead sheep had been lying here for at least three months or more. Perished in the winter and dried by the summer. The stench and the blowflies didn't deter the eager hands that shook the fleece from the bones and brushed the blowflies away at the same time. Their work exposed the maggots to the deadly sun, from which they cringed in the onslaught. The crows cawed out joyfully, as the rotting flesh was to be their feast when left behind by the eager hands. For the dead wool, when sold in all its stinking glory would put food on the table, petrol in the tank and smoke back into the lungs of the two men.

'Dass all Unc!' cried Bill, sweating profusely as he hoisted the last of the five fully packed bags into the back of the ute.

'Gawd, diss place stinks,' called out Barney, not realizing he had been right in the middle of the stench for the last two hours.

'Let's bullyaka then Unc,' said Bill with a satisfied smile on his face.

'Yeah, you have boyyah till your day now,' smiled Barney as he edged his way through the gates and past the farmhouse. He wanted to thank the farmer for giving him permission to pick his dead wool.

There was no life around except the dogs and he wanted to get away from them quickly as possible. The drive back was even slower than the drive coming out, for he and Bill did quite a job back there.

'How much we get for this lot?' asked Bill.

'Orrr, dunno. Might be hundred dollars, might be more,' said the old fella with a twinge of tiredness in his voice.

'Never mind Unc. Long as my yorgah get some money, she'll be happy,' said Bill.

'The first thing um gunna do, is have a shower an' tell Florrie to get some mutton flaps,' he said, feeling the hunger pangs starting to attack his stomach. He was also beginning to realize that the stench was quite powerful in the cab of the ute.

'I hope Aunty Florrie made that big damper. I wanna get some off youse,' said Bill feeling the same.

'Nearly home soon,' said Barney, not worrying about the radiator as he put his foot down on the pedal.

'Hey, Unc, what that watjella said back at his farm. Something 'bout four million dollars. I thought he said four million sheep was dead. I was happy cruel, look,' laughed Bill.

'Naw,' Barney said, laughing. 'Four million Lotto draw last night.'

'What if you had four million dollars Unc? What you do?' asked Bill

'Well,' laughed Barney, 'first thing I do is give my kids a million each.'

'What you an' Aunty Florrie gunna do with your million?' asked Bill laughing.

'Um gunna take Auntie Florrie to dat French River place, somewhere. And next we be goin' to see that Nyungah bloke. You know he was locked up in jail for twenty years an' come out to run his own country. Wass his name?' asked Barney.

'Or yeah Unc, I know. Or … Nelson Mandela. Yeah Unc, dass him. Anyway Unc, what you wanna meet him for?' wondered Bill.

'Look young Bill, all I wanna do is shake his han' an' tell him he horse of a Nyungah orright. After bein' locked up alla time. Come out an' be boss of his own country. He moorditj orright.'

'But he not Nyungah Unc. He South African,' Bill explained to his old Uncle.

'He still moorditj anyway,' said Barney. They were now driving through town and slowly making their way to the Woolbuyers. As he pulled up outside Willie the Woolbuyer's shed, Bill said to his old Uncle, 'Never mind Unc, you sit here an' rest. I'll take em into Willie's.' Barney watched his young nephew unload and take the old wool into the woolshed. It wasn't all that long before Bill came out with a smile on his face. As he passed the cheque to Barney, Bill said, 'We got one hundred dollars for that lot, one dollar a kilo he gave. Dass orright, unna.'

Barney was pleased. He headed for the bank where they cashed it. He gave forty dollars to Bill, whilst he in turn, kept sixty—fuel for the car. He dropped Bill off, who didn't live all that far and then headed home for a shower.

'You get em newspaper?' asked Florrie as Barney stepped inside.

'What you wanna paper for?' he asked. 'Anyway um gonna have a shower. Here boyyah, cause you goin' down town. An' get me some flaps,' he said passing the money to her.

After he'd showered and got himself cleaned up, he sat and had a cup of tea. It was peaceful and quiet. He kept wondering why Florrie wanted that paper. Barney couldn't read or write and he often got Florrie to read for him. He knew she was a good reader. Even at the ripe age of seventy. *Moorditj Yorgah*, he thought. Florrie came in carrying the shopping and put it on the table.

'Gawd, still warm outside,' she said.

'You get em paper?' he grunted.

'Course,' she said, grabbing the newspaper and taking off into the bedroom. Barney watched as she stopped to pick up her reading glasses and then watched her back disappear into the other room. Within minutes, the warm peaceful and quiet humidity of the early evening was shattered by a piercing scream.

'Choo, aye wassa matta?' shouted Barney, jolting back to reality and running into the bedroom. He froze in his tracks as he saw his wife sprawled on her back across the bed, white as a ghost shouting, 'Gawd, gawd. Thank you Granny Maud!'

Barney was speechless. Granny Maud had died forty years ago. When he and Florrie first got together as pups. Granny Maud had always called them that, and she was eighty when she died. Their first child was two then.

'I think I win plenty of boyyah!' was Florrie's only response when she came to. She composed herself and told him about the other day. She was lying on the bed, having a cry and thinking of Barney—old as he was—always going out to pick dead wool to put food on the table. Then she looked up and saw the spirit of Granny Maud, clapping her hands and smiling at her, then she disappeared. After that Florrie walked down town and saw on a poster at the newsagent's in big bold letters 'FOUR MILLION DOLLARS' to be won that night. She went in and bought a ticket. She had just checked her numbers with the paper, and she had gotten six numbers correct.

Still trembling, he asked, 'What Granny Maud got to do with it?'

Florrie told him when she had the last two children, Grannie Maud's spirit was by the bed, smiling and clapping as she was giving birth.

'Look at our beautiful children now. Granny Maud only brought good luck to me,' she whispered. She was thinking of Barney and the kids. Especially Barney—to take 'im to see the black man, who was put in jail an' came out to be boss of his own country, before they both passed away.

Barney grabbed and hugged her. With tears in his eyes, he whispered in her ear, 'He not Nyungah, he South African!'

1996

LISA BELLEAR
1961–2006

Lisa Bellear was a Goenpul woman of the Noonuccal people of Minjerriba (Stradbroke Island), Queensland. A notably political poet, she was also a visual artist, academic and social commentator, being involved in Aboriginal affairs nationally. She was an executive member of the Black Women's Action in Education Foundation and a volunteer broadcaster on 3CR community radio for eleven years on the 'Not Another Koori Show'.

Her collection of poetry *Dreaming in Urban Areas* was published in 1996. Bellear also conceived and co-wrote the promenade-style theatrical work, *The Dirty Mile: A history of Indigenous Fitzroy* (2006). She performed her work nationally and internationally, and was widely published in journals, newspapers and anthologies. An avid photographer, Bellear took thousands of photographs over the many years she spent engaged with Indigenous affairs, both politically and socially.

Women's Liberation

Talk to me about the feminist movement,
the gubba middle class
hetero sexual revolution
way back in the seventies
when men wore tweed jackets with   5
leather elbows, and the women, well
I don't remember or maybe I just don't care
or can't relate.
Now what were those white women on about?

What type of neurosis was fashionable back then?   10
So maybe I was only a school kid; and kids, like women,
have got one thing that joins their schemata,
like we're not worth listening to,
and who wants to liberate women and children
what will happen in an egalitarian society   15
if the women and the kids start becoming complacent
in that they believe they should have rights
and economic independence,
and what would these middle class kids and white women do
with liberation, with freedom, with choices of   20
do I stay with my man, do I fall in love with other
white middle class women, and it wouldn't matter if
my new woman had kids or maybe even kids and dogs
Yes I'm for the women's movement
I want to be free and wear dunlop tennis shoes.   25
And indigenous women, well surely, the liberation
of white women includes all women regardless ...
It doesn't, well that's not for me to deal with
I mean how could I, a white middle class woman,
who is deciding how can I budget when my man won't   30
pay the school fees and the diner's card club simply
won't extend credit.
I don't even know if I'm capable
of understanding
Aborigines, in Victoria?   35
Aboriginal women, here, I've never seen one,
and if I did, what would I say,
damned if I'm going to feel guilty, for wanting something
better for me, for women in general, not just white
middle class volvo driving, part time women's studies students   40
Maybe I didn't think, maybe I thought women in general
meant, Aboriginal women, the Koori women in Victoria
Should I apologise
should I feel guilty
Maybe the solution is to sponsor   45
a child through world vision.
Yes that's probably best,
I feel like I could cope with that.
Look, I'd like to do something for our Aborigines
but I haven't even met one,   50
and if I did I would say
all this business about land rights, maybe I'm a bit
scared, what's it mean, that some day I'll wake up
and there will be this flag, what is it, you know

red, black and that yellow circle, staked out front   55
and then what, Okay I'm sorry, I feel guilt
is that what I should be shouting
from the top of the rialto building
The women's movement saved me
maybe the 90s will be different.   60
I'm not sure what I mean, but I know that although
it's not just a women's liberation that will free us
it's a beginning

      1996

Woman of the Dreaming

My sweet woman of the Dreaming
Where is your soul,
I need to surround your body
With my spirit, the spirit
Of the embodiment of love   5
      anger
      pain
      disparate neutrality

My sister, lover, friend,
Let your soul and my soul   10
Fall in love

But love is so remote,
The gum trees are whispering
The Yarra Yarra is polluted
Koalas on Phillip Island are   15
So stressed that they too will
Be another victim of the
Invasion

1990, the beginning of the
Haul towards the new century   20
Where do you fit in my sister
No one but you know you
No one but me knows the love
I have for the world but …
More apt the love I have   25
For you
      Sweet
      Strong
      Determined
      Misunderstood   30

Woman of the dreaming
Find your soul,
And peace and love and
Eternal fire and spirit will
Connect with our ancestors   35
And our land
Will begin to smile, again.

1996

Urbanised Reebocks

In a creek bed at Baroota
I lose myself amongst
the spirit of life of
times where people
that is Blak folk   5
our mob—sang and laughed
and danced—paint-em
up big, red ochre
was precious ... go on
remember-hear the   10
sounds of flattened
ground and broken gum
leaves—

My feet slip out of their
urbanised reebocks/   15
of sadness, which
hides its loneliness
behind broken reebans[1]

Uncloaked feet hit
the earth ...   20
And it's okay
to cry

1996

Taxi
For Joan Kirner

splashed by a passing cab,
and another and another
there's rules you see;
don't. stop. for.

---

1 Author's note: 'I coined this word reeban—it comes from combining the words reebocks and raybans. I love wearing these types of shoes and sunglasses.'

black women, accelerate   5
past black men
and pensioners on pension day
can't trust,
trash
got no cash   10
we're all *nuisances*
reminders of an unjust
world, where the poor,
people of colour
are at the mercy   15
of even taxi drivers.

1996

MICK DODSON
b. 1950

Mick Dodson was born in Katherine, NT, and is the brother of Patrick Dodson (qv). He is a member of the Yawuru peoples of the southern Kimberley region, WA. A lawyer, academic and advocate, Dodson worked with the Victorian Aboriginal Legal Service (1976–81) and became a barrister in 1981. He joined the Northern Land Council as senior legal adviser in 1984 and became director of the Council in 1990. He is a member of the United Nations Permanent Forum on Indigenous Issues and was a founding director of the Australian Indigenous Leadership Centre, as well as a member and chairman of AIATSIS.

From 1988 to 1990 Dodson was Counsel assisting the Royal Commission into Aboriginal Deaths in Custody and he was Australia's first Aboriginal and Torres Strait Islander social justice commissioner with HREOC, serving from 1993 to 1998. In 2003 Dodson was appointed Inaugural Professor of Indigenous Studies at the Australian National University and convenor of its National Centre for Indigenous Studies.

We All Bear the Cost if Apology is Not Paid

The Commonwealth Government has finally responded—in part—to the National Inquiry into the Separation of Aboriginal and Torres Strait Islander Children from their Families. While there are some laudable initiatives that will have tangible effects, there exists a matter of much greater significance, which the Government's response fails to grasp.

In its response, the Government fails to appreciate that the way forward for all Australians has as much, if not more, to do with spiritual repair as with material programs.

Australians cannot escape the uncomfortable truth that policies and practices of the past were inherently racist. 'Half-caste' children, and others, were taken from their families for no reason other than the colour of their skin.

Despite the best motivation of the individuals involved in administering these policies, or their belief that what they were doing was in the best interests of the children, the facts remain that the aim was the destruction of a group of people—the Aboriginal people. No amount of welfare or well-modulated phraseology can remove this reality.

The package announced by the Minister for Aboriginal Affairs, Senator John Herron, focuses principally on the welfare-related recommendations, insultingly dismissing as 'not applicable' the fundamental principle of self-determination. It excludes any indigenous organisation from participating, in any formal way, in the monitoring of government application of the recommendations.

The package omits any attention to fundamental issues of compensation and it excludes the recommendations on training and learning that would ensure schools' curricula include compulsory modules on the history and effects of forcible removal. This flies in the face of the minister's statement that 'we must learn from the past so that we do not allow such circumstances and policies to happen in our community again'. If we don't teach, how can we learn?

Indigenous people repeatedly told the inquiry that an apology would make an enormous difference to their ability to overcome the traumas they have suffered. Without an expression of real regret evidenced by a national parliamentary apology the package is fundamentally flawed.

The justifications for refusing to offer an apology are spurious straw-clutching. There is no legal impediment to stop such an initiative. Further, the Government's argument that a national apology is untenable, given the large proportion of Australians who have arrived in the past 20 years, is fallacious and does not reflect the views of many Australians.

Today's Australians are not being asked to accept individual guilt, but collective responsibility. Ethnic communities have offered their apologies to indigenous people. Their mood is captured in the remark of Mr Randolph Alwis, the chairman of the Federation of Ethnic Communities Councils of Australia, who recently said that 'we are part of the current society and society is a continuum. Anything we can do to help the reconciliation process, we will do.'

Above all, the Government's refusal to apologise stands in sharp contrast to the plethora of formal apologies from parliaments around Australia, churches, community groups, ethnic organisations, schools, local governments, unions, leading non-government organisations, and the thousands of individual Australians who have signed petitions, written letters and declared their sorrow. Indeed, these groups, and many individual Australians, have felt compelled to make it clear that they directly endorse the Human Rights and Equal Opportunity Commission's recommendation that there be a national apology.

The Government also has reasserted its rejection of indigenous people's right to compensation. The Government made it clear in its initial submission to the inquiry that it did not consider compensation appropriate. The national inquiry considered this, along with a wealth of expert advice, and concluded that an essential component of reparation for past wrongs was monetary compensation.

It is regrettable that the Government's view has not changed. An absence of any statutory compensation fund is already resulting in recourse to the courts at significant legal cost to taxpayers and potentially significant compensation payments.

However, there are some positive initiatives. In targeting health, counselling services and family reunion, the Government shows that it appreciates the long-term impact of removing Aboriginal and Torres Strait Islander children from their families, on the wellbeing of those families and communities.

Programs to expand indigenous link-up programs will provide much needed practical support for the bringing together of families torn apart by past government policies. The provision of more than $39 million to enhance counselling and mental health services for people affected by separation also will help.

Aboriginal people know what it means to be poor—and know that material assistance is not irrelevant. But we also know it is not material wealth that makes a family. If there is a lesson to be learned from our families being broken apart, it is about love, understanding, and the seeking and giving of forgiveness.

These are values that could make an Australian family of all people within this country. Many know this. The Commonwealth Government's failure to understand has resulted in a failure at the heart of its response. As a consequence, we are all the poorer.

1997

ALEXIS WRIGHT
b. 1950

Alexis Wright is from the Waanyi people from the highlands of the southern Gulf of Carpentaria. She has worked in government departments and Aboriginal agencies across four states and territories as a manager, educator, researcher and writer. Wright coordinated the NT Aboriginal Constitutional Convention in 1993 and wrote 'Aboriginal Self-Government' for *Land Rights News*, later quoted in full in Henry Reynolds' *Aboriginal Sovereignty* (1996). Her involvement in Aboriginal organisations and campaigns has included work on mining, publications, fund raising and land rights both in Australia and overseas. As well as writing essays and short stories, Wright is the author of *Grog War* (1997), an examination of the alcohol restrictions in Tennant Creek, and two novels, *Plains of Promise* (1997) and the multi-award-winning *Carpentaria* (2006), the first work by an Indigenous author to win the Miles Franklin Award outright. She edited *Take Power Like This Old Man Here: An anthology of writings celebrating twenty years of land rights in Central Australia, 1977–1997* (1998).

From *Plains of Promise*
Chapter 6: The Timekeeper's Shadow

[…] It was a dangerous time to travel alone over the land: it was waking-up season. Elliot's journey back through the Channel Country and along his Dreaming line, intermeshing between snake-rivers to the Great Lake was carried out in the Dry. It was at this time that whatever powerful essences lay submerged all around rose from the earth. You needed to take extra precautions to remain safe. He was careful to eat sparingly from a limited amount of available food, so that he would not create any noticeable odours which the spirits would notice. Suspicious of every movement around him, even a leaf fluttering in the breeze, he starved himself to avoid the risk. The pathway he followed was dimly visible in his mind as a narrow, hazy tunnel. Should he penetrate its walls, even though soundless to his ear, this would create disturbance amid the serene surroundings and awaken the restful state of the spiritual environment and bring forth its malignant powers.

The most perilous time of all came early in the evening, when the dying sun beamed its last light onto the sandhills and over the dead grassland. This was the time you needed to take cover, when the last screeches of the black cockatoos with their red tails died away and the land was quiet. It was best to sit it out for the night. Beyond his camp, Elliot watched the bush pigeons fossicking amongst dry twigs in the red, glowing grasses. Although he lay with some sense of security beneath a gidgee tree, his father's totem, he was brooding about how he could get rid of the pigeons. No point in being cautious on the one hand then gamble in your camp at night.

Over the passing of many nights he repeatedly whispered to the pigeons, urging them to take flight and seek the safety of cover. Sometimes the birds took a moment and made head-wobbling movements as if they took notice of his words and actions, but they did not fly off. Mainly they ignored him. At first he tended to dismiss their lack of intuition, but as days of travel grew into weeks and he sat swathed in his sweat under a tree where the breeze did not penetrate, he heard the echoes of the great spirits thundering in the distant hills and started to have second thoughts about the nature of birds. He changed his attitude towards their presence. He felt he was right to do so, for he was trained in religious knowledge of the land by the thoughts of the elders, through a straight line of law since time began and the land and everything in it had been created. It was his duty to do his utmost to maintain harmony in the world that owned him.

As each day passed on his long journey he began to lose sight of the reality of St Dominic's and his own place in the Mission. He tried in vain to recall people's faces, the inside of his father's dwelling … try as he might he could not do it. It was like lifting his weight in lead. He had become obsessed by the pigeons. Before dusk each day he tried every evasive angle he had been taught—movements which were now an instinctive part of his nature—to try to rid himself of the birds. He had always been able to outsmart anyone: at St Dominic's people knew this side of Elliot's nature well. Some bore scars as reminders of times they had tried to call his bluff.

Try as he might, he could not escape the pigeons. He never saw them during daylight. It was only at dusk, when he made his camp, that they appeared. Sometimes he hid from them in low bushes. At other times he buried himself in the deep sand of a dry river bed, hiding there for hours until it was dark. He arose from his makeshift grave only to find the pigeons looking at him from a short distance away. By now, the birds were cooing and scratching the dirt right next to the place where he slept. They would be gone in the morning, but Elliot never saw them leave.

The night is broken into stages in the Hot. Early on the ground retains the stored energy of the sun and radiates uncomfortable heat—it is impossible to lie on this hot ground and sleep. Hours later, it cools: the dry, brittle earth sighs and expands in vast yawns. This is the signal for creatures and men, big red stony devils, to lie stretched out asleep on their sleeping mother. It is the time of the creaks and moans of the great spirits awakening. Rocks, trees, hills and rivers—all are awake at this time. Released from their sedated daytime state, the spirits of the land travel from place to place. The air, the sky is alive with the ancestral spirits of the land. As Elliot endured another night of restless sleep, he knew it was best to sing their songs and urge them towards good feelings.

No one was able to look after the land any more, not all of the time, the way they used to in the olden days. Life was so different now that the white man had taken the lot. It was like a war, an undeclared war. A war with no name. And the Aboriginal man was put into their prison camps, like prisoners in the two world wars. But nobody called it a war: it was simply the situation, that's all. Protection. Assimilation … different words that amounted to annihilation. The white man wanted to pay alright for taking the lot. But they didn't want to pay for the blackman's culture, the way he thinks. Nor for the blackman's language dying away because it was no longer tied to his traditional country … now prosperous cattle station or mining project. The white people wanted everyone to become white, to think white. Skin and all. And they were willing to say they will pay out something for that, even though they believed what happened was not worth much. They could not actually see the value for their money—not like buying grain or livestock.

Yet no one could change the law—so Elliot muttered to himself as he crossed the whiteman's roads or stepped across tyre marks made by vehicles that had been bogged at river crossings. In spite of the foreign burrs and stinging nettles along the river banks—nothing foreign could change the essence of the land. No white man had that power.

Elliot visualised the hands of white people writhing with some kind of illogical intent to misuse and swallow up what was not on a map imprinted in the ancestry of their blood. Hands that hung limp when the land dried up. That buried dead children, set tables with no food to eat. Hands that tried to fight the fires that destroyed the crops and livestock they valued so much. The essence of their souls. He saw the same hands gesturing with self-centred righteousness, a backhand flick to explain hard times, without thought of the true explanations for disaster from the land itself. Good season, bad season! Their palms opened to beg for more government money to keep their stranger life afloat. Kill off whatever got in the way of it. Put it down to bad luck when things were bad. Put it down to good luck when things went right. A simplistic way of ignoring their own ignorance. Sit in one spot and eat it all away. A laconic race living on its wit's end in order to voice its demands and ordered others to fall into line.

The night might have been enjoyed once. He thought of the days when the spirits and the black people would have spoken to each other. But the blackman's enforced absence from his traditional land had inspired fear of it. They had to alter old, ongoing relationships with the spirits that had created man and once connected him to the earth.

As the weeks passed, Elliot the Traveller became convinced he would not live to be an old man. Cattle lay dead beside the mud-cracked waterholes of the dry riverbeds. Kangaroos and wallabies lay nearby. He had been sent at the wrong time. The restless spirits exchanged thunderous blows of anger, tying earth and sky into knots. *Wrong! Wrong! Wrong!* They raced up and down the sky in the pitch-black night. Giant arms struck out with a fearful force, felling giant ghost gums which nearly killed him as they crashed to the ground.

Why had the elders sent him in the first place? Yes, he was convinced they had hatched a plan to get rid of him. *'You won't get me,'* he repeated to himself a thousand times a day. He was no longer distracted by their attempts to cloud his thinking—for it must have been they who had taken away his memory of St Dominic's. Why did they want him dead? For the first time he imagined he saw deception in his own father's face. *This is a lot of trouble you have gone to,* he screamed. *Why? Why here and not there?* If the elders did have some sinister plan for him, Jipp the self-appointed augur would not have been any the wiser. Elliot traced and retraced every detail of his life for clues.

Perhaps it was his tendency towards violence. Surely not, when even the most demure of young women with babies in their tummies stomped through the village yelling at their husbands after they had quarrelled with them—'You wait! I'll be coming for you with a big knife! As soon as I get some money I am going to buy a knife for you.' While the husband, looking like a piece of well-kneaded dough, trotted along after her at a safe distance. Then she yelled again: 'to rip your guts out!' And you could believe it would happen. And alongside, her two-year-old, shaping up his little fists, kicked each leg back towards his father to demonstrate he was on his mother's side and he meant business, too.

No, it was not his violence. His magic then? Almost everyone in the community was wary of his knowledge of magic. When he was younger he would run and complete a somersault in mid-air, land on his feet and do it again up and down the road between the village and Mission. He made tobacco tins glow in the dark. Children begged him to show them. Watching, their mothers' eyes nearly popped out of their heads and they chased their kids away with sticks. He balanced stones on the tops of sticks and made them twirl around. The old men found interesting stones to challenge him. He beat them each time. He could sketch faces to the exact likeness, and left the portraits blowing around in the wind. That nearly frightened people half to death. Their fear was a source of amusement to him. They believed he was trying to steal their souls to serve himself. That he might be in secret collusion with the spirit world.

Elliot believed he could count on one hand the number of occasions when he had infringed the law during his thirty years of life. Trivial matters. Nothing to deserve this punishment. So what could it be? Perhaps some great danger threatened his people and his own life was considered inconsequential, a trivial matter in the greater scheme of things. Did the community fear of more suicides override one sacrifice? Had they agreed that he should provide that sacrifice? Who could know the true malevolence of Ivy Koopundi—or the combined force of her people, the guardians of the majestic spiritual being? Could their power, in some explicable way, stretch out to kill anyone, anywhere? Were they able to make those deaths appear as suicides? What pitiful chance did he have of confronting this power?

So, Elliot told himself, he was soon to become the sacrificial lamb for Ivy Koopundi. Why had not somebody simply murdered her in the middle of some moonless night? It would have been easy enough. He should have thought of it himself. He had no difficulty in recalling the way her sly face watched him everywhere he went. Jumping in front of him from right to left, left to right, the whole day, trying to send him crazy. Why had he not recognised the same sly look on the faces of Pilot and May Sugar and those other two old grannies? It was all as plain as day to him now.

Yes, it was her. He had been careful that she, above all, should have no knowledge of his travelling—yet there she stood in the dark shadows the morning he left. Further back, he recalled the day Old Maudie died, and the sidelong glance she had thrown him on her way through the village, a glance that chilled the base of his neck. She was a different kind. Not happy like his own people, who could joke about life, no matter what. They might be treated like dogs, but they could laugh just the same. They came from the spirits, and to the spirits they would return. That was the law. Always look above. Ivy played another role, and laughing at life was not part of it.

So be it. If this journey led to death then he must allow it to happen. But the pigeons ... were they a warning to him, a contradiction of prediction?

1997

From *Carpentaria*
Chapter 1: From Time Immemorial

[...] The ancestral serpent, a creature larger than storm clouds, came down from the stars, laden with its own creative enormity. It moved graciously—if you had been watching with the eyes of a bird hovering in the sky far above the ground. Looking down at the serpent's wet body, glistening from the ancient sunlight, long before man was a creature who could contemplate the next moment in time. It came down those billions of years ago, to crawl on its heavy belly, all around the wet clay soils in the Gulf of Carpentaria.

Picture the creative serpent, scoring deep into—scouring down through—the slippery underground of the mudflats, leaving in its wake the thunder of tunnels collapsing to form deep sunken valleys. The sea water following in the serpent's wake, swarming in a frenzy of tidal waves, soon changed colour from ocean blue to the yellow of mud. The water filled the swirling tracks to form the mighty bending rivers spread across the vast plains of the Gulf country. The serpent travelled over the marine plains, over the salt flats, through the salt dunes, past the mangrove forests and crawled inland. Then it went back to the sea. And it came out at another spot along the coastline and crawled inland and back again. When it finished creating the many rivers in its wake, it created one last river, no larger or smaller than the others, a river which offers no apologies for its discontent with people who do not know it. This is where the giant serpent continues to live deep down under the ground in a vast network of limestone aquifers. They say its being is porous; it permeates everything. It is all around in the atmosphere and is attached to the lives of the river people like skin.

This tidal river snake of slowing mud takes in breaths of a size that is difficult to comprehend. Imagine the serpent's breathing rhythms as the tide flows inland, edging towards the spring waters nestled deeply in the gorges of an ancient limestone plateau covered with rattling grasses dried yellow from the prevailing winds. Then with the outward breath, the tide turns and the serpent flows back to its own circulating mass of shallow waters in the giant water basin in a crook of the mainland whose sides separate it from the open sea.

To catch this breath in the river you need the patience of one who can spend days doing nothing. If you wait under the rivergum where those up-to-no-good Mission-bred kids accidentally hanged Cry-baby Sally, the tip of the dead branch points to where you will see how the serpent's breath fights its way through in a tunnel of wind, creating ripples that shimmer silver, similar to the scales of a small, nocturnal serpent, thrashing in anger whenever the light hits its slippery translucent body, making it writhe and wrench to escape back into its natural environment of darkness.

The inside knowledge about this river and coastal region is the Aboriginal Law handed down through the ages since time began. Otherwise, how would one know where to look for the hidden underwater courses in the vast flooding mud plains, full of serpents and fish in the monsoon season? Can someone who did not grow up in a place that is sometimes under water, sometimes bone-dry, know when the trade winds blowing off the southern and northern hemispheres will merge in summer? Know the moment of climatic change better than they know themselves? Who fishes in the yellow-coloured monsoonal runoff from the drainages, with sheets of deep water pouring into the wide rivers swollen over their banks, filling vast plains with floodwaters? The cyclones linger and regroup, the rain never stops pouring, but the fat fish are abundant.

It takes a particular kind of knowledge to go with the river, whatever its mood. It is about there being no difference between you and the movement of water as it seasonally shifts its tracks according to its own mood. A river that spurns human endeavour in one dramatic gesture, jilting a lover who has never really been known, as it did to the frontier town built on its banks in the hectic heyday of colonial vigour. A town intended to serve as a port for the shipping trade for the hinterland of Northern Australia.

In one moment, during a Wet season early in the last century, the town lost its harbour waters when the river simply decided to change course, to bypass it by several kilometres. Just like that. Now the waterless port survives with more or less nothing to do. Its citizens continue to engage in a dialogue with themselves passed down the generations, on why the town should continue to exist. They stayed on to safeguard the northern coastline from invasion by the Yellow Peril. A dreadful vision, a long yellow streak marching behind an arrowhead pointing straight for the little town of Desperance. Eventually the heat subsided. When the Yellow Peril did not invade, everyone had a good look around and found a more contemporary reason for existence. It meant the town still had to be vigilant. Duty did not fall on one or two; duty was everybody's business. To keep a good eye out for whenever the moment presented itself, to give voice to a testimonial far beyond personal experience—to comment on the state of their blacks. To do so was regarded as an economic contribution to State rights, then, as an afterthought, to maintaining the decent society of the nation as a whole.

2006

MELISSA LUCASHENKO
b. 1967

Melissa Lucashenko is of European and Indigenous Yugambeh/Bundjalung heritage. Born and educated in Brisbane, Lucashenko studied at Griffith University, graduating with an honours degree in public policy. She worked for a short time in Canberra for the Department of the Prime Minister and Cabinet before moving to Darwin and then returning to Brisbane. At Griffith University she began PhD studies on the experiences of Aboriginal women at work. She left her studies to take up full-time writing, and has since written two adult novels, *Steam Pigs* (1997) and *Hard Yards* (1999), two young adult novels, *Killing Darcy* (1998) and *Too Flash* (2002), essays, stories, and a political study, *Policy and Politics in the Indigenous Sphere* (1996).

From *Steam Pigs*
Chapter 6: Revolution

[…] There's a few kids hanging around outside the brick community centre, including one of Shane's friends in a landrights T-shirt eyeing Kerry's bike. Sensible girl, she's got a bloody great lock on the front wheel, but still, a kid can dream. Sue smiles hello at him, but he looks at her blankly, not recognising her and stoned off his head anyway. Jesus, you're a bit young for it aren't you mate, she thinks, and what'd Maureen say if she knew ya weren't at school? Inside she peers around the corner into the hall, then knocks on Kerry's door.

'Hang on, I'll be out in a sec. Who is it?'

'Um, Sue. From karate, you probably don't remember me … did you know there's kids outside looking over yer bike?' The door opens to reveal Kerry pulling her bike boots on.

'Oh, Sue! Yeah, I remember, how are ya? And I know the Centre kids are there, they're waiting to be picked up.'

'Pretty good. I s'pose. Did you go to Nepal?'

'Nah, ended up in Indonesia instead. Bit different, I know, but the money ran out quicker than I expected, and Bali's closer. Come in and sit down, do you want a coffee?'

'Yes please, white no sugar. Were you going somewhere?' still diffident about approaching the woman she didn't know at all well, and wondering about the merits of Bali versus Nepal. If all the blokes looked like Made, built like brick shithouses, she'd take Bali anyday.

'I told young George that I'd take him for a ride on Harriet if he went to school every day last week, and he did, amazingly enough, so I owe him a run into Beenleigh. But he can wait a minute.' Kerry sees Sue puzzled. '... oh, Harriet's the bike; Harriet the Harley,' she explains.

A cup of coffee in hand, Sue sinks into Kerry's armchair in the little room. Blond, tattooed Kerry has an openness and friendliness that puts her at ease, and they chat comfortably for ten minutes about bikes, Eagleby and the course Kerry's about to run. The unlikely social worker lights a cigarette and peers at Sue more closely for a moment.

'Hey, I've got a brilliant idea. Why don't you give us a hand with the conflict resolution?'

'Me? I was hoping for some tips from *you*.'

Sue didn't mention the fight her and Rog had the other night, when he'd thrown her up against the wall of the lounge, screaming abuse square in her face. She couldn't work it out at all, it was like another person. Not like Rog at all and anyway he was sorry after, bought her flowers and everything.

'Well, we're going to be doing stuff about self-esteem and body image, and part of the body image is about using your body to *do* stuff, not just to look at. I've got a Chinese friend coming down to teach some acrobatics one night, that sort of thing. So you could teach the women some basic karate moves, hey, what about it?'

Sue becomes enthusiastic with a little prompting. Karate is one thing she does feel confident about in front of strangers, and she's been helping Lou with the kids' class a bit lately too, so she knows what it's like to teach. Every Tuesday night for six weeks, it means shuffling her training around, but sounds like fun. She might meet some people she can relate to, as well.

'But where's it gonna be? There's karate here on Tuesday nights.'

'Oh, I'll hold it at my place, I reckon. I moved down here, you know. I've got an old Queenslander in Beenleigh.'

'Yeah, alright then. Sounds like fun. Maybe Roger'd like to come and help too.'

'Oh, my house is women's space, mate. Sorry. No men allowed, unless it's special circumstances, and especially not for stuff like this.'

'Oh ... how does that work, though?' Sue asks sceptically. 'What if some bloke tried to come in, what would ya do?' Kerry looks faintly amused, but takes Sue's question seriously nonetheless.

'Well, it depends. Step one is, you explain the reasons women sometimes need to be on our own, away from men. And if that doesn't persuade him Inter-lech-ally, usually if you use the right tack, and defuse the situation by listening you can convince people to do just about anything. And if not,' she cracks her knuckles over her head melodramatically, 'then we kick the living shit out of em from here to Hobart, until they abjectly apologise on their knees, cravenly begging our forgiveness. Which of course we give them.' Kerry laughs at the girl's face. Sue is a bit stunned by the idea of women telling men they weren't allowed to go somewhere; if anyone but Kerry had suggested it she would have been unconvinced. Somehow though, coming from her it sounded almost reasonable. *Wild*. Most of the men she'd grown up with would give you a flogging for less. Wow. But should she tell Rog? And what would he say about her hanging around with this skinny feminist with the weird tats?

They swap phone numbers, then Kerry heaves her boots off the desk. 'Look, I better take George for this run before he slits his wrists. Why don't you come in again tomorrow and we can make some plans. Oh, hang on, tomorrow's no good, I'm going up the bush. Come in on Monday, why don't ya?'

Sue explains about her new job.

'Alright, well, I'll give you a ring over the weekend then, and we can start talking about the course, OK?'

'Yeah, sure.'

And with that, Kerry and Sue walk outside to the growing bunch of envious early teens who are waiting to see George's moment of glory. Kerry fires the bike up and the adolescent boys all just about cum at the sound, thinks Sue contemptuously. The kid hangs on to Kerry's leather jacket and they burn off up the road past the cemetery into town, leaving Sue to wander back home, thinking about her new job, and whether she could afford a bike herself. Have to be japcrap of course, but still—Brrrrrrrrrrrrmmmmmmmmmmmmm, burn the ute off, that'd really give Rog the shits! Pictures of bikes roaring in her head, Sue traipses back across the road, thinking about what Kerry's said, oblivious to the newly-sown seeds of revolution.

1997

JOHN MUK MUK BURKE
b 1946

Born in Narrandera, NSW, of a Wiradjuri mother and an Irish father, John Muk Muk Burke spent many years teaching music and art in schools in New Zealand, Darwin and outback NT. He has lectured at the Centre for Aboriginal Studies at Northern Territory (now Charles Darwin) University and worked with Aboriginal inmates at the Goulburn Correctional Centre. His novel, *Bridge of Triangles*, won the David Unaipon Award in 1993. He is also the author of *Night Song and Other Poems* (1999).

A Poem for Gran

Flatwalk field of Suffolk—
Your insular chalk walls are crumbling.
The last of summer's apples
Are tumbling from your trees;
Your larders are fully laden   5
With earth-grown food—
A goodly preparation
For the cold and coming winter.

For your winter winds do whistle
Over flat fields, squat villages   10

And important towns.
And everywhere, sensible people are preparing.

The hay is gathered in
For the sheep's hard winter
And the hay is gathered in   15
For the street's hard sound
And the hay is gathered in
For the apples in the attic.

All over drifts the first smoke
Of winter's falling.   20
From a soft room of lavender
A little girl is calling.
Born at the ingathering
Of the good things of the earth.

And from overhead we see the red house   25
On the high street, the river turgid,
The tower Norman. Solid trees and lonely lanes.
And overhead the sky is grey and all around
Is England.

                                                              1999

JENNIFER MARTINIELLO
b 1949

A writer, artist and academic born in Adelaide of Arrernte, Chinese and Anglo-Celtic descent, Jennifer Martiniello has lectured in education at the Canberra Institute of Technology and the University of Canberra and worked with Indigenous communities in regional NSW and Victoria. In 2005 she was the public officer of the Indigenous Writers Support Group in Canberra and a member of the Publishing Advisory Committee of Aboriginal Studies Press at AIATSIS. She has edited a number of anthologies, including *Black Lives, Rainbow Visions: Indigenous sitings in the creative arts* (1999), *Writing Us Mob: New Indigenous voices* (2000) and *Talking Ink from Ochre* (2002), and is the author of a collection of poetry, *The Imprint of Infinity* (1999).

Uluru by Champagne

you
are a flame in the blue
dome of heaven
eternal
bubble of evanescent   5
earth, the mother rising
in the spirits of her children
the land your

magic
spun   10
between suns
horizon to horizon

you are
blue earth, red sky, deep shadow

the imprint   15
of infinity on my soul

1999

Emily Kngwarreye[1]

your face
is the grace a harsh life
bestows on its survivors, each crease
a bar whose notes, escaping their dirge,
run for the high octaves like a bird   5
to a joyous freedom once the doors
of the cage are broken

deep-coloured as the millennia
sediments that scar the cliff faces of sacred country
your face is as ancient a bed to flowing water   10
carving its agelessness into the land the way
wisdom enscripts its elusive dance upon
humanity

and I watch you
slowly measuring out the journeylines with a finger   15
brushed with red earth and hear the dust
that others only see as a place to put their boots
open its voice and speak,
see your hand on the cave walls where they
have held the ochred spirit in the rock for all   20
eternity, and watch how the sun shifts
to accommodate your shadow, effortlessly,
day after day without tiring

I watch you bend
your face to greet the waterhole, see   25
how your laughter is caught up in the transient

---

1 Emily Kngwarreye (c. 1910–96) was an internationally acclaimed Aboriginal artist from the Utopia
Community in the NT.

ripples and released without possessive grasping
to share you with reed, tree,—how you
and it are the same manna
born in the same creation   30

I see ... beyond the verticals
and horizontals of skin the hundred boys who've
died in custody and whom you've mourned, the warp
and weft of sorrow in your face for all the young women
whose eyes do not know their country or their mothers   35
but whose children still belong to your body—how your skin
stretches to embrace their homecoming with every
carefully recorded story, mother, son, daughter,
place and time—the same way your smile
stretches other boundaries   40

sometimes beyond comprehension
and lesser visions restrained to the finite byte
of desert stopover, campfire talk, a desperate camera-clutch
at a surreal otherworld that fail to distinguish how you
rise from earth, become   45
ancestor, mother, daughter, grandmother, granddaughter,
terrain, sacred physicality—fail to see
how the one spirit makes you blood and rock, well
and water

your face wears the intaglio of embattled anguish,   50
betrayal, theft, deceit, massacre and grief survived—
and when I remember the zealot piety and passion
of ANZAC, two world wars, Korea, Vietnam,
I remember also that you witnessed all of them
for nine generations and more; and as I watch you   55
bend to trace creation in red earth with a finger
more purposeful than Michaelangelo's Sistine god's
I see a light more eternal kindle in those you teach,
see each one, mirror-like, reflect the tireless radiance
of an inevitable grace   60

2002

KENNY LAUGHTON
b 1950

Kenny Laughton was born in Alice Springs and is of Arrernte descent. He is a Vietnam veteran who served two tours of duty as a combat engineer between 1969 and 1971. On his return to Australia and subsequent discharge from the armed services, Laughton went home to Alice Springs where he spent the next twenty years working for the

Commonwealth, the NT Public Service and also in the private sector. He is the editor of *The Aboriginal Ex-Servicemen of Central Australia* (1995), and the author of *Not Quite Men, No Longer Boys* (1999), an account of his military experiences in Vietnam, and a poet.

The Tunnel Rats of Phuoc Tuy[1]
Ode to 1 Field Squadron

They sent us here to be tested in battle,
To uphold traditions, forged by Aussies before,
To a war with no boundaries, uniforms or direction,
The one they would call the 'unwinnable war'.

We sweated and fretted through rivers and thick jungle,   5
Through rubber, 'wait-a-while' and bamboo.
Not quite men but no longer boys,
But would they remember us, the 'Tunnel Rats of Phuoc Tuy'.

We walked with the foot soldier and rode with the tracks,
Through paddy-fields and villages, with our world in our packs.   10
We faced the Long Hais[2] and saw our mates die,
In death's bloody, unexpected, explosive roar.
Through minefields and traps that clung to the hillside,
Like incurable, festering, cancerous sores.

We wept as we loaded our mates onto choppers,   15
For their last ride, through a South Asian sky.
We were choked with emotions, our feelings ran high,
What else could we say but 'mate, goodbye'.
Not quite men but no longer boys,
But would they remember us, the 'Tunnel Rats of Phuoc Tuy'.   20

We honed our skills on stealth and detection,
Through villages, bunkers and tunnels galore.
We soon became noticed for our strange affliction,
Of the many safety pins we wore.
But still we delivered through Monsoon or dry,   25
Splinter-teams and mini-teams at the ready,
'Where's the F.E.s?' we would hear someone cry.

Like rats we would crawl through chambers of tunnels,
In search of the cunning, elusive V.C.
But like D445 they would run and survive,   30

---

1   Phuoc Tuy, a province in the south of Vietnam, was a prominent base for Australian soldiers during the Vietnam War.
2   A range of hills in Vietnam.

Like 'will-o-the-wisps' you see.
Not quite men but no longer boys,
But would they remember us, the 'Tunnel Rats of Phuoc Tuy'.

Now that it's over and much has been said,
On valour, courage and heroic deeds.   35
My mind still wanders to the old squadron lines,
Where many a tale could be told.
Of soldiers and sappers who all did their jobs,
And some paid the price for being so bold.
They gave of their lives in the field of battle,   40
And long may we honour our illustrious dead.

Through time's abyss, I still remember,
The sign in the troop lines that read
And I quote with pride and a lump in my throat,
'Through these gates pass the greatest F.E.s in the world' unquote.   45
Not quite men but no longer boys,
But will they remember us, the 'Tunnel Rats of Phuoc Tuy'.

                                                                          1999

KIM SCOTT
b. 1957

Kim Scott has written novels, a biography and a children's picture book, as well as poetry, stories and criticism. He was born in Perth, and is a descendant of the Noongar people. Scott graduated from Murdoch University. After teaching English for some time in urban, rural and remote secondary schools, including at an Aboriginal community in the north of WA, Scott began researching his family history. This led to his first novel, *True Country* (1993), which, along with *Benang: From the heart* (1999), explores the problem of self-identity faced by light-skinned Aboriginal people and examines assimilationist policies during the first decades of the twentieth century. In 2000, Scott was the first Indigenous writer to win the Miles Franklin Award, for *Benang*, sharing the prize with Thea Astley. *Kayang and Me*, a collaborative autobiography with senior Aboriginal woman Kayang Hazel Brown, was published in 2005.

From *Benang*
We Move ...

I had a new game. I had never been one for games, but I was unusually thrilled, I was giggling like a child with the pleasure it gave me to share this one with Uncle Will. I could see, even within the composure and dignity he liked to feign, that it startled and excited him.

At the same time—and this helped his appearance of composure—he was I think stunned, and in awe of such freedom.

Previously I had performed it solely for the pleasure of seeing the terror, and—later—the *indignation* it aroused in Ern.

I simply indulged in my propensity to drift. In the mornings I would attach strong fishing line to a reel on my belt, anchor one end of it to the house and, stepping out the door, simply let the land breeze take me. I rose and fell on currents of air like a balloon, like a wind-borne seed. The horizon moved away so that the islands no longer rested on its line, but stood within the sea, and it seemed that the pulsing white at the island's tip was not a mere transformation induced by collision, but was a blossoming and wilting at some fissure where sea met land.

It was indeed a very long time after this—but it may have begun here—that I realised that I had come back from the dead, was one of those few. I may well be djanak, or djangha—so much so that I stumble at what is the correct dialect, let alone how I should spell it—but even then I had not completely forgotten who I am. I floated among the clouds, and even with a bleached skin, and an addled memory I nevertheless saw the imprint of the wind upon the turquoise ocean. I remembered the call of quails in the dune grasses, and thought of curlews crying from moonlit chalky paths, and the footprint such a bird would leave.

It was as if sunlight told me of the sameness of granite and sand, and—in the evenings—flickering firelight fed the fire of my life, of my breathing.

But I was telling of when Uncle Will and Uncle Jack had returned for me, and of when I was accustoming myself to this experience of drifting. I studied the pathways and tracks which ran along the coastal dunes, and saw the white beach as the sandy, solidified froth of small waves touching the coast. I noted how rocks and reef and weed lurked beneath the water's surface, and saw the tiny town of Wirlup Haven and how Grandad's historic homestead—as if shunned—clung to a road which was sealed and heading inland.

So it was not purely mindless, this floating on the breeze. It required a certain concentration, and I chose it not just for the fun, but also because I wanted to view those islands resting in the sea, and to get that aerial perspective. I couldn't have said why.

The wind ruffled my hair as I rode its currents toward the islands. At first I worried when I saw boats or any sign of human life marking land or sea, but such sightings were rare along that isolated stretch of coastline and, after a time, I realised that I could not be seen at all, except by my family.

Grandad used to stare in shock. It scared him. I loved that.

Uncle Will said he envied my unburdened existence. More pragmatically, he suggested I take another line, and try fishing as I drifted across the ocean.

I liked it best when the breezes were soft, and I watched whales, dolphins, the schools of salmon moving below me. Late in the day the breeze blew me back to the house.

The very first time he found me so tiny and out of earshot in the sky, Uncle Jack hauled me in like some sort of airborne fish. A sharp tug upended me, and then I was bent double, my limbs flapping with the force of such a retrieval into the land breeze.

'Shit, you made a mess of the line,' I said.

He snorted. 'You fuckin' silly little shit. What? You kartwarra, that it? You're something special, you know.' He was insistent and angry. 'I tell you you gotta go right back, you got something special there coming out. I can see where you come from all right. You oughta give away that reading and all those papers for a while.'

He wanted to take *all* of us?

Uncle Jack wanted to take us all driving. He wanted to show me some places. We could drive, and camp. We'd take Ern with us.

'Will?'

Uncle Will nodded.

Uncle Jack reckoned that the main roads more or less followed traditional runs; along the coast to where his Aunty Harriette had been born. The roads went inland from there, up to Norseton, and back to here. It's the waterholes, see. They used to follow the waterholes.

Rain still falls, water still gathers.

'Bring your papers with you if you like,' he said. 'Do all that. You can even fly yourself high as a kite, if you like, if you still wanna. No matter.'

'The main roads follow a traditional run,' he had said. 'And, you know, we showed all those white blokes.' He looked at Uncle Will. 'Your father, he was shown by your mother, and her mother. And there you were wanting to be a pioneer.'

It disturbs my clumsy narrative even more, of course, this sudden and contemporary journey. It disturbed me at the time also. I was scared, but seeing the reluctance in Ern's face convinced me it was the thing to do.

We drove for the afternoon, humming along the sealed road. A 'run', I kept thinking; we once walked where now we skim? The wind roared outside our small and stuffy capsule.

I remembered the little Uncle Will had written—it was not much more than notes scattered among Ern's well-organised papers. It was all about his father, as, perhaps, is my own.

Uncle Will had begun a little history of this region, and of his family. His motivation was the publication of a little booklet, a feeble local history, to which he had taken exception. He had written:

> We may see how greatly facts are distorted and these people are most misleading in their trying to put the arrival of their parents in the new field before many others, for the sake of being known as descendants of the first pioneers.

It was incomprehensible to me: Uncle Will, who had been refused 'Susso' in the Depression and told, instead, to go to the Aborigines Department for rations; Uncle Will, who had barely escaped being sent to a Mission or Native Settlement. Uncle Will desperately wanted to name his father as among the very first to 'settle' at Gebalup, and he scarcely wrote of his mother. Yet it was she who gave him his rights to be here.

He was of 'the first'.

I thought of how Uncle Will walked. Proudly, cautiously; like one provisionally uplifted, whose toes barely gripped the earth.

Grandad had written very little, yet he had organised and collected an array of material. Uncle Will had written a few pages from memory, and that was all he had. But I saw the evasion, the desire to compete and to say he was as good as anyone and that this seemed the only way possible. In his rather formal, affected language, there was this hint of an alternative:

> Can you understand, dear people, why I'm rather diffident about discussing the early history of Gebalup as I knew it as a boy? The descendants have given their forebears images which they wish to see and present to the public in their most favourable light. It would be a continual source of acrimony were I to join in their discussions. So I think it much better for me to write all my thoughts down for the perusal and study of my younger relatives.

But then he'd faltered, and after a few hundred words had stopped.

My father had written nothing, and had just begun to speak to me when I killed him. Uncle Will was family, my father had said. Even your grandfather. That's all you've got, your family. Even if, sometimes, it hurts to have them.

Of course, this was not in any of the material I had read to my grandfather, the so-close-to-smug-in-his-victory Ernest Solomon Scat.

We camped close to Uncle Will's birthplace on our first night away. It was among ancient sea dunes, and nearby, behind a fence, there was a dam which, Uncle Will informed us, collected fresh water from a small spring.

The four of us sat around the campfire, sipping beer. It was a cold night and I was clumsy with the vast bulk of my clothing. I had wrapped a long scarf several times around both myself and a log, partly for the warmth, but also because, as Uncle Jack reminded me, drinking grog inevitably set me drifting off 'something cruel'.

'Somewhere here, eh? I was born somewhere around here,' said Uncle Will, suddenly.

'It was a hot day,' he said. We allowed him the authority to tell us of his birth. We assumed the story had been handed to him and not that he was possessed of a most remarkable memory.

When Uncle Will was born the sides of the tent had been lifted and tied to catch any movement of the air.

Fanny and old Sandy One arrived at the camp, and then Sandy One went to find the other men and left the three women to attend to the birth.

What other men? *Three* women?

Uncle Will and Uncle Jack had to explain to me who all these people were. Be patient, have patience, their sighs said.

Harriette and Daniel? I knew about them, Will's parents. Daniel Coolman of the missing lip and great bulk who was sown in a mine. Harriette, a shadowy but already powerful figure in my little history.

Dinah and Pat? I didn't know them. Uncle Pat, they told me, was Daniel's twin brother. Dinah was Harriette's sister. Aunty Dinah was the other daughter of Fanny and Sandy One Mason.

I worried, as any reader must also do, at this late and sudden introduction of characters. Except that for me it was not characters, but family.

'Yeah, well, there's lots all of us don't know,' said one of the old men.

And then it was definitely Uncle Jack who spoke. 'It's hard to know where to begin—except with each place we come to, really. Where we are right now.'

It was hot, back then, by the tiny pool, here; the heat snapped twigs from the trees, and they bounced off the heavy canvas roof of the tent. Fanny and Dinah murmured to Harriette.

Deep and rasping breaths. The soak's water is still. Campfire smoke grows straight to the sky. The women's breath is very warm, and there is so much moisture, all this liquid pooling beneath the trees.

The place's spirit continued to billow. Fanny felt so grateful.

As the wet child took its first breath they heard the leaves above them clacking and rustling. Will was rolled in white sand.

'This sand is so fine,' Uncle Will said, looking into our faces and letting it run through his fingers, 'it's like talcum powder.'

When Daniel took the child in his arms the women could not help but smile, he so thick and burnt and gnarled and the baby just a bundled heartbeat, mewing and clutching.

Daniel was happy. 'Now, this is the first white man born here. No doubt about that.'

Uncle Jack was smiling at Uncle Will, teasing him.

So where was Uncle Jack born?

He said he'd tell me that later. When we got back to the other side of Wirlup Haven. He hadn't been lucky enough to know his parents like Will had.

Harriette, Daniel, Dinah and Pat had come across from Dubitj Creek way (as you can imagine, I spent a lot of time consulting a map as we drove), where they had been carting goods to the goldfields. There's water all through there, the old men told me, and it was true that my map showed many small and temporary waterholes to which the main road clung. But a new railway line from the capital city had depleted the need for teamsters, and there was various troubles to get away from.

They tried roo shooting which—in those days—gave them enough cash for what they needed.

The truth is, the Coolman twins were happy. It was a decent life. Moving slow; hunting, drinking. There was always the chance of gold. They had wives who knew the country; who found water, food, a place to camp. The women could do everything. They could work like men, feed off the land, embrace their men and make them strong. And Sandy One Mason, their father-in-law, that enigmatic fellow they laughed at between themselves, was known by people all around this way; pastoralists, old miners, carriers, all of which could prove helpful when and if they needed to get work again.

There was no fear of attack, as was prevalent with some travellers. When the Premier Man John Forrest had come this way less than thirty years before, he and his party had kept a rostered watch each night. A publication of 1900, *In Darkest Western Australia*, devotes several pages to the threat of attack by the *blacks*. But when Daniel and Pat met any who were not like themselves they stood close behind the women. It was what Sandy One had advised them. Their faces would echo the expressions of those speaking this peculiar language, as they half-listened and tried to understand.

They gathered kangaroo skins. Or rather, the women gathered them. A trip back to Kylie Bay every few months meant they were making money. Do you wish to hear how they suffered; of their endurance, hardship, deprivation? In fact it was almost too easy a life. It was practically a relief to run out of grog and so they purposely deprived themselves, brought less of it with them—and even that they sipped with their wives.

They moved between the coast and the goldfields; between the old and the new telegraph lines; between the railway to the north and the ocean to the south. Finding where they could take a heavy cart. And, always, there might be gold.

Drinking. Fucking. They wandered, following gossip and getting Harriette and her sister Dinah to take them as far as the goldfields, where they thought they saw their women's people slumped in the dust, rotting from the inside out. The women brought them back, always, to no further than a day or two from the ocean.

No gold. Then suddenly you needed a licence to sell roo skins. They found themselves 'Gebalup' way, near the outer limit of the women's country, and fell in with the Mustle and Done families. The *landed gentry* of this story.

The four of us sat around the fire until late in the night. Perhaps it was the beer, but I felt very heavy, as if burdened. Old people surrounded me.

'Listen to the voices in the trees,' said Uncle Jack.

In the firelight the three men looked exceptionally old, ancient beyond their years. Grandad's face glistened with the tears which now so often came to him. Uncle Jack and Uncle Will's arrival had given him some protection from me, and I had not harmed him for months.

The intervals between Grandad toppling, and being propped up again, grew longer. The eyes of my uncles reflected the fire. I remember noticing my own hands, and being frightened at how old they looked in that light.

1999

BARBARA NICHOLSON
b. 1935

A senior Wadi Wadi woman from the Illawarra district, NSW, Barbara Nicholson was born on the reserve at Port Kembla. As a mature-age student she graduated from the University of Newcastle. Outspoken on issues of land rights, assimilation and criminal justice, Nicholson has been active in many Aboriginal organisations. Her poetry has appeared in *The Strength of Us as Women: Black women speak* (2000).

The Bastards

'You don't take that land,' they cried, they yelled, they wailed
at the men in the military suits and feathered hats.
'Go away and get off my land, get off my land, *my land.*'
But they didn't listen,
listen to the laws of this land,   5
didn't listen to the rock-carved declarations of sovereignty,
didn't listen to the dreaming
and they didn't go away
and they took the land, took the land, took the dreaming away.
Bastards.   10

'You don't take that woman,' he cried, he yelled, he wailed
at the men in the moleskin pants and cork-rimmed hats.
'Is not right marriage, is wrong skin, is not *your woman.*'
But they didn't listen,
listen to the laws of this land,   15
didn't listen to aching hearts of warriors who knew and lived
    the ancient law,
didn't listen to the screaming
and they beat her
and they took her, they raped her, took the woman away.
Bastards.   20

'You don't take my people,' they cried, they yelled, they wailed
at the men in the redcoats and braided caps.
'Is not our law, our law says must not kill, is not OUR LAW.'
But they didn't listen,
listen to the laws of this land,   25
didn't listen to the terror or the ache or the agony that wrenched
    every face,
didn't listen to the screaming
and they took them,
they put them in chains, they butchered, took the people away.
Bastards.   30

'You don't take that kid,' she cried, she yelled, she wailed
at the men in the pinstripe suits and fedora hats.
'Come back here with my babies, don't take my babies, my babies,
    my babies.
But they didn't listen,
listen to the heartache   35
didn't listen as she ran, arms stretched out in longing, embracing nothing,
didn't listen to the moaning,
and they gloated.
and they took them, put them in homes, took the babies away.
Bastards.   40

'You don't take them boys,' they cried, they yelled, they wailed
at the men in blue with the chequerband caps.
'They've done nothin', leave them alone, done nothin' we say.
    Leave them alone.'
But they didn't listen,
listen to the injustice,   45
didn't listen to truth, six young lads doing nothing, just going home,
didn't listen to the moaning,
and they beat them, and they locked them away, and they killed them.
Bastards.

'You don't take that land,' we say, we yell, we holler   50
at the men in black flowing robes and curly white wigs.
'It's our land, always was, always will be. *It's our land.'*
But they don't listen,
listen to equality,
don't listen to truth, to human rights, to land rights,   55
don't listen to our law,
and they take our land, and they graze it and mine it and fuck it up
    forever.
Bastards.

                                                   2000

RICHARD FRANKLAND
b. 1963

Richard Frankland is a singer-songwriter, playwright and film-maker of Gunditjmara/
Kilkurt Gilga descent. He has written poetry, young adult fiction and musical theatre.
Born on the coast of south-west Victoria, Frankland worked as a field officer during the
Royal Commission into Aboriginal Deaths in Custody, which led to his appearance as
a presenter in the award-winning Australian documentary *Who Killed Malcolm Smith?*
(1992), which he also co-authored. His other film credits include writer/director for
Harry's War (1999). Some of his songs have been recorded by Archie Roach (qv). His
novel *Digger J. Jones* was published in 2007.

Two World One

I'm a two world one
I live in two worlds
One time I must have lived in one

But tears fell and a baby taken
Under some law they said   5
A law from one world but not the other

I'm a two world one
I walk down two roads
One time I must have only walked down one

But surely a mother's heart was broken   10
At a birthing tree or birthing room
When I was taken

I'm a two family one
I live with two families
One is black one is white   15

But surely heritage is no barrier to love
Even though the papers scream
About the two hundred years of hurt and shame

I'm a two world one
I can see inside two worlds   20
But one day I'll only have to see in one

2001

KERRY REED-GILBERT
b. 1956

The daughter of Kevin Gilbert (qv), poet Kerry Reed-Gilbert is a Wiradjuri woman from central NSW. She has worked as a consultant on Indigenous culture, history and heritage, and as a human rights activist. Her photography has appeared in numerous exhibitions across Australia. She has edited a number of anthologies of Indigenous writing, including *The Strength of Us As Women: Black women speak* (2000). Her books include *Black Woman, Black Life* (1996) and *Talkin' About Country* (2002).

Let's Get Physical

Let's get physical
The man cried, five in the morning.
They lined up side by side. Row by row.

Let's get physical
The boss man cried as he started them off,   5
on their walk for miles.
In between rows they did walk.
Backs bent, too tired to talk.

Let's get physical
The white man cried as he watched them,   10
pick his cotton, make his money,
to put in his bank.

Let's get physical
The white man cried.
he'll never know,   15
the Koori pride,
that makes that man,
bend his back between his rows.

Koori pride is what it is,
that makes that Blackman bend his back,   20
to pick that cotton, to pay his rent,
to feed his kids.

Welfare cheques not for him.
A honest day's work says he'll win.
Kids' belly full that's all that matters.   25

Let's get physical
The white man cried, he doesn't look
to see the pride in the Blackman's eyes.

     2001

VIVIENNE CLEVEN
b 1968

Vivienne Cleven was born in Surat, Queensland, and grew up in western Queensland, homeland of her Aboriginal heritage, the Kamilaroi nation. She left school at thirteen to work with her father as a jillaroo, working on stations throughout Queensland and NSW. Cleven won the David Unaipon Award in 2000 for her novel *Bitin' Back* (2001). Her second novel, *Her Sister's Eye* was published in 2002. In 2005 she adapted *Bitin' Back* for the stage.

From *Bitin' Back*
Chapter 7: Make Him a Man

I head down to Booty's backyard shed.

The pig dogs sprawl at the door, scarred heads restintween big paws. I squint me peepers at the biggest of em. *Is it my magination or is that dog startin to look like his master? Funny thing that, how dogs can look uman. Them big ol eyes sorta drill ya down like. Yep, that dog lookin jus like Booty. Hey, lookandsee, a woman gettin mighty myall in the head.*

A closer look tells me there's a deep gash down the side of its gut. *Poor buggers, chasin pigs ain't healthy work.*

The bitch brings her head up n starts a low growl in the back a her throat. Ignoring her I keep walkin to the shed, blinkin me eyes to adjust to the dark. Me nose picks up the smell a beer, sweat, dust … n somethin else. Somethin thick, somethin that feels like it smotherin a woman, like a hot n heavy hand closin round me throat. Then it hits me—it's fear.

I take in the room whit careful eyes. Booty sits back on the dirt floor holdin a stubbie n bustin his guts at Nevil. Trevor's perched on a empty molasses tin, watchin Booty n Nevil, his eyes flickerin back n forth.

I feel sweat pop out on the back a me neck, the heat in the shed is fierce. I get a load a Nevil, shirtless n pissin sweat as he moves round a sack of potatoes that hang tied from the beams. He cuts it round the sack like a dancer, his eyes peeled on it as he jabs n hits whit all his strength.

'If that were a fella he'd have your guts by now—have ya busted from arsehole to breakfast time!' Booty roars, gettin to his feet n goin over to Nevil. 'Mid-section, son. You gotta bring this fucka to his knees! Otherwise this fucka's gonna bring you to *ya* knees, got it!' Booty pelts forward and hits the bag so hard it swings back, drivin him backwards. 'Ain't no fucka ever got away from this here punch!'

Booty holds his fists in the air, like he's standin in the middle of a big time boxin ring.

I nod me head toward him then wander over to Trevor.

'Hello, Missus Dooley,' he greets me whit what looks like relief.

'Hey there. Now what the hell's goin on here?' I wipe the sweat off me neck.

'Booty's teaching Nevil how to box. He reckons it'll make a man out of him. He shrugs his shoulders and winces each time Nevil jabs the sack. I guess that's the way of life out here in the bush.'

'Yeah, no use bein a girl round these parts. Gotta look after yerself, nobody else will.' I hold in a laugh as I watch the way Booty struts round the shed. His fat gut hangs out over his shorts, his bare feet move along like he can hardly carry his own weight, and his big frame moves across the room like a constipated goanna. *Yeah, that's good ol Boot for ya.* He comes over to us swingin his fists and stops in front a Trevor.

'On ya feet, son!' he barks.

'Oh, gee,' Trevor casts me a look of desperation.

Just as I'm bout to unhinge me trap to tell Booty to leave him be, I hear loud laughter comin from the shed doorway. Big Boy and Grunta saunter in. Big Boy carries a box a piss. Grunta's got a blue heeler on a chain. Big Boy's eyes sweep cross the room n come to rest on Trevor.

Booty nods at Big Boy, 'Here, son, git ya black arse over here n teach this migloo how to handle hisself.'

'Oh gee listen, Booty, I'm no good at this sort of thing,' Trevor says, wringin his hands n lookin down at his boots.

'Talk shit, son.' Booty hauls him to his feet. 'Get that fucken shirt off, will ya.' He pokes at Trevor's tee-shirt.

'Booty, he don't wanna do this. Leave him be.' I shake me head. But it's too late, Booty's on a drunken high, and Big Boy's gettin high on the possibility a smashin somebody's face in.

Nevil turns to look at Trevor but Trevor is lost in this mad moment, most probly can't see or hear anythin. *Fear does that to ya.*

Grunta ties the dog to a post n comes to stand beside me. 'Who he?'

'That's Trevor, a *friend* a mine.' I lay down me cards. *If there be hurtin goin on whit that poor boy then I'm gonna be the one whoppin arse. Ain't like he's a scrubber. Not like this lot, born whit fists in the air.*

'Geez, them boots n socks for real or what?' Grunta points at Trevor's knee socks n ridin boots.

'Yep, I told him to wear em like that. Good, eh?' I curl up me mouth n wait for Grunt's reaction.

'Solid, Missus D.' *He knows the score.*

Booty whispers somethin into Big Boy's ear then turns and whispers into Trevor's ear. I feel the back a me neck crawl. I don't like it. Booty can get a bit fist happy n not know when to give up.

I throw Nevil a sour look. He stands starin, hands on hips, eyes slitted. He knows what his uncle's doin. So do I.

Trevor, white-faced, shakin like a mongrel dog jus swallowed ten-forty, swings round n gives me a please-help-me look.

'That's enough!' I walk toward them. *A woman seed nough blood in her lifetime already. This little fella they gonna kill.*

Booty steps in front a me. 'No one's gettin hurt, Mave. Jus teachin the boy some tricks,' he says, beer fumes comin outta every pore.

'If anybody hurt Trevor then they fight me—Mavis Dooley!' I throw a fist in the air, all gammon like cos that's what it's all bout. A gammon game. Cept it ain't like that for this mob—Big Boy, Grunta, specially Booty.

Not willin to put me to the test, Booty pats me on the shoulder. 'Come on, Sis, how ya think he gonna get on down at the Two Dogs? They'd make mincemeat a him. Alls I'm doin is tryin to teach him a few things. No one gonna get hurt.'

'They better not, Booty. Cos I holdin you sponsible for this.' I poke his chest, then walk over n sit on the molasses tin and watch as Big Boy n Trevor dance round each other. Trevor looks like he some ol clodhopper, his feet movin heavy like on the ground. *He don't stand a chance. These fellas gonna flog him stupid.*

'Stop! Come here, Trev.' I motion him to come close.

He looks puzzled as he scans me face. 'Yeah?'

I look round to make sure no one can hear. 'Now listen. That Big Boy's gonna try n hurt ya. I like Big Boy, but that's not the point. The point is ya couldn't even win a fight whit me, son. But I can't stand back n watch you pulped like a orange. Now take those bloody boots off ya feet n listen to this.' I give him all me hard-earned tricks. Everthin I ever learned to survive. *There's quite a few of em.* After our talk he walks back to Big Boy mebbe whit a small hope. *Booty n his shit talk! Teachin em how to fight. Geez, only Booty!*

Grunta eyeballs me. 'What was that bout?' He bends down n hauls a stubbie outta the box.

'Nuthin for you to worry bout.' I purse me lips n step up on the molasses tin.

'Higher, fuck ya!' Booty runs round circlin the boys. 'What ya, a fucken pussyboy!' he yells at Trevor.

The more I watch him the more I don't like it. He's singled Trevor out for special treatment. *Booty treatment. That means hurtin in his books.*

'You right, Trevor. Just do as I tole ya.'

'Girl, fucken big city girl!' Booty taunts.

It's all a bad mistake. I shouldn'a let em go on like this. Ain't right. Me n me big trap. Poor ol Trevor. I jump off the tin n run toward the boys. 'Break it up, Booty!' I shout, flappin me arms. 'It's gone too far.'

Big Boy turns to look at me, a killer smile on his face. At that moment Trevor throws a wild punch and, like in a slow motion movie, it lands on the side a Booty's head.

Cccrraaacckkkk! Booty's gob flips open and a deep, high *arghwwoooo* comes out, soundin like a injured bull. His arms fall behind him as his big fat frame wobbles n crashes to the dirt. *Whhhumummpp!* I feel me gut drop, I struggle for air, sweat rivers me face. *Fuckery!*

Big Boy gawks at Trevor, his mouth open wide, his eyes bulgin outta his head like he gonna explode. Grunta rushes forward, stubbie in hand, and stares down at Booty like he can't believe his own eyes.

Nevil, his shirt on now, hurries over to stand beside me and gapes at Trevor then Booty.

Me, well, I'm ready to have a heart attack! Ain't nobody ever put Booty on his arse! Nope, none a the fellas round Mandamooka or anywhere else for that matter would even dream a standin up to Booty's big, hard fists. Cept for this skinny, brown-eyed white boy in front a him. He the first. Ever.

Me insides churn, me hands shake n I feel the piss buildin up in me bladder. Trevor has his hand cross his mouth, as like to stop hisself from screamin whit terror. Yeah, terror. Can see it in the boy's watery eyes.

Booty, not missin a beat, gets to his feet, stunned n half stupid lookin. A trickle of blood runs down the side a his ash-coloured face. He turns round to Trevor.

I realise whatever's gonna happen now is right outta me hands. I close me eyes and see Trevor hanged from the beams, stripped right down to his shorts, and bein pummelled like the punchin bag as Booty goes to town on him.

Then, hearin a sharp gasp, I turn to Nevil who holds onto his chest like it's gonna collapse in on him.

'He didn't mean to,' I hear Nevil almost bawlbabyin to Booty.

'Dead meat fer sure,' I hear Big Boy mutter.

'Bad move, bro,' I hear Grunta say to Trevor.

'Nnnnnooooo!' I scream and rush at Booty, blockin him from Trevor.

'Outta the way, Mavis.' Booty pushes past, over to Trevor.

Yep, can see it all: blackfella bashes white fella to death in a dog shed. Mavis Dooley—liar, Tim Tam eater, poofter protector, stood by n watched while the white fella carked it. Yeah, that's what the Bullya News'll be sayin.

Booty's hand drops on Trevor's shoulder. *Yep, even ripped the boy's arm clean outta its socket.* Then Trevor takes a stumbly step back, his face by this time white as Missus Warby's sheets. *Yeah, the boy's face was ripped off, skin pale as a ghost it were.*

Trevor opens his mouth to speak but all that comes out is a squeak. Loomin over Trevor's fear struck body, Booty, sweat pourin down his face, lets out a low growl, 'Fucken punch n a half on ya, Sonny Jim!' then explodes into loud laughter.

The boy lives! I can see it now: white fella bashes Booty Dooley in his own shed. Yep, even knocked him to the ground! To look at he ain't much, but ... man, he can whop anyone! Not to be fucked whit! I can hear all the town gossipin at once.

I look at Trevor all beamin n relieved as he takes a stubbie from Grunta's hand. *Proved hisself. That he sure did!*

Booty puts an arm round me. 'Mavis, you sure know how to get a pussy n turn him into a tiger.' He laughs n slaps me on the back.

What can I say? All I done tole Trevor was to run away when Big Boy started to throw punches at him. I never tole him to belt Booty one. Gee, a woman's not that mad n all. I run a hand cross me hot face, dust clogs me mouth n sweat drenches the front of me dress. *A woman gonna call it a day.*

'I'm off, boys.' I move towards the door. Well, at least Nev seems back to normal n Trevor's still kickin, phew. I walk out into the eye-achingly bright day when a voice behind me stops me in my tracks.

'Missus Dooley, thanks, thanks for everything.' Trevor walks toward me with a smile, his face returnin to normal colour.

'Why thank me, son? I ain't done nuthin fer ya. Anyway, how'd ya get that punch on Booty?'

'Oh that was a mistake.'

'Jesus! Well, don't go tellin any a them that,' I reply, suddenly realisin I like the boy. Like his ways. *City boy or not.*

'I'm not that stupid,' he laughs. Then in Booty's voice he booms, 'What d'ya think, I'm a pussy now?'

'I wouldn't make a habit of doin that either.' I continue on out the gate.

2001

NOEL PEARSON
b 1965

An Aboriginal activist and community leader, Noel Pearson is a member of the Bama Bagaarrmugu from the Kalpowa and Jeanie River area in the south-eastern Cape York region. He was born in Cooktown and grew up at Hope Vale, a Lutheran mission on the Cape York Peninsula, and graduated with an arts/law degree from the University of

Sydney. In 1990 Pearson co-founded the Cape York Land Council, and was Executive Director until 1996. He was also a legal adviser for ATSIC. He continues to advise a number of Indigenous organisations in Cape York, and is an advocate for self-determination and land rights for Indigenous people. In 1997 he was named an Australian Living National Treasure. He is well known for his media commentary on public affairs.

The Need for Intolerance

[…] I turn now to Paul Keating's[1] legacy on Aboriginal policy. In relation to his acknowledgment of the truth of our colonial history, Keating was correct. The Redfern Park speech was and continues to be the seminal moment and expression of European Australian acknowledgment of grievous inhumanity to the Indigenes of this land. The Prime Minister had spoken on behalf of all Australians and to the extent that he used the rhetorical 'we' in that speech, he had of course not claimed the individual responsibility of Australians for the actions of the past, but rather a collective owning up to the truth of that past and to its legacies in the present. The Prime Minister had explicitly said that it was not a question of guilt, but one of open hearts. How could this acknowledgment have been better put?

As much as I could never understand the reactions and campaigns on the part of the right in relation to Paul Keating's Redfern Park speech, I could never understand the subsequent incessant campaign on the part of the left seeking an apology from John Howard.[2] The truths of the past in relation to the stealing of children and the destruction of families were already the subject of prime ministerial acknowledgment. And that acknowledgment came without prompting and could not have been more sincerely expressed. The pointless campaign for an apology from John Howard, to the extent that it expresses the importance which people attach to reconciliation, is understandable, but to the extent that it is touted as one of the most important questions in Aboriginal policy, it underlines for me the distinction between being progressive and progressivist. Paul Keating's Redfern Park speech was progressive. Seeking an apology from John Howard is progressivist and is not the main game in terms of what is important in Aboriginal policy.

Paul Keating's stand on native title was not just progressive—it was in turn liberal in its respect for the law and property rights and rejection of racial discrimination, and conservative in its fidelity to the legal traditions and institutions that gave us Mabo. The prescriptions of the political right in this country towards the native title property rights of Indigenous Australians would have horrified Friedrich von Hayek.[3] They proposed the very legislative discrimination and governmental appropriation of property that von Hayek stood firmly and clearly against.

1   Paul Keating (b. 1944), Labor politician and Prime Minister of Australia (1991–96). His influential 'Redfern Park Speech' was delivered in Sydney on 10 December 1992.
2   John Winston Howard (b. 1939), Liberal politician and Prime Minister of Australia (1996–2007).
3   Friedrich August von Hayek (1899–1992), economist.

Paul Keating recognised the High Court's decision in Mabo as a 'once in a nation's lifetime' opportunity to make peace between the old and the new Australians. Native title proffered the basis for what he called 'peace' and could be the cornerstone for the settlement of fundamental colonial grievance.

Without Paul Keating's *Native Title Act* this cornerstone that had been hewn by Eddie Mabo, Ron Castan and their colleagues would have been lost to the nation. The cornerstone would have been turned to dust if protective federal legislation had not been put in place by the Keating government. The *Age* editorial got it right when it said that the *Native Title Act* 'may yet be judged the most profound achievement of Paul Keating's political career'. If it had not been a career of so many achievements I would not hesitate to endorse the view of the *Age*. Let me make only two brief observations about the negotiation and passage of the *Native Title Act*.

Firstly, to Don Watson's description of Gareth Evans' performance[1] in the Senate as a 'tour de force he was born to deliver one day', I say Amen. On his feet for forty-eight of the sixty hours it took for the debate to be had in the Senate, Evans turned in what must count as one of the greatest, if not *the* greatest performance in Australian legislative history. The sheer complexity of the law, the policy and the politics which Evans commanded was staggering.

Secondly, no other leader—not then and not in the past—would have had the will, the courage and the fidelity to get the *Native Title Act* through parliament and to keep faith with its indigenous beneficiaries other than Paul Keating. Even Evans, someone who had been a supporter of Aboriginal causes since his early days, was one of many people in the Cabinet who would have chosen to drop us. Evans rose to the occasion and made his outstanding contribution because of Paul Keating's leadership.

With the opportunity of Mabo having been seized by the federal Labor government it was time for a necessary redefinition of what it is to be socially progressive in Aboriginal affairs.

2002

WESLEY ENOCH
b. 1969

Born on Stradbroke Island, Queensland, Wesley Enoch is a playwright and director. He has been the artistic director of Kooemba Jdarra Indigenous Performing Arts, an associate artist with the Queensland Theatre Company, and a resident director with the Sydney Theatre Company. Enoch is the author of the plays *Black Medea* (*2005*/2007) and *The Story of the Miracles at Cookie's Table* (*2006*/2007). With Deborah Mailman and Hilary Beaton, he co-authored *The 7 Stages of Grieving* (*1995*/1996).

---

1   Don Watson (b. 1949), speechwriter for Paul Keating and prominent journalist; Gareth Evans (b. 1944), Labor politician and Australian Foreign Minister (1988–96), played a primary role in the passage of the *Native Title Act* through the Senate in 1993.

From *Black Medea*
Medea Speaks

MEDEA: Look at me … I had everything … and now I've got nothing. He's left me; he didn't even have the guts to say it to my face … he's left me. Spirits give me the strength for what I have to do tonight. I don't ask for your blessing just the strength to do it. Take away any doubt.

You heard his promises to me … You know what I gave up to be with him—a father, a brother, a mother, a country … I carried him, I nursed him when he was sick, I held him in the middle of the night, I begged for food to feed this family … and now he's left me. Shouldn't I be angry? Shouldn't I take what's mine? I gave him all the happiness he has; I have the right to take it back. I gave him my life; I want a life in return. I honoured him, obeyed him, gave him a son … Let the spirits decide who is right in this argument.

The spirits have witnessed everything in this Land. They've been here long before Jason and Medea and they'll be here long after what I do tonight. Let them judge me … Tonight I am coming home. Let the spirits decide if I'm an outcast. Let no person stand in my way.

FALLING IN LOVE

OLDER MEDEA: You got to imagine a settlement on the edge of the desert, full of kids and dogs and nothing much else. A dusty little corner of the world where the girls can't fall in love with a boy cause they're related and they have to get promised to a man, like in the old way. You got to imagine some of the girls sitting on the verandah of the canteen when the city men come in from the mine—then lining up to take their turn in the back seat of the company Toyota. If he's had a shave, a shower and brushed his teeth, he's in with a good chance. They share around the one good dress, dance all Friday night until it's soaked in sweat, wash it the next morning, dry it in the midday sun so some other girl can do it all again on the Saturday. And so it goes on until the poor thing fades away, falling apart in the hands of a man.

MEDEA: But he's different. A traveller, picking up some work on his way through. They say if you find yourself in this part of the world you're either running away from something or in search of it. He seems to be doing both … No one thinks about marrying these blokes … maybe have a kid but they don't expect him to hang around.

JASON: But she's different. She has dreams of living in a big house with a garden, in a place where the sand doesn't creep in under the door. She's been promised to this bloke with the right skin but she knows he's never going to give her what she wants. He's never going to get her out. So she's been waiting …

MEDEA: He ran away from his father. Had enough of feeling useless, watching his mother get thumped, watching his father's moods. He wants to see the world. He doesn't care if he never goes back to where he came from.

JASON: She's been waiting to run away.

MEDEA: He smells of soap and aftershave.

JASON: She smells of ambition.

OLDER MEDEA: You got to imagine these two falling in love and how the other girls got cut cause they were so jealous. How he promised her a star of her own. How he took her in the sand dunes on a blanket in the night. There, under the stars, in the desert they promised each other. He took her, and she followed him. She promised never to leave him.

You make these kind of promises cause you can't imagine a world where they wouldn't be true. Young love tends to shoot its mouth off.

You got to imagine what her parents thought, how they told her she was promised to this other bloke, how they reminded her of who she was and where she came from. How they told her if she walked out that door she could never come back. How her brother went after them in a borrowed car and how Jason punched him to the ground.

MEDEA: I'll follow wherever you go. I'll walk with you and make a home in your shadow. I will regret nothing I do for you. I'll spill my own blood before I see a drop of yours. All you have to do is ask and I will make the deserts bloom.

OLDER MEDEA: You got to imagine the two of them travelling, from the deserts to the rainforests, from the mountains to the salt water. Imagine, when they finally get a house in the city, in this house here, and settle down to raise a family. How he feels trapped. How he starts to hit her.

[MEDEA touches JASON's hair.]

[BLACKOUT]

[MEDEA hugs JASON from behind.]

[BLACKOUT]

[JASON stands by the fridge, MEDEA stands by the sink.]

[BLACKOUT]

[MEDEA is sitting in the sand.]

[BLACKOUT]

[MEDEA and JASON exchange looks.]

MEDEA: Point me where I should go, which way I should call home. Every road leads away from you … The doors I opened for you, closed for me … Go home to my country, to the desert?

JASON: Go back to your family.

MEDEA: And say you didn't need me any more … The road out of that settlement only goes one way. You want me out, but where, where? I'm on the run, Jason. That's nothing new, but where are you sending me? I gave up belonging somewhere. The desert was where I belonged, but I swapped it. The dances and songs my granny taught me, that was my dowry. I bought your love, gave up everything I had to be with you.

JASON: I didn't ask you to give … Why give up everything? If I had a place … You know your language, you know where you come from. You have a place you fit in. You follow me and I'm looking for things you've already got. Where will you belong now?

MEDEA: With you.

JASON: You used me to get out. Go back, crawl back and ask forgiveness. You treat your family like a burden, you're never happy, you're always wanting something more. Never happy with what you got. Now I got nothing more to give you.

MEDEA: I've sacrificed for you.

JASON: And what've you got to show for it?

MEDEA: A home, a husband and a son.

JASON: The son is all we have now.

MEDEA: Where will I go, Jason? This is my home.

JASON: No, your home is somewhere else.

MEDEA: When I go down the street people stare at me. They know I'm from somewhere they've never been … I walk confident cause I know where I come from and they're scared. I remind them of what they don't have. I've known the spirits to come up through my feet and take my body when I'm dancing. But not here. I gave him my body and everything that was mine I gave to be with him. And now I …

[MEDEA *lets the sand run through her fingers.*]

MEDEA CURSES

MEDEA: Give me a hair and a finger nail and I will curse you Jason. Something with your sweat in it and I will curse you. Everything you have done to me, come back to haunt you ten-fold. I want you to feel empty. The emptiness I feel without you. I want you to wake up every morning and feel a part of you is missing. I want you to search and everywhere you look to see me … whenever you close your eyes, to see me. Let the spirits hear me curse … Let everything you love hurt you.

Wherever love is inside of you let it cause you pain, make you double over in the street. Let the desert wind whisper madness in your ear and the sun beat down to boil your mind. Let every time you love be like a knife between your ribs. Let no type of love be safe from my curse, not the love of a woman nor the love of a son.

May you find all the words for pain. From the sharp hard jabs to weeping bedsores. But don't misunderstand me, I want you alive, I want you to feel this emptiness for as long as you live. I want you to carry the torment to your death bed, alone and unloved. I want you to regret your life and at your burial I want your bones separated, your name spoken and your face displayed on every street post, so your spirit will wander aimless without a home.

Then you'll have time to think how you wronged me.

2002

SAMUEL WAGAN WATSON
b. 1972

Samuel Wagan Watson has Irish, German and Aboriginal (Bundjalung and Birri Gubba) ancestry. He is the son of Sam Watson (qv). Wagan Watson has won state and national awards for his poetry and prose, and prior to being a full-time writer was a salesman, public relations officer, fraud investigator, graphic artist, labourer, law clerk, film industry technician and actor.

In between writing and working on community projects, including poetry in the built environment (his poetry adorns the Eleanor Schonell Bridge in St Lucia, Queensland), Wagan Watson acts as a guest speaker, workshop facilitator and mentor in the creative arts. *Of Muse, Meandering and Midnight* (2000) won the 1999 David Unaipon Award. A later collection of poetry, *Smoke Encrypted Whispers* (2004) won the Book of the Year Award in the NSW Premier's Literary Awards for 2005.

Recipe for Metropolis Brisbane

Serves: Nearly 3 million people (give or take a generation)

Ingredients:
    1 utopian landscape with a blue river
    a mixture of European cultures seasoned with convicts
    200 years of conservative politics
    1 trillion tons of bitumen, steel, glass, concrete and treated timber
    garnish of exhaust

1. Peel the utopian landscape of most of its flora, fauna and Indigenous flavour. Place what remains in an obscure melting pot on medium heat.
2. Stir in the mixture of European cultures seasoned with convicts. Other cultural flavours may emerge in the process. They can be included or excluded. Cover and allow to simmer for over two centuries.
3. Every 10 years, add some conservative politics and gradually pour in the 1 trillion tons of bitumen, steel, glass, concrete and treated timber. Stir until the blue river turns brown.
4. Firstly, your dish will gel into *Brisbane Town*; drain and stir until it becomes *Brisbane City*; cover, allow to simmer.
    Include the rest of the politics until the desired thickness of *Metropolis Brisbane* is achieved.

Cook's note: Metropolis Brisbane is served best with the aroma of lead exhaust, sprinkled over the dish!

2002

For the Wake and Skeleton Dance

the dreamtime Dostoyevskys murmur of a recession in the spirit world
they say,
the night creatures are feeling the pinch
of growing disbelief and western rationality
that the apparitions of black dingos stalk the city night, hungry   5
their ectoplasm on the sidewalk in a cocktail of vomit and swill
waiting outside the drinking holes of the living
preying on the dwindling souls fenced in by assimilation

the dreamtime Dostoyevskys ponder
as dark riders in the sky signal a movement   10
for the wake and skeleton dance

it's payback time for the bureaucrats in black skins
and the fratricide troopers before them
with no room to move on a dead man's bed

is it all worth holding onto these memories   15
amidst the blood-drenched sands?
better to forget?

the dreamtime Dostoyevskys feel the early winter
chilled footsteps walk across their backs in the dark hours,
the white man didn't bring all the evil   20
some of it was here already
gestating
laughing
intoxicated
untapped   25
harassing the living
welcoming the tallship leviathans of two centuries ago
that crossed the line drawn in the sand by the Serpent
spilling dark horses from their bowels
and something called the Covenant,   30
infecting the dreamtime with the ghosts of a million lost entities
merely faces in the crowd at the festival of the dead,
the wake is over
and to the skeleton dance the bonemen smile
open season on chaos theory   35
and retirement eternal for the dreamtime Dostoyevsky

                                                                        2004

White Stucco Dreaming

sprinkled in the happy dark of my mind
is early childhood and black humour
white stucco dreaming
and a black labrador
an orange and black panel-van   5
called the 'black banana'
with twenty blackfellas hanging out the back
blasting through the white stucco umbilical
of a working class tribe
front yards studded with old black tyres   10
that became mutant swans overnight
attacked with a cane knife and a bad white paint job

white stucco dreaming
and snakes that morphed into nylon hoses at the terror

of Mum's scorn   15
snakes whose cool venom we sprayed onto the white stucco,
temporarily blushing it pink
amid an atmosphere of Saturday morning grass cuttings
and flirtatious melodies of ice-cream trucks
that echoed through little black minds   20
and sent the labrador insane

chocolate hand prints like dreamtime fraud
laid across white stucco
and mud cakes on the camp stove
that just made Dad see black   25
no tree safe from treehouse sprawl
and the police cars that crawled up and down the back streets,
peering into our white stucco cocoon
wishing they were with us
                                                                          2004

Cheap White-goods at the Dreamtime Sale

if only the alloy-winged angels could perform better
and lift Uluru; a site with grandeur
the neolithic additive missing from that seventh wonder of the
    world expo,
under the arms of a neon goddess, under the hammer in London,
murderers turning trustees   5
a possession from a death estate
maybe flogged off to the sweet seduction of yen
to sit in the halls of a Swiss bank
or be paraded around Paris' Left Bank
where the natives believe   10
that art breathed for the first time;
culture, bohemian and bare and maybe brutal
and how the critics neglect the Rubenesque roundness of a bora-ring
unfolded to an academia of art
yes, that pure soil in front of you   15
the dealers in Manhattan lay back and vomit
they're the genius behind dot paintings and ochre hand prints
rattling studios from the East Side to the Village
and across the ass of designer jeans
porcelain dolls from Soho wanting a part in it so bad   20
as the same scene discards their shells upon the catwalks
like in the land of the original Dreaming
comatose totems litter the landscape
bargains and half-truths simmer over authenticity

copyright and copious character assassination on the menu   25
sacred dances available out of the yellow pages
and
cheap white-goods at the Dreamtime sale!

2004

DENNIS McDERMOTT
b. 1946

Dennis McDermott grew up in Tamworth, NSW. He was born to a mother of Sydney's Gadigal–Eora people and an Irish–Scottish father. A psychologist, poet and researcher in Indigenous health, he is the author of a collection of poems, *Dorothy's Skin* (2003), as well as criticism and essays.

Dorothy's Skin

At fourteen, my daughter knows why *The Old Couple* on the
　　　　beach, not *The Tiger*
leaps at her from her Christmas gift. She likes Dali. I don't,
　　　　except for one image
that I flip pages for, until I realise they've left it out: *Lifting*   5
　　　　the Skin of the Water
to See the Dog Sleeping in the Shade of the Sea. Down the road
　　　　from Tamworth,
from Christmas at my mother's, Goonoo Goonoo paddocks
　　　　wear bright, bad toupees.   10
Surreal colour wraps Wallabadah hills from ridge to
　　　　highway, like an over-packaging
of something subtle. *Look there!* Kath Walker would stop
　　　　you. She'd peel back the veil
of leaves so you'd see the slender swamp orchid growing   15
　　　　up the paperbark. *Kath*, then,
in the seventies, on my visits to Stradbroke Island—
　　　　Noonuccal land—before she became,
or reclaimed, *Oodgeroo*. I still don't know whether she
　　　　lifted a layer, or added another.   20

When I met Oodgeroo, I met my mother: not just Dossie's
　　　　poise, eyes and Lindt-like
skin, but the funny-bugger with a steak knife, buried, a
　　　　serrated intensity that
unsettled me—a boy of elocution lessons and an easier ride,   25
　　　　a man of lighter brown
travelling, whose tab of overt intolerance came in at insults
　　　　and one lost girlfriend.
I wasn't there when indignity did its daily round—rarely
　　　　blunt, rather, a pointed   30

needling that cut near the core, left wounds that broke their
        stitches every morning
I did know that the sharp steel about Oodgeroo was also
        about my mother. On campus—

UQ—a doctor's daughter from Ingham or Innisfail, some   35
        sugar town, told me Queensland
houses on their skyscraper stilts were the perfect metaphor
        for non-Indigenous Australia's
perch on the land. Then she described the GTO, that
        seventies model of sexual intimacy   40
popular where she came from: *Gravy Train On—Wooh-Wooh!!*
        —the only girl she knew
her age, in her town, that hadn't been gang-raped. I had no
        reason to disbelieve her.
I thought about targets: when you're a candidate for grief,   45
        keep moving. I knew some of
the men's stories: my sister's man, jumping from a moving
        car on a lonely Tassie road
to miss a bashing; my sister's son, dodging a splintered
        pool cue in that high-culture   50
high-altitude, cold and broken town, Orange; but not the
        women's. When we were kids
mum kept us in motion, in baths and out, to school and
        back: the devil had a thing about
motors on the idle. Doss draped protective layers on us all: 55
        cardigans, scholarships and
singing lessons, and more manners and mannerisms than
        the middle-class we aped.

I like Queensland houses. I want and don't want to lift the
        skin of settlement   60
If Oodgeroo were alive, I'd take Doss to Straddy. Maybe
        they wouldn't hit it off—just
fight like the sisters they seem. Yet they might walk
        alongside each other, an old couple   ·
on the beach. Oodgeroo could lift the skin of sea and land   65
        —when, and when not,
to harvest oysters—show mum the swamp orchid, tell her
        of the Grannies
that walk some nights, stories she's never heard. In the
        Link-Up office, counsellors talk   70
to me in supervision of taking clients, their stolen
        generation clients *home.* Everyone

seems to know just where the fucking place is. Doss Lennis
         from old Newtown, black
with steam-train soot, respect-full *Dot*, from the Ladies   75
         Auxiliary, Tamworth RSL—
mum's many layers peel so slowly. The West Indian cover
         is an old friend. Eighty four
years along—long wait—I hear the word 'Aboriginal'
         creep into a self-descriptive   80
sentence. Dorothy's skin is so thick and yet so thin. Where
         can I find those red shoes
you simply click to teleport you home?

                                                                              2003

LARISSA BEHRENDT
b. 1969

Born in Cooma, NSW, of Kamilaroi and Eualeyai descent, Larissa Behrendt is an academic, lawyer and writer who graduated from Harvard Law School with a doctorate in 1998. Her thesis was later published as *Achieving Social Justice: Indigenous rights and Australia's future* (2003). Since 2001 she has been professor of law and director of research at the Jumbunna Indigenous House of Learning at the University of Technology, Sydney, and has published extensively on property law, Indigenous rights, dispute resolution and Aboriginal women's issues. Behrendt has held numerous positions on legal and creative arts bodies. Her novel *Home* (2004) won the 2002 David Unaipon Award and a Commonwealth Writers' Prize (2005).

From *Home*
Chapter 1

1995

My father told me that the name of the town meant 'the meeting of the rivers' in the old language. We had set out from Sydney in the fresh hours of the morning, leaving the tame quarters of suburbia, crossing over the mountains, until the landscape bled into undulating black soil plains. The afternoon crept up on us, the distant mountain formation offering a craggy, blue-haze backdrop. Barbed-wire-fenced paddocks held flocks of cotton-wool sheep, undisturbed by our passing.

It is three o'clock in the afternoon as my father parks his car in the main street, bumper pointing at the steps of the well-worn Royal Hotel. The retiring sun sparkles red and gold, the light catching in flashing opal colours. A hot wind blows across the concrete, mortar and wood packing grit in every crevice it brushes over—between bricks, the cracks of window frames, between teeth.

I decide that I will go to the post office. If I send a card today, it will reach my mother by Tuesday. Although that's the day that I'm planning to return, I can see her delivering a trim pink smile of thanks ('Oh, Candy'), and she will be pleased that I have remembered her. I can also see my father dismissing this with an 'Oh, Can-deese', as he rolls his eyes.

The air-conditioning in Dad's large sleek car—I can stretch my legs out in front and not touch anything—had protected me from the aggressive heat and light film of swirling dust. I have always preferred the feeling of warmth on my skin to controlled too-frigid temperatures. I enjoy the stifling heat that now clings to my legs, underneath my skirt, embracing my face, as I walk across searing concrete. The post office is built with old burnt-red bricks and garnished with a wide verandah and white flourishes, defying the starching weather and the stretching time.

Inside, the sails of the ceiling fans click slowly, rhythmically. I pick a faded postcard from the wire stand, disappointed that there were none more parochial, less rustic (*Greetings from Big Rig Country* or a flock of sheep: *I miss Ewe*) to send on to my best friend Kate. I look over a display of books laid out on a table, publications of the local Historical Society, mostly photocopies stapled together between colourful cardboard. I decide on a collection of old newspaper articles about the area and a book of one resident family's memoirs. They arrived in 1904, the year my grandmother was born here. I know my father will comment on my impulse-buying. I've bought something at every stop we've made today. Dad loves to dramatise how much money I spend, as though each coin is extracted from his own pocket.

On the back of my postcard of the town centre, sun-scorched and faded, I write—*Hi Mummy, Hot and dusty; lots of sheep. By the time you get this, I'll be home. Love Candy*—and take my purchases to the counter where a homely, wrinkle-faced woman with curled grey hair waits.

'All this way from Sydney?' she asks. I suddenly feel conscious of my suit and my leather shoes that clip confidently across the wooden floor.

'Yes. I guess you can pick a tourist.'

'We get to know the faces in here. Are you staying a while or driving through?'

'I'm staying for the weekend.'

'Well, there's lots of interesting things to see around here. There are the fisheries down on the river and there's a pioneers' museum.'

'I'm here to visit family,' I reply.

'Really?' she answers, her interest piqued. 'If they're locals, I probably know them.'

'Well, the family names are Lance and Boney.'

'Hmmm. Doesn't sound familiar to me. Do they live in town?'

'No, just outside.'

'Oh,' responds the woman, her mouth making a tight circle as she peers more carefully at me and then, quickly regaining her smile, processes my purchase with renewed efficiency. I have surprised her. She would know 'just outside town' means the Aboriginal reserve. She was fooled by my light skin and has mistaken me for exotically Spanish, Brazilian or Italian. I'm used to this reaction but still it annoys me each time, like a distracting hangnail. I don't mind being mistaken for someone from somewhere else, but I mind when the realisation that the dark features are Aboriginal is met with disappointment, confusion or even disgust. I mind when the person observing me feels betrayed by my lightness.

I return to the car and sit with my door open, the stagnant heat still floating against my skin. I know my father will be in the pub for a while. Uncle Henry will convince him to have just one more drink to quench his city thirst. Dad will relish the excited welcome he'll receive as faces, known and unknown, crowd around for a free drink. Only such attention could make my father so flush with generosity.

I'm too shy to enter the bar even though I know Dad will be distracted and detained for a while. He'll be talking about his work at the Department of Aboriginal Affairs and feeding everyone snippets of information about friends and relatives also living in Sydney. I suddenly feel over-dressed and self-conscious in my dark blue cotton suit, something that I would wear to court or for a meeting with a client. I've already attracted the gaze from a group of four locals relaxing on the hotel verandah. I can't be sure whether they're looking at me—so obviously not of this place—or my father's flashy new car. Perhaps both.

I open one of the books I've just bought. The page falls to the writings of a clergyman who, accompanied by a 'black boy', travelled through the area in the late 1880s. He had written:

> And yet, it was a privilege to be a pioneer, for this is the life that has helped to develop characteristics that make for a real greatness. Friendships, courage, indominatable perseverance in the face of difficulties were the privileges of our pioneers.

I close the book and think about the woman in the post office and her stagnant, glazed expression that had, for just a moment, rejected me. A glance held only for a split-second, but the message so unmistakable. Perhaps she didn't know what it was that her look revealed, what it was that I saw.

My light cocoa skin wrapped around my mother's European features have allowed me to slip unnoticed into social circles, my presence never enough to make others feel guarded. Not like Kingsley, my brother, who, much darker, can never slip by. There is a price for this free access. I hear the things they assume will pass me by, things that would otherwise be said when I'm not there. I'm treated in these moments as though light skin is different, tougher than the person who wears it. 'But you are not a real one,' thin pink lips will tell me, to excuse me. 'You're different.'

But I keep these interactions—these looks, exclamations, excuses and hints of disgust—bottled within me. The words—'not a real one'—work into my skin like splinters, making me feel as though I have Kingsley's own dark skin wrapped around me. It is, of course, easier for me. I have these word-splinters under my flesh but Kingsley is undisguisable, cannot be masked. No one will mistake him as an exotic southern European. I feel guilt about the way I can slip in and out, but I also have a deep envy of Kingsley when dark hands shake his in greeting while darting eyes flit over me with unspoken suspicion.

My father emerges from the pub with a cheerful Uncle Henry by his side, just like veterans on Anzac day, and I am distracted from my brooding. I rise and embrace my gravely handsome uncle, who had, in his youth, been a football player for one of the Sydney teams. Henry's athleticism, all these decades on, still clings to him.

'Ah, Bub, look at you,' he exclaims as he pulls me against his chest.

'Oh, Uncle Henry, it is so good to see you.'

'Your father's been telling me that you're causing all kinds of trouble in those law courts in Sydney. God only knows we could use your skills around here.'

'He exaggerates. I'm just plodding away,' I respond, both embarrassed and pleased by my father's boasting.

'I kept all those postcards you sent me from Paris. Showed them to everyone around here who'd listen. Proud of you, I am.'

'It's easy to see why you're my favourite uncle.' I savour the flushed feeling his attention creates in me.

He holds my arm. 'It took your father too long to bring you out here,' he glances at his cousin with a reproachful eye.

'Henry is taking us out to dinner. We'll go check into the hotel and rest up before then,' my father replies sheepishly.

2004

STEPHEN HAGAN
b. 1959

Stephen Hagan is a descendant of the Kullilli people of south-west Queensland. His early years were spent living in a fringe camp on the outskirts of Cunnamulla but when he was seven the family moved to the town. While employed by the Department of Foreign Affairs, he was posted to Colombo and to Calcutta, where he worked with Mother Teresa. He now teaches at the University of Southern Queensland. As well as journalism, Hagan has written *The N Word: One man's stand* (2005), recounting his fight to have the word 'Nigger' removed from the name of the 'Nigger Brown Stand' at the Toowoomba sports stadium, and a children's book, *Melly and the Bilby* (2006).

From *The N Word*
Introduction

The game started upfront with two large packs of forwards trying to dominate each other. After the initial ten minutes' softening-up period was over, the nimble outside backs started to see more of the ball and were able to create a little bit of their magic out wide. When our team scored first, adjacent to the goal posts, the ground broadcaster's voice came clearly over the public-address system, 'That try scored at the "Nigger" Brown end of the oval takes the score to four points to nil with the kick to come.'

I looked at my wife Rhonda and she frowned in disbelief. In unison, we turned toward the apex of the wooden grandstand to our right and looked at the sign—E.S. 'Nigger' Brown Stand—which the announcer had referred to moments earlier. I glanced around at my relatives before casting a look at other spectators standing close by. There was no discernible reaction from any of them.

Within minutes the broadcaster made another announcement, 'Just a reminder to drinking patrons that the bar is now open in the "Nigger" Brown Stand. Also additional toilets can be located immediately under the "Nigger" Brown Stand.'

Since arriving in Toowoomba a couple of years earlier, Rhonda and I had become increasingly distressed by the word 'nigger' emblazoned on the grandstand's sign.

We had all been excited at seeing my nephews on the field but now, as on previous occasions, Rhonda and I were struggling to maintain our interest in the game. In hindsight, we should have gathered our young children, Stephen and Jayde, and left the ground. Instead we stayed till the end, feeling more and more frustrated as we endured further references to the 'Nigger' Brown Stand on the public-address system.

The game finally finished and our team ran off the ground as victors. Relieved, we grabbed our things and made our way to the car with the children, shaking our heads and wondering whether anyone had ever challenged any authorities about the sign.

In my younger days I had played representative rugby league and had always been an avid supporter but as we left the ground on that wintry June day in 1999, I realised the time had come to make a stand.

This family outing had not turned out as planned and instead it would prove to be a defining moment in our lives.

On 20 March 2002, the Australian Associated Press article published in the *Herald Sun* reported:

> A bid by an Aboriginal activist to remove the word 'Nigger' from a football grandstand has been thrown out by the nation's highest court.
>
> High Court Justice Mary Gaudron said the word 'Nigger' on the sign was no more offensive than the word 'Pinky' on a cement mixer. 'Let us assume for a moment that I'm "Pink"—and it's not an unreasonable assumption—and I'm offended by a sign that says "Pinky's Porkies", she told a Brisbane sitting of the High Court.
>
> Justice Gaudron rejected Canberra constitutional barrister Ernst Willheim's submission that there was a link between the sign on the grandstand with the word 'Nigger' on it and racism.
>
> The case was brought to court by Stephen Hagan, an ATSIC regional councillor from Toowoomba, west of Brisbane …

I stopped reading for a few seconds to catch my breath, not quite sure what to expect next.

Outside the court today, Mr Hagan said he was disappointed the High Court had not granted him leave to appeal and would now take his case to the United Nations' Committee on Racial Discrimination (sic) in Geneva.

'Now it's been formalised that you can have a public sign with the word Nigger on it,' he said.

'Why are they [judges] talking about a pink truck when they are talking about the word Nigger.

'I'm absolutely astounded that they don't see that Nigger is offensive.'

Costs were also awarded against Mr Hagan, who had no idea how he would pay for his legal forays.

'It could be $100,000, it could be $200,000, it could be $20,000 ... but I'm flat out paying my petrol bill back to Toowoomba, so I don't know how I'm going to pay $100,000.'

Similar headlines, flashed over national newspapers, television and radio broadcasts, greeted me the day after the ruling. Going to the High Court of Australia had proved to be an unsuccessful attempt to dispose of what I believed to be the only sign bearing the word 'nigger' on any public sports grandstand in the world.

Friends and critics, both privately and publicly, asked why I proposed to take the case to the United Nations. Many said I should abide by the umpire's decision and let it rest. As I pondered these comments I too began to question my motives. What was it that made me want to fight against the odds when all around me were giving up?

After days of procrastinating as to my next move I recalled the words my father once said to me when I was growing up in Cunnamulla, 'I never called any white person sir or mister because no white person ever called my father sir or mister.' In those words I was at last able to make some sense of the stubborn streak that has been part and parcel of my life. Researching a little deeper into my past, I discovered that I'd inherited that wilfulness.

I was one of the third generation of Hagan men who'd been born on the wrong side of the tracks. The rise from poverty to respectability and distinction by the first two generations was impressive. Beside the achievements of my predecessors, my own journey may not rate. However, I believe my struggle was a journey they too would have undertaken had they been presented with similar circumstances.

That aside, I took on the authorities because I also sought to honour my promise to Rhonda to ensure the sign was removed. I had a vision of my children playing on the oval with children of other races, free in the knowledge that they would not have to confront a relic of a racist past.

The United Nations would be my last legal option. After successfully filing the application to the Committee on the Elimination of Racial Discrimination all I could do was wait. As I waited, I searched the past for answers.

2005

JIM EVERETT
b. 1942

Jim Everett is a member of the Plangermairreenner clan of the Ben Lomond people, of the Cape Portland nations in north-east Tasmania. He has been active in Aboriginal affairs, lectured in Aboriginal heritage and history, and produced radio and television. Everett is a poet, playwright and short story writer. He has co-edited a collection of Tasmanian Aboriginal poetry, *The Spirit of Kuti Kina* (1990), and short stories, *Weeta Puna: The moon is risen* (1992).

planegarrartoothenar

planegarrartoothenar grew up in meenamatta country. his clan is the
plangermairreenner, along with the plindermairhemener, and the
tonenerweenerlarmenne clans they make-up the ben lomond nation. his
people know mount ben lomond as turbuna, it marks the boundary between
meenamatta and the stony creek country to the west. oyster bay country   5
connects to the south-east from where the coastal waters stretch north to the
north-east people's country. to the south-west are the big river people who
often travel through meenamatta country to enjoy coastal foods, and the long
white beaches with clear water inlets. many clans gather along the coast to
celebrate, and corroberee to tell their stories.   10

planegarrartoothenar's father, prignarpanar, often takes his family to the
sea for lobster and muttonfish, warreners and other shellfish. prignarpanar
will hunt wallabies and wombats along the coastal scrublands, while
planegarrartoothenar goes with his mother, maytyenner and his sisters,
collecting swan eggs in the lagoons, and to hunt possums in the trees.   15
planegarrartoothenar's sisters, pooreretenner and teemee are wonderful tree-
climbers, they catch many possums, swiftly dashing them from the tree-tops
to the ground where maytyenner is waiting for them with her waddy.

wherever planegarrartoothenar's family journey there is water. the family
always respect water because it gives life to all living things that nurture   20
them, and other living things. water is the connector across all clans,
people, birds, animals, plants, and even the rocks and grounds. prignarpanar
teaches planegarrartoothenar about water, how it travels in the clouds, until
as rain it washes the country and brings life into their world. he teaches
planegarrartoothenar about the water that travels under the ground, under   25
meenamatta, until it comes up in a spring to join the creeks and rivers.
planegarrartoothenar has come to understand that all life must have water,
and that it is the nectar of the great spirit moinie, and the water spirit, ria
warrawah.

with planegarrartoothenar i travel meenamatta country camping and   30
refreshing my connection with my clans. water is everywhere within the life of

this place. when i was young, my family travelled to many places far away from
meenamatta country, returning to flinders island while i was still a young man.
my journey had really begun. finding my identity involved visits to where my
roots are, and where country is central to who i am. like planegarrartoothenar, 35
i have been learning about water and why it's so important to country, and
the all-life of meenamatta. when i camp on meenamatta country i think
about the many families that live in this place. for more than 35,000 years the
meenamatta clans, and many other clans have lived on this big island now
called tasmania. their stories live in the country and in the spirit of the whole 40
land and everything here.

planegarrartoothenar and his family travel along the creeks going through the
blue tiers where i sometimes camp with friends, or on occasion, alone. when i
walk the tracks that go through the blue tiers i can sense the family enjoyment
of this place, with full moon creek running across it, and forests with native 45
peppers and meenamatta tomatoes.

i camp in many places on meenamatta country, and along the bay of fires and
the blue tiers, and further north to waterhouse island. our people live in all of
these areas where prignarpana, maytyena and their children, pooreretenner,
teemee and planegarrartoothenar come to visit their family clans. everywhere 50
my family camps on country, right across the north-east of tasmania, they
connect with the spirit of the whole land and everything here.

we talk about our old people when we camp here, remembering the past with
our present, creating visions for our future. being here on meenamatta country,
and all the big clan country of the north-east and south along the coast to 55
oyster bay clans, going west to turbuna, we know ourselves. this country with
its all-life make up who we are, as does the country have our identity, and
we are family. this place is where I visit planegarrartoohenar and his family,
finding memories of our connection that go beyond time and space. here,
i find my grandfather and grandmother, my parents, and my brothers and 60
sisters. meenamatta country is me as i am it, living in the natural world that is
not acknowledged or respected by all people of today.

meenamatta country takes me beyond the colonial construct, beyond
landscapes and development, it takes me to freedom. planegarrartoothenar is
my brother, as are pooreretenner and teemee my sisters, they are my teachers 65
in the spirit of all-life. prignarpanar and maytyenner are my family teachers,
bringing the past into a timeless story for me to understand who i am.
here is my peace, my freedom from the colonial dome of thinking, and the
restrictions of a conditioned society that is firmly based in its market-place.

prignarpanar and maytyenner, pooreretenner and teemee, and 70
planegarrartoothenar are always here on meenamatta country. my youngens,
jamie, aaron, ebonee, and larni, are always here too, with me on meenamatta

country. this place is our home, our roots that connect with the all-life of
country. we are connected through our bloodline, our all-life waterline. it
is here that we join with our clans to celebrate being together in timeless   75
memory, this creation by moinie, who's spirit is always here. we are one family
in the all-life, with waterlines that journey in our arteries and veins, the cycle
of recycle in timeless space of no space, where there exists no past, present or
future. our today is forever, yet in time i am with planegarrartoothenar forever.

2006

TONY BIRCH
b. 1957

Melbourne-born academic and author Tony Birch has published poetry, fiction and
creative non-fiction. He has worked as a writer and curator in collaboration with
photographers, film-makers and artists, and as a writer in the areas of Australian urban and
social history and 'contact' histories. He also lectures in creative writing. *Shadowboxing*, a
series of ten linked short stories, was published in 2006.

The True History of Beruk

'MY WORDS', BERUK-NGAMAJET—1835

Captain Cook marched—
in jacket and brass button
Buckley[1] stood ragged
in possum skin at Muddy Creek
Batman[2] came looking
with glass, beads, powder
and mirrors in a wooden boat
around the sea

Buckley spoke his old tongue—
the visitor is not ghost
he is not ghost
look at Batman's face
do not touch his skin
his bread or his house
do not touch his house

Beruk[3] spoke the truth—
whitefellow shoot us
down like kangaroo
whitefellow come

---

1   William Buckley was an escaped convict who lived with the Wathaurong tribe for 32 years, adopting their
    way of life, language and having a family of his own.
2   John Batman, an Australian farmer and businessman, and one of the first settlers of the Melbourne area. He
    made a private treaty with Aboriginal elders of the Yarra region in 1835 (declared void by Governor Bourke).
3   William Barak (qv).

by and by
and shoot us
shoot us down

whitefellow come
and shoot us down

CORANDERRK—1866[1]

(i)
30 April 1866
[Cost of acquiring land from and incarcerating 'the blacks']

Flour	108,610 lbs.
Tea	2,991 lbs.
Sugar	28,617 lbs.
Tobacco	1,983 lbs.
Rice	3,024 lbs.
Oatmeal	450 lbs.
Soap	3,181 lbs.
Meat	787 lbs.
Blankets	1,175 pairs
Serge Shirts	548
Twill Shirts	464
Jumpers (boys)	183
Petticoats	424
Chemises	111
Tomahawks	142
Pint Pots	180
Quart Pots	100

'The condition of the station is eminently satisfactory.'

(ii)
And in that year the Protector celebrated before God and Queen. He rejoiced with ink—'The blacks have become, if not civilised, very interesting, social and industrious.' They have decorated the tolerably well-furnished, neatly swept, and very comfortable huts with pictures taken from the *London Illustrated News*. 'Here,' proclaimed the Protector, pointing a finger in the direction of the gates of Buckingham Palace, 'your mother, the Queen of Victoria, she watches over you.' And that night the Protector wrote 'they are no longer savages'.

(they have become)
seven children reading simply and clearly
fourteen males and four females
taking lessons from the bible

---

1   Coranderrk Aboriginal Reserve was established in 1863 near Healesville, Victoria.

fifteen boys and eleven girls
at study in the schoolhouse

(they have become)
three bullocks, five cows and one calf
seven acres of land fenced in
two acres of oat and three of potatoes

(they are now)
six huts built
diligent subjects
dutiful souls

(they are)
working men receiving each week
sugar, 2 lbs
tea, 3 oz
flour, 5 lbs
tobacco, 1 fig.
(they are additionally several deceased natives, including some children.)

We rejoice, in conclusion, that in this Year of The Lord (1866), William Barak of the Yarra Yarra tribe, married Annie, of the Lower Murray in a Christian ceremony.

CORANDERRK — 1881

And so William was put on a coach for Melbourne, carrying his son, David, in his arms. When they arrived at Richmond they were left to themselves—in the dark and cool, and late into the night. William arrived with nothing—was left with nothing. He carried the boy to his heart through the streets where heavy brick and stone denied the footsteps of William's father, and the footsteps of his own childhood. David clung to his father, William's love stayed with his son—until he fell. And when the boy was dead William returned to Coranderrk alone. He arrived 'home' to the manager's welcome of dry bread, weak tea and the Bible. In the following year William appeared before the governors. He told them the story of his own people. He told the story of his loved son, David. When his testimony had ended all that they could bother to ask, these sombre-suited civil servants, was 'Was this a wild country when you were born?—Are you too old to work?—[and] Do you have undershirts provided each year?' William did not know his age, but was sure that he had worked hard for these men—all to build his own house of freedom. His wife was dead. His son—dead. The Protectors knew nothing of the boy, who was now with William—David's skin with William's skin—his name murmured a song on William's lips—his spirit ebbing through the body of his father.

'PAINTING BY KING BILLY: LAST OF THE YARRA TRIBE' — 1890

William paints with a soft voice. He paints with indigo, rouge and charcoal. He paints the emu, the serpent, dancing men, the women in cloaks. William paints for God. He witnesses the future and paints the past for a shadow with the name

Private Collection. He paints for the glass and stone temples of the city. William rests his paintbrush awhile and poses in a starched white suit—William resting with hands in pockets. The caption reads: 'William, the friend of the white men—with white men friends, all smiling too'. William hunts. William dances. William tells his story. Listen to him:

> I will be all gone
> all gone soon
> I will be gone

And then William becomes gone. Beruk sheds his white suit, discards his brush, his indigo, rouge and charcoal. As the city sleeps Beruk walks away, leaving the spirit of William behind. The colony mourns him dead—William Barak—'the last of his tribe'. William no more. He is Beruk. And he is here.

BERUK WATCHES MELBOURNE FROM THE SKY—1945

Half the world is a bombsite—the spoils of liberation. A is for Amen and V is for victory, signalled to those on the move—searching for the dead—seeking a home among the ruins. H is for the Holocaust and Hiroshima. H is for hydrogen—a civilised solution for disorder. All are equal before the bomb, but the burning flesh of Europe and Asia does not smoulder in Batmania. Ours is a city of cold light and dead shadows. Tombstone towers reach for the sun, casting their darkened skeletal frames over fields of gold reduced now to a sludge of shifting grey. The veins of the city are empty and still. Beruk follows the story of his footsteps, away from the temples to the ground of Coranderrk. He looks for his people—toiling in the shadow, they have become shadows also. He looks for his father. He looks for his son. Beruk searches for William, who comes to him in his white suit. 'It is not time,' William tells him. 'When the bed of the river rises to meet us, it will be time.'

BERUK VISITS THE RIVERBED—2005

Beruk moves quietly through the canyons of the city—all is stone still now. He passes the winking lights—imitating life. He listens for machines grinding to failure. Beruk observes his reflection in the flaws of glass, now inhabited by the petrified few. Women offer themselves. Men spit abuse. While dead children drift silently by, on a journey from the river to the ocean. Beruk slips into the water, beneath the heavy metals—the leaching arsenic, iron oxides, poisons and the death throes of toxic fish. Below the monster hulls of ships the current carries Beruk onward and down, to where the riverbed of the Wurundjeri awaits his return. Beruk calls into the darkness—singing his travels until his feet meet the floor of 100,000 lives once lived. In the beauty and blackness of the riverbed Beruk greets his son, David. He then greets his father—the *Ngamajet*. They sing, feet raising a rhythm of shifting earth:

> we will be gone
> all gone soon
> we will be gone

and we will come
we will come
and be

we will be

2006

TERRI JANKE
b. 1966

Terri Janke was born in Cairns, Queensland, and is a descendant of the Wuthathi/
Yadaighana and Meriam people. She is a solicitor, and her Sydney-based law firm, Terri
Janke and Company Pty Ltd—which focuses on Indigenous arts and intellectual and
cultural property—is the first Indigenous law firm to be owned by a woman in Australia.
She is the author of the novel *Butterfly Song* (2005), legal texts, poetry and short stories.
She is also the co-author of a children's picture book, *What Makes a Tree Smile* (2003).

Exotica

Give me high-arched eyebrows. Lips of red and a clean fresh face. Paint me into
fashion. Don't give me abstract. Glow me in gauche and frost me in fuchsia but
don't mix in any realism. I don't know who I am and I need you to interpret
me, to give me strength and direction. For what am I without you? A lump of
flesh. A lump of stinking flesh. Can it be your pleasure to paint me? Capture me
or reinterpret me. Make me something special and exotic. Tell me what I think.
I want to be told. A portrait lasts a thousand years. A portrait tells a thousand
stories. A thousand stories are worth a thousand memories. Can artistically shape
me as more than a memory? Can you paint my dreams?

There is nowhere I can hide in his presence. He is like a wave. I am just a shell,
one of many on the beach. No-one owns me. No-one wants to hear the words
in my head. The water rolls me in to the shoreline, ebbing away as I madly cling
to the sand. Dumped again.

The first eye. He is the ebbing tide, the sand at my feet. I watch him move.
He emerges out of the water, flicks his long hair, smoothing it with his hand,
like a seal's coolness, his moves sleek and agile. The salty water smells so pure
and clean. As I walk towards him, I step on shells so small several of them would
fit on my little fingernail. When we kiss the taste of the ocean escapes from his
mouth and invades my tongue. Fish swim in the shallows, like glittering jewels,
the kind they sell in a costume jewellery store. Fake and plastic. Cheap and gone
by the next season. Easy to lose or break.

I want him to know me, to touch me. To paint me in shades of happiness and
then curve my form with the arc of his hand.

Everyone else has gone out so I decide to pamper myself. I paint on fresh nail
polish. I let the crème fuchsia colour dry and go hard so that the colour shines.

I turn on Donna Summer and sing along pretending to be on stage in front of a large and admiring audience. I don't know the words to the next song so I go and look at myself in the mirror. I admire my painted pearly hands, testing out the many different ways I can show them off. I can put my hands up to my face, or point a finger when someone asks directions, or I can manage a cheeky wave.

Outside, I collect hibiscus flowers from the garden, selecting a random mixture of red and orange. The night sky is on its way, and the heat of summer stirs. Back inside I break the flowers from the stem and hold them carefully in my manicured hands. The curly edged leaves are still attached. The yellow stuff from the stamens sticks to my fingers. I hold in my palm another small bud, not yet open. Rolling it like a ball I squash it between my palms.

When I turn on the tap over the bath the cool water flows strongly. It swirls and hums as it travels through the pipes, reminding me of the ocean. I undress and imagine that I am a beautiful island princess living in a tropical paradise. The water reaches ten centimetres from the top of the bath so I turn off the flow.

I throw handfuls of my selected bounty into the bath until the orange, red, green and yellow pieces form a whirlpool, going round and round with my hand as I stir and stir. I unpick and peel three more flowers. Red petals and green leaves. The sticky yellow bit floats. The scent is sweet. In front of the full-length mirror I observe my form and shape, how much it has changed in the past three years. That familiar straight up and down flat chest has given way to two small breasts. My waist goes in and curves out around my hips and the hairs between my legs are feathery soft.

I light a candle scented with lavender, the orange flame light is warm like a heart. I slip down into the tub with a sigh. Here is the place where I can feel that special feeling. I pretend it is a pool in some exotic rainforest. The candle is the sun, and somewhere I can hear birds.

Water caresses my hairline, my lips and then my nose. I taste it in my mouth. I am beautiful, like a mermaid, free to know the calming secrets of water against the intimate parts of my body. My whole head pushes down and under and when I resurface I see the flowers floating. I move my body, my legs and hips to make the flowers dance. The petals are now very wet and heavy, they cling to my breasts, forming adornment on two peaks that rise up out of the water. Cool freshness surrounds me. Hibiscus heaven.

I remember that it felt like I had invented fire. The nightclub lights were firecrackers. My thin legs stomped on the dance floor and the DJ, up there in that funny box-like structure, smiled like the devil, high above the pulsating crowd. I moved my feet. *Dance, dance, dance!* There was only that one word I kept repeating. *Dance, dance, dance!* The music slapped me, soaked me, raved me. I was a tune. I was the first-ever dancer absorbed in the language of movement, pure passion. *Dance like you can't dance no more!* I drank in the music, slammed it like tequila, into my bloodstream.

And then came the snake man dancing slippery, sweat tipping his hair. He looked good in those jeans and when he danced it was like the space could not contain him. His eyes looked small like two pins and then I felt his breath against my neck. The disco ball created a solar system, turning and changing the colours around us from red to blue, purple to green.

Later, back at his place, I pulled off his shirt, making the buttons pop. I crushed my new black dress, flicking it across the room like a broken kite. I burned as his tongue moved, slowly at first like a cat, then a pure tiger face, growling at my gate. I felt the heat across my belly a body on fire, and I commanded the flames to dance once again.

Paint sticks to your fingers.
Paint gets in your hair.
Paint gets under your fingernails.
Paint edges flake and burn when next to a naked flame.

2006

JARED THOMAS
b 1976

Jared Thomas, a Nukunu man from the southern Flinders Ranges, SA, is a novelist, playwright, poet, teacher and academic. He has worked as the manager of the Indigenous Arts and Culture Division of Arts SA, and has coordinated Nukunu People's Council cultural heritage, language and art projects. He is the author of two plays—*Flash Red Ford* (1999/unpublished) and *Love, Land and Money* (2002/unpublished)—and the young adult novel, *Sweet Guy* (2005).

The Healing Tree

This one here's a real good tree. This eucalypt with the red stem. You chew on it and it keep you good all winter, boy. You chew. Taste good, iny? If you real sick you dig out these roots. See, they soft and hold lots of medicine. You mash up the root, mix it with some yawi and drink it down. When the old people used to get sick, arthritis and that, we'd boil up water and mix some of it in with 'em, in their baths, take away their aches and pains good and proper. Yep, this yirta here's a real good medicine tree, cure almost anything, even a broken heart.

Alf sat on the front porch of Cyril Lindsay House, Aboriginal Sobriety Group Hostel, looking out from the cloud of a freshly lit cigarette. Every day since arriving in Adelaide from Melbourne, Alf looked at the hills thoughtfully, wanting to be cradled by them. Alf had not returned to Adelaide or his home, Baroota, for twenty years but still he remembered his way back, the stretch of road that meets the rise of the ranges, the first glimpse of the gulf over the hill, just about every tree and turn along the way as if he had been there just yesterday. He recalled the smell of his home, the scent of the sea and dust skipping through the salt and buck bush. He remembered the trees, the gums and native pines sitting by the soft edges of the creek bed or contorting through the rocks and slate of the hills. Alf especially remembered his father's uses for the trees. He closed his eyes and concentrated on the aroma of lemon-scented gum, wafting from the nearby South Terrace Park Lands. In his mind's eye he could see the creek bed that he used to play in as a boy. It was full of frogs and yabbies and he was just about to grab a yabby when a ball of phlegm, sour with tobacco, hit the back of his throat and pulled his thoughts back to reality. 'Fuckin' pulyus,' muttered Alf between fits of coughing. He caught a lungful of air and then spat on a rose bush before taking another long draw on his cigarette.

Alf appreciated the mornings he spent alone on the porch as the other hostel residents slept. It was his only opportunity for peace and quiet, a glimpse of the normal life of an old man. When the boys woke they would start talking about where to score drugs, a drink, a fight, a woman. They found most of these things in the action videos that hostel residents watched from morning to night. Alf thought of all the residents as boys, boys pretending to be criminals, boys finding comfort and security in stories of bank robberies they'd got away with, women they'd had, fights they'd won, made-up reputations. Alf listened and was entertained by the stories of fast cars and women, schemes, plans and robberies. He was most excited by the stories of the boys in the Aboriginal Sobriety Group Boxing Program and their dreams of title fights. Alf knew it wasn't worth preaching to the boys at the hostel about clean living, his own track record didn't exactly stand as a good example. In his youth he'd spent almost more time behind bars than out of prison and there he was, a 55-year-old man, in a hostel, no home or kin to go to and without time on his side. When the boys talked about fast cars and women he just told them, 'Well good luck if you catch them things.' Spurred on by Alf's lack of belief in their plans, the boys promised Alf that one day they'd get that fast car, the pretty woman. Alf knew he had wasted too much time dreaming about those things.

Some days Alf enjoyed playing along with the boys, telling them a few stories of his own. Alf told one young fella, Jamie, about the time he fought Lionel Rose.

'Lionel Rose was going to retire, see, but then he seen me flog three bouncers in a Kalgoorlie pub. Next thing I knew Rose's manager was there, real rich and a fancy talker he was too, like Don King. And this Don King–type fella told me that he'd give me this briefcase full of money if I fought Rose. There was a lot of money in that briefcase.'

'So what'd you say to him, Alfy, what did you say?'

'Well a man would do anything for a drink when he's thirsty, eh, so I told 'im that if he bought me a few beers right then and there that I'd bust up Lionel Rose real bad.'

'And did ya, Alfy, did ya bust him up?'

'Well by the time that fight-night come I was real fit. I looked Lionel in the eye like a wild tiger when I jumped in that boxing ring …'

'Then …'

'Then what?'

'Then what did you do?'

'Then I jumped out of that boxing ring.'

'And?'

'Then I jumped on my bike and I rode all the way to Alice Springs before noticing that my chain was missing.'

'Hey Alfy, you're full of shit!'

'Well you're the dumb prick who believed I'd fight Lionel Rose, what you reckon I am, some crazy old bastard?'

A few days ago, after picking up a new tweed jacket from the Salvation Army shop, Alf started making his way down Hindley Street to Rundle Mall. When he saw the Exeter Hotel on Rundle Street Alf was reminded of a true story about his younger days that he could share with the hostel boys. Before deciding to enter the pub, Alf stood and watched people enter and exit as one would watch another crossing an old and high rickety bridge. Confused, he walked out of the Exeter with a pint of lemon squash and took a seat at one of the pub's footpath tables. Alf couldn't believe the types of people who were being served inside the pub; fellas with coloured hair, women with no hair at all. Alf thought of the changes that had happened since he had last been in Adelaide, a time when dark coloured men, unless they happened to be Indian, could not be seen let alone get served at the Exeter or any other hotel for that matter.

That night Alf recounted his memory of the Exeter to the boys back at the hostel.

'I remembers when me and some fellas visited Adelaide and we ducked behind the Exeter Hotel and wrapped towels around our heads. Wobblin' our heads from side to side we walked into the hotel and said to the publican, 'Two bottle of beer thank you very much, two bottle of beer.' Unawares that we were thuras, the barman handed over the grog when we gave him the bunda, see. Then me and the fellas went and got charged up at the park. True as God we were only boys but that barman thought we was real Indian men.'

Alf knew better than anyone that getting away with tricks like impersonating an Indian man to buy grog was the beginning of his end. At the age of twenty Alf was dousing himself in grog every day and thinking himself wiser than all in his drunken stupor. He was less wise as a man than he was at age ten, when he listened to his elders and took responsibility for his actions. The old people ordered Alf to stop drinking and they were prepared to exile him from his community if he didn't heed their advice. One old uncle took it upon himself to teach Alf a lesson in order to save Alf from himself.

Alf's uncle woke him up early in the morning by clanging two of the many beer bottles that were scattered around Alf's bed on the bare, hard dirt. Alf was still drunk and thirsty for water when he stirred but Alf's uncle wouldn't let Alf have a drink from his waterbag or Nhatapilka, the nearby creek. Instead Alf's uncle held his waterbag selfishly to his side and dragged Alf up Kaparinya, the hill at Port Germein, overlooking the gulf. Alf was near dead when he reached the top of the hill and as soon as Alf sat exhausted on the ground at the top of the hill he asked for some yawi. Alf's uncle took a long mouthful of water from his waterbag and then just stood laughing at Alf. 'Why won't you let me drink?' asked Alf. The uncle wouldn't answer Alf's question, telling him only to be quiet or else he would be punished more severely than what was already in store for him.

Alf sat on that hill for the best part of three very hot days without drinking or eating. Alf's uncle wouldn't let him sleep on the first night. Alf just had to sit there thirsty and patient, upright on the hill overlooking the ocean. In the morning, the uncle sipped from his waterbag, teasing the thirsty Alf. In the afternoon while keeping an eye on Alf, the uncle went down to the sea to swim and fish. Alf was so parched that he tilted back his head to let his sweat roll to his lips. In the evening the uncle ate his fish and drank some water in front of Alf while only sharing one cockle with him.

Alf woke wearily the next morning with his head slumped upon his chest. As the day wore on he could hear his heart thumping harder and the heat rising hotter through the earth beneath him with every breath that he drew. Noticing Alf's exhaustion, his uncle took the opportunity to sneak up to Alf and place a beer bottle in front of him before sneaking away. The uncle, out of Alf's sight, whistled to catch his attention. Alf's head lifted gingerly to see his uncle drinking from his waterbag through a haze of heat. As Alf's head slumped down to avoid torture and humiliation he caught sight of the beer bottle full of liquid in front of him. Alf lurched for the bottle and let the contents overflow into his mouth. Seconds later he dropped the bottle to the ground and began spewing.

As Alf's stomach shuddered and spew hung in streams from his mouth, his uncle walked over to him, taking the bottle that he had filled with seawater and holding it to Alf's face. The uncle played the trick another time on Alf that day and once again he drank the seawater that he thought was beer and again he spewed. Late in the night the uncle allowed Alf three cockles and from his waterbag poured three splashes of water into Alf's cupped hands for him to drink. As Alf lay down to sleep he listened to the water lapping against the shore and visualised waves of fresh water crashing upon his tongue. With each wave that he imagined, a tear flowed free.

Alf woke the next morning to find another beer bottle placed in front of him and his sneaky uncle standing over him and drinking greedily from his waterbag. Alf wanted to drink the contents of the bottle but instead pushed it over. Later that day, thinking that he was going to die, Alf raised his eyes to find his uncle's eyes fixed upon him and another beer bottle, full of liquid placed before him.

'It's all right,' said his uncle, 'You can drink it, it's yawi.'

But Alf did not believe his uncle and would not touch the beer bottle. Alf's uncle tried to convince him that the liquid within the beer bottle was safe to drink but still Alf wouldn't touch it. Eventually, feeling sorry for Alf and convinced that Alf would never again touch a beer bottle, the uncle cradled the exhausted Alf in his arms and let him drink his fill of fresh water from the waterbag.

Alf didn't drink grog again. Not for another ten years, until after the 1967 referendum. Grog was the new religion and Alf visited its church every day. He could always find his spirituality in the bottom of a glass or a can but still couldn't pick up a beer bottle. And when the old people told him to stop drinking he cheekily replied, 'I'm not drinking, I'm just sipping.'

Sick of everyone telling him what to do, Alf took off to the bright lights of Sydney and Melbourne. The only thing he found there was more drinking, crime and time inside.

Daily Alf sits on the porch of Cyril Lindsay House and it still feels like he is inside a prison. Some days it feels like his uncle is punishing him again. Alf believes he is sitting on that hill waiting for death. His old bones ache and his lungs cry. Sometimes he listens to the stories of the boys. Sometimes they take his mind off his sickness, his heartache and dreams that just flashed by. He waits for an old friend to take him home. The old friend never comes. These days he dreams only of the yirtas, the trees. All he wants to do is chew on their leaves hungrily, hoping they'll fix his broken heart.

2006

TARA JUNE WINCH
b. 1983

Tara June Winch is of Wiradjuri, Afghan and English heritage and lives in NSW. *Swallow the Air* (2006), a collection of short stories that can be read as a novel, won the 2004 David Unaipon Award.

From *Swallow the Air*
Wantok

Johnny takes me away, together we run the white-sanded beaches, and we eat mangoes and pick coconuts and wade through swamps to pull up lily roots and eat them as sugar rhubarb. Even if we're sitting there in Caroline Street or walking up Vine to the park, we've escaped with each other and the rest of it—the Block and the city rise up and drift away like vacant echoes.

We follow the train tracks to Central, we rake in the city and buy hot chip rolls with gravy, we go west and discover streets that even Johnny didn't know existed; there we play hockey games with wooden stakes and beer cans. Johnny says it's not the same as in Waiben but it's still fun. In Waiben he says they use tree branches and they carve their own balls from wood. He says Waiben is his real home, where his father lives. We talk of the beaches and our old folk, them and something missing.

Johnny Smith was born four months before me; we worked it out, exactly to the day. He was born in Sydney though, not Waiben. He hasn't been to Waiben yet, but he knows that it is his home. Johnny said he was going to get initiated, but Justine was in lock up so she couldn't come to mourn the spirits. He reckons he's still going to go up and get cut. He says people call it Thursday Island, cos Thursday is pension day see, the best day of the week, and that's why they call it that, cos it's so good up there that everyday is just like pension day.

When I first came to Joyce's he'd tried to crack onto me. I remember us sitting in his room at Joyce's, him blowing bong smoke through the gap of the window. The way he looked at me, it was nice, a gentle look, but I told him to piss off, told him all men are bastards.

'You're my girlfriend, hey? Me and you?'

'Piss off. All men are bastards. Don't reckon you're any exception!'

'Nah, girl, you've just heard that from TV and stuff, magazines've brainwashed ya. That ain't true. Look at me—I'm no bastard!'

'I *know* all men are bastards. Even if you're not, even if you're just too young to be a bastard—don't worry you will be one day.'

We stir each other up, joking. We know we are just best friends.

He always tells me about when his uncles have travelled through the Block, come and stayed with Joyce even. She'd make them a big pasta feed and they'd tell him all about the Torres Strait. He told me the same stories.

He says in the islands lots of people live in houses on high stilts, perched up in the leaves of pawpaw trees and towering black palms. He says that you can reach out from your window and pick off a ripe mango. Just like that.

He takes my hand like always and we scramble up the palms and hack down coconuts with a machete, we run down to the rocky beaches and cast off our canoe, we fish all day, following the reefs and tides and winds. We read the ocean looking for dugong, we beachcomb for turtle. We visit the other islands and trade food and sing songs. We dance with palm branches and deri flowers, like we are spirit people. We rest in the houses as warm tropical storms light up the bruised sky. We lie out on the high balconies and watch the ocean turn to ink. Osprey hawks soar in from the deep, they plummet feet first into the stirring water, when they hit it they fold their wings downward and lift up into the air, a fish slipping in their claws. They return home, like us, to nests. Their nests are like houses, stacked high above the water line atop rock outcrops in the hot billowing wind. We rest.

In the late evening when we wake, I take *his* hand and lead him to my mum's country, to the lake. We wade through the delicate water, the moon spilling on our colourless bodies. Brolgas ruffling their wings against water ribbons, making the muddy bath flinch in coiling waves. We dig hollows in the wet sand and become snakes, silting though the swampy streams, creating mouths and rivers. We make fires, hunt red kangaroo and wrap ourselves in the warm skin and sand. We sleep.

We run back to Joyce's house, and hang out on the little veranda. Johnny's cousins come round and we listen to music under the sunshine. Daylight blanching our dreamings, the gritty air fuming back to our noses, engines starting back in our listening, and we remember what we're all really seeing. Beach lines of gutters, trunks of layered windows, metal wings fleeing the sky, and dinner on the stove. We don't mind, because anytime we can leave in our minds.

It isn't bad when we come back; we notice little similarities to our dreaming places. The cabbage palms, the fire pit, the family.

I suppose that's what makes it, family, and I suppose we don't see the faces in our dreams yet. We promise each other to find them, the faces, to go to our homelands for our people, for ourselves. We are best friends. Johnny says I am his *wantok*, his black girl ally. I tell him that he reminds me of my brother. And he says he is my brother, always.

2006

GLOSSARY

All reasonable endeavours have been made by the editors to ensure appropriate translations of language words. In the instance where the author of an entry had not identified the language group their words were from (or had not provided their own glossary), the editors have taken the liberty of suggesting it was from the country in which that author was born (if that was stated by the author). Unfortunately, language translations could not be obtained for all words published in this anthology, which further demonstrates the harsh realities of the impact of colonisation on Aboriginal language and culture.

Alcheringa (Arrernte): term for the Dreamtime or creation period

Assimilation: the view that Aboriginal people should be removed from their own cultures and absorbed completely into Anglo-Australian culture, often reflected in government policies during the twentieth century

Biamee: a creator spirit in south-eastern NSW; also Biami

billabong: a waterhole by a river or creek

blackfella: slang used by Aboriginal people for their own people

boob: a small jail cell

boomerang: wooden instrument used for hunting, and also used as a percussion instrument when two are hit together

bora rings: an initiation or ceremonial site; also rings of bora

boyyah (Noongar): money

brolga: a large grey crane

bullroarer: a wooden instrument whirled around the head, often for ceremonies restricted to initiated men

bullyaka (Noongar): take off

bundji: brother/sister (in law)

bungarra: goanna

bunyip: a mythical spirit, often referred to as evil, which dwells in creeks, swamps and billabongs

chubel (Noongar): spear

churinga stone: sacred stone

clapstick: common name for wooden sticks struck together during ceremonial songs

coconut: Aboriginal slang term used for those people who are dark skinned but are considered by some to think or feel like white people

cooee: to shout out, usually to find someone or to locate the caller (thought to be from the Dharug nation of Sydney)

coolamon: wooden carrying dish; also coolamen, cooliman

corroboree: ceremonial gathering with song and dance

damper: traditional bread made from wheat and cooked on coals or in the ground

deadly: cool, good

didgeridoo/Yidaki (Yolngu): a large wind instrument made from hollowed-out hardwood trees and originally used in northern Australia (the Top End) by men

dijwun: this one

doak (Noongar): throwing stick

Dreamtime: the time of creation for Aboriginal people; also the Dreaming

dubakieny (Noongar): steadily, slowly

Duramula: Father/Creator

fella: Aboriginal slang for a person of either gender

fringe-dweller: person living on the fringe of a town or city

full-blood: term used by colonial cultures and authorities to differentiate between degrees of perceived Aboriginality

gerbah (Noongar): alcohol

gin: derogatory term used historically for an Aboriginal woman

girdi girdi (Mardujara language): hill kangaroo

gubba: usually derogatory generic slang term for a white man used by Aboriginal people in NSW and Victoria

gubberment: Aboriginal slang for government

gudeeah (Noongar): white person

gulja (Mardujara language): a mixture of tobacco and ashes

gunyah (Dharug): a shelter made from bushes and bark

half-caste: term used by colonial cultures and authorities to differentiate between degrees of perceived Aboriginality

inji stick (Noongar): decorated stick used in ceremonies

Integration: the view that Aboriginal people and their cultures should be allowed to live alongside Anglo-Australian culture, often reflected in government policies during the later twentieth century

kaal (Noongar): fire

kadaitcha: term used widely among Central Australian groups to refer to a form of secret killing and other related rituals; also an Arrernte expression meaning 'evil person walking about'

kartwarra: mad, bad in the head

kia: yes

kienya (Noongar): shame

Koori: generic term used by Aboriginal people for themselves in much of NSW; also Koorie (in Victoria) and Goori (parts of northern NSW)

koort (Noongar): weak

kuliyah (Noongar): yes

lubra: derogatory term used historically for an Aboriginal woman or girl

Mabo: Eddie Koiki Mabo (1932–92)

Mabo judgment: A highly significant judgment of the High Court of Australia in 1992 (*Mabo v Queensland [No. 2]* (1992)), recognising claims by Eddie Mabo and others for common law ownership of their traditional lands at Mer Island, and more generally recognising the fiction of *terra nullius* in the acquisition of Australian territory by Britain

message-stick: wooden stick with a message carved into it, passed between clans and nations to transmit information or a message

miggloo: generic term used in Queensland for a white person

minditj (Noongar): stick

mission: pocket of land controlled by various religious factions to contain Aboriginal people under the policies of Protection and Assimilation; similar areas run by government agencies were called reserves

mob: an Aboriginal clan, nation, language group or community

moorditj (Noongar): deadly, in the sense of cool, good

mulga: acacia woodland or scrub

muntj: have sex

murrandu (Mardujara): goanna

Murri: generic term for Aboriginal people in Queensland

myall: derogatory term used to describe an Aboriginal person who is simple

Native Title: concept in Australian law which recognises the ownership of land by Aboriginal peoples, first enacted in Parliament in the *Commonwealth Native Title Act* 1993 following the Mabo judgment of 1992

Nebalee: great man of the heavens; also Neboolea

Ngarrindjeri: Aboriginal people (and their language) from the lower Murray River and Western Fleurieu Peninsula, SA; also Narrinjeri

nietjuk (Noongar): who

Noongar: Aboriginal people (and their language) from south-western WA; also Nyoongah, Nyungah

octoroon: term used by colonial cultures and authorities to differentiate between degrees of perceived Aboriginality

Protection Act/s: acts of state and territory governments authorising state authority over Aboriginal cultures and communities, generally in force from the late nineteenth century to the mid-twentieth century

Protection Boards: government boards created to administer Aboriginal people and communities under the terms of the Protection Acts

Protector: officer of the Protection Board authorised to implement Board policies within state districts; the Chief Protector was the head of the Protection Board

quadroon: term used by colonial cultures and authorities to differentiate between degrees of perceived Aboriginality

quarter-caste: term used by colonial cultures and authorities to differentiate between degrees of perceived Aboriginality

Rainbow Serpent: a creation spirit

reserve: government-run compound used to hold Aboriginal people separate from the rest of the community and free up land for grants to new settlers; similar areas run by church groups were called missions

right skin: different spiritual and kin groups that determine the relationship of one Aboriginal person to another, and therefore who they can marry

self-determination: Aboriginal self-governance without external influence

stolen generation/s: term used to describe the Aboriginal and Torres Strait Islander peoples forcibly removed from, and denied further access to, their families and communities under government policies between 1869 and 1969

terra nullius: a Latin expression derived from Roman law meaning 'nobody's land'

Uluru: one of Australia's most significant sacred sites and the world's largest monolith (formerly known as Ayers Rock); situated on the lands of the Anangu people in Uluru – Kata Tjuta National Park, NT

vox nullius: see *terra nullius*; 'nobody's voice', a coinage to suggest that, like Aboriginal rights to land, Aboriginal languages and voices did not warrant attention

waddy: hunting stick or war club

walkabout: travel embarked upon by Aboriginal people for the purpose of death and funeral ceremonies, cultural ceremonies, bartering, food, water and so on

watjella (Noongar): white person; also whitefella, wetjalas

White Australia policy: unofficial name for government policies restricting immigration into Australia to Anglo-Celtic people, particularly during the late nineteenth to mid-twentieth centuries

wilgi (Noongar): specially prepared paint for ceremonies

womba: mad

woomera: spear thrower

wurlies: shelters made of branches or leaves

yabby: small freshwater crayfish found in south-eastern Australia

yongah (Noongar): kangaroo; also yonga

yorgah (Noongar): woman; also yorga

yortj (Noongar): penis

yumbah (Noongar): children

yowie: a large ape-like human, believed to roam in some parts of Australia, especially southern NSW; also yuwi

SELECTED READING

William Arthur and Frances Morphy (eds), *Macquarie Atlas of Indigenous Australia* (2005)

Bain Attwood and Andrew Markus (eds), *The Struggle for Aboriginal Rights: A documentary history* (1999)

Faith Bandler, *Turning the Tide: A personal history of the Federal Council for the Advancement of Aborigines and Torres Strait Islanders* (1989)

Roger Bennett (ed.), *Voices from the Heart: Contemporary Aboriginal poetry from Central Australia* (1995)

Anne Brewster, Angeline O'Neill and Rosemary van den Berg (eds), *Those Who Remain Will Always Remember: An anthology of Aboriginal writing* (2000)

Alexander Brown and Brian Geytenbeek, *Ngarla Songs* (2003)

Maryrose Casey, *Creating Frames: Contemporary Indigenous theatre, 1967–1990* (2004)

Ann Curthoys, *Freedom Ride: A freedom rider remembers* (2002)

Jack Davis and Bob Hodge (eds), *Aboriginal Writing Today: Papers from the first national conference of Aboriginal writers* (1985)

Jack Davis, Mudrooroo, Stephen Muecke and Adam Shoemaker (eds), *Paperbark: A collection of black Australian writings* (1990)

Josie Douglas (ed.), *Untreated: Poems by black writers* (2001)

Kevin Gilbert (ed.), *Inside Black Australia: An anthology of Aboriginal poetry* (1988)

Heather Goodall, *Invasion to Embassy: Land in Aboriginal politics in New South Wales, 1770–1972* (1996)

Michele Grossman et al. *Blacklines: Contemporary critical writing by Indigenous Australians* (2003)

Anita Heiss, *Dhuuluu Yala (Talk Straight): Publishing Indigenous literature* (2003)

Anita Heiss and Penny van Toorn (eds), *Southerly: Stories without end*, vol. 62, no. 2 (2002)

Barry Hill, *Broken Song: T.G.H. Strehlow and Aboriginal possession* (2002)

Bob Hodge and Vijay Mishra, *Dark Side of the Dream: Australian literature and the postcolonial mind* (1991)

Jack Horner, *Seeking Racial Justice: An insider's memoir of the movement for Aboriginal advancement 1938–1978* (2004)

Sylvia Kleinert, Margo Neale and Robyne Bancroft, *Oxford Companion to Aboriginal Art and Culture* (2000)

John Maynard, *Fight for Liberty and Freedom: The origins of Australian Aboriginal activism* (2007)

Peter Minter (ed.), *Meanjin. Blak Times: Indigenous Australia,* vol. 65, no. 1 (2006)

Aileen Moreton-Robinson (ed.), *Whitening Race: Essays in social and cultural criticism* (2004)

Howard Morphy, *Aboriginal Art* (1998)

Philip Morrissey, 'Aboriginality and Corporatism', in Michele Grossman (ed.), *Blacklines: Contemporary critical writing by Indigenous Australians* (2003)

——'Stalking Aboriginal Culture: The Wanda Koolmatrie affair', *Australian Feminist Studies,* vol. 18, no. 42 (2003)

Mudrooroo, *The Indigenous Literature of Australia: Milli Milli Wangka* (1997)

——*Writing from the Fringe: A study of modern Aboriginal literature* (1990)

Martin Nakata, *Disciplining the Savages: Savaging the disciplines* (2007)

Bruce Pascoe, *Convincing Ground: Learning to fall in love with your country* (2007)

Hetti Perkins, *One Sun One Moon: Aboriginal art in Australia* (2007)

John Ramsland, *Remembering Aboriginal Heroes: Struggle, identity and the media* (2006)

Henry Reynolds, *The Law of the Land* (1987)

——*The Other Side of the Frontier: Aboriginal resistance to the European invasion of Australia* (2006)

Michael Rose (ed.), *For the Record: 160 years of Aboriginal print journalism* (1996)

Jennifer Sabbiono, Kay Schaffer and Sidonie Smith (eds), *Indigenous Australian Voices: A reader* (1998)

Selina Samuels (ed.), *Australian Writers 1975–2000* (2006)

Adam Shoemaker, *Black Words, White Page: Aboriginal literature 1929–1988* (1989)

Penny van Toorn, *Writing Never Arrives Naked: Early Aboriginal cultures of writing in Australia* (2006)

Alexis Wright (ed.), *Take Power Like This Old Man Here: An anthology of writings celebrating twenty years of land rights in Central Australia, 1977–1997* (1998)

Jack Davis: Keith Chesson, *Jack Davis: A life story* (1988); Gerry Turcotte, *Jack Davis: The maker of history* (1994)

Mick Dodson: 'The End in the Beginning: Re(de)fining Aboriginality' in Michelle Grossman (ed.), *Blacklines: Contemporary critical writing by Indigenous Australians* (2003)

Patrick Dodson: Kevin Keefe, *Paddy's Road: Life stories of Patrick Dodson* (2003)

Richard Frankland: 'Conversations with the Dead' in *Blak Inside: 6 Indigenous plays from Victoria* (2002)

Kevin Gilbert: Pauline McMillan, 'Kevin Gilbert and "Living Black" ' in *Journal of Australian Studies,* no. 45 (1995)

Vincent Lingiari: Alexis Wright (ed.), *Take Power Like This Old Man Here: An anthology of writings celebrating twenty years of land rights in Central Australia 1977–1997* (1998)

Narritjin Maymuru: Howard Morphy, Pip Deveson and Katie Hayne, 'The Art of Narritjin Maymuru' (CD-ROM) (2005)

Sally Morgan: *Arthur Corunna's Story* (1990), *Mother and Daughter: The story of Daisy and Gladys Corunna* (1990), *Sally's Story* (1990). Delys Bird and Dennis Haskell (eds), *Whose Place? A study of Sally Morgan's 'My Place'* (1992)

Doug Nicholls: Mavis Thorpe Clarke, *Pastor Doug: The story of an Aboriginal leader* (1965), *The Boy from Cumeroogunga* (1979)

Oodgeroo Noonuccal: Kathleen J. Cochrane and Ron Hurley (illustrator), *Oodgeroo* (1994); Adam Shoemaker (ed.), *Oodgeroo: A tribute* (1994)

Charles Perkins: Peter Read, *Charles Perkins: A biography* (1990)

Doris Pilkington: *Under the Wintamarra Tree* (2002)

Bob Randall: *Songman: The story of an Aboriginal elder of Uluru* (2003), *Tracker Tjugingji* (2003)

Kerry Reed-Gilbert: (ed.) *Message Stick: Contemporary Aboriginal writing* (1997)

Kim Scott: *The Dregersaurus* (2001)

Alf Taylor: *Winds* (1994), *Rimfire* (2002)

Pat Torres: *The Story of Crow: A Nyul Nyul story* (1987)

David Unaipon: Mary-Anne Gale, 'Giving Credit Where Credit is Due: The writings of David Unaipon' in Gus Worby and Lester Irabinna Rigney (eds), *Sharing Spaces: Indigenous and non-Indigenous responses to story, country and rights* (2006); Sue Hosking, 'David Unaipon: His story' in Philip Butterss (ed.), *Southwords: Essays on South Australian writing* (1995)

Samuel Wagan Watson: *Hotel Bone* (2001), *Itinerant Blues* (2002), *Three Legged Dogs and Other Poems* (2005)

Glenyse Ward: *Unna You Fellas* (1991)

Eric Willmot: *Australia: The last experiment* (1987), *Below the Line* (1991). Lyn Jacobs, 'Mapping Shared Spaces: Willmot and Astley' in Gus Worby and Lester Irabinna Rigney (eds), *Sharing Spaces: Indigenous and non-Indigenous responses to story, country and rights* (2006)

SOURCES AND PERMISSIONS

The following works of reference have been used, and are acknowledged here instead of in individual biographies:

Reference works

D. Horton (ed.), *Encyclopaedia of Aboriginal Australia* (1994)

S. Kleinert and M. Neale (eds), *Oxford Companion to Aboriginal Art and Culture* (2000)

Who's Who in Australia (present and past editions)

Websites

AustLit: The Australian Literature Resource: www.austlit.edu.au

Australian Dictionary of Biography online edition: www.adb.online.anu.edu.au

Barani: www.cityofsydney.nsw.gov.au/barani/

Black Words, Aboriginal and Torres Strait Islander Writers and Storytellers subset of AustLit: www.austlit.edu.au/BlackWords

Kev Carmody: www.kevcarmody.com.au/biography.html

Gary Foley's Koori History website: www.kooriweb.org/foley/indexb.html

HREOC website: www.hreoc.gov.au

Magabala Books: www.magabala.com

National Archives of Australia: www.naa.gov.au/fsheets/fs225.html

Extracted texts

Mary Ann Arthur: General Correspondence CSO11/26 file 378, Archives Office of Tasmania, 10 June 1846

Walter George Arthur: General Correspondence CSO11/26 file 378, Archives Office of Tasmania, 15 July 1846

William Barak: *Argus*, 29 August 1882

Larissa Behrendt: *Home* (2004). Copyright © Larissa Behrendt. Reprinted by permission of the University of Queensland Press

Lisa Bellear: *Dreaming in Urban Areas* (1996). Copyright © The Estate of Lisa Bellear. Reprinted by permission of the University of Queensland Press

Bennelong: Letter to Mr Philips, Sydney Cove, New South Wales, 29 August 1796. Original lost, copy held at National Library of Australia. NK4048, MS 4005

Tony Birch: *Meanjin*, vol. 65, no. 1 (2006). Copyright © Tony Birch. Reprinted by permission of Tony Birch

Gerry Bostock: *Meanjin*, vol. 36, no. 4. Spring (1977). Copyright © Gerry Bostock. Reprinted by permission of Gerry Bostock

Kitty Brangy: B313/1, item 42. National Archives of Australia, NAA

Thomas Brune: *Flinders Island Chronicle*, Papers of George Augustus Robinson, ML A7073, vol. 52, Mitchell Library, Sydney

John Muk Muk Burke: *Night Song and Other Poems* (1999). Copyright © John Muk Muk Burke. Reprinted by permission of John Muk Muk Burke

Burnum Burnum: from Marlene J Norst, *Burnum Burnum: A Warrior for Peace* (1999). Copyright © Marelle Burnum Burnum. Reprinted by permission of Marelle Burnum Burnum widow of the late B. Burnum

Bessie Cameron: *Argus*, 5 April 1886

Kev Carmody: from Paul Kelly, *Don't Start Me Talking, Lyrics 1984–2004* (2004). © Paul Kelly and Kev Carmody. Reprinted by permission of Allen & Unwin Pty Ltd

Jimmy Chi: *Bran Nue Dae* (Currency Press and Magabala Books, 1991). Copyright © Jimmy Chi, Mick Manolis, Steve Pigram, Garry Gower, Pat Bin Amat and Bran Nue Dae Productions 1991. Reprinted by permission of Currency Press Pty Ltd

Monica Clare: *Karobran: The story of an Aboriginal girl* (1978). Copyright © Les Clare 1978, 1983, 1985. Reprinted by permission of Hale & Iremonger Pty Ltd

Vivienne Cleven: *Bitin' Back* (2001). Copyright © Vivienne Cleven. Reprinted by permission of the University of Queensland Press

William Cooper: Melbourne *Herald*, 15 September 1933

Jack Davis: 'The First-born', 'The Black Tracker', 'Warru', 'Integration' from *The First-born and Other Poems* (1970). 'Walker' from *Jagardoo: Poems from Aboriginal Australia* (1978). Copyright © The Estate of Jack Davis. Reprinted by arrangement with the licensor, the Estate of Jack Davis, c/– Curtis Brown (Aust) Pty Ltd. *No Sugar* (1986). Copyright © The Estate of Jack Davis. Reprinted by permission of Currency Press Pty Ltd

Graeme Dixon: *Holocaust Island* (1990). Copyright © Graeme Dixon 1990. Reprinted by permission of the University of Queensland Press

Michael Dodson: *Age*, 18 December 1997. Copyright © Michael Dodson. Reprinted by permission of Michael Dodson

Patrick Dodson: Welcome Speech, 4 June 1993. Copyright © Patrick Dodson. Reprinted by permission of Patrick Dodson

Wesley Enoch: *Black Medea, Southerly,* vol. 62, no. 2 (2002). Published in *Contemporary Indigenous Plays* (Currency Press, 2007). © Wesley Enoch 2005, 2007. Reprinted by permission of Currency Press Pty Ltd

Jim Everett: *meenamatta lena narla puellakanny* an arts collaboration between Jim Everett and Jonathan Kimberley (2006). Copyright © pura-lia meenamatta (K.J. Everett) 2006. Reprinted by permission of K.J. Everett

Lionel Fogarty: 'Decorative Rasp, Weaved Roots', 'Ecology' and 'Shields Strong, Nulla Nullas Alive' from *Yoogum Yoogum* (1982). Copyright © Lionel Fogarty. Reprinted by permission of Lionel Fogarty. 'For I Come—Death in Custody', 'Kath Walker', 'Dulpai—Ila Ngari Kim Mo-Man' from *New and Selected Poems: Munaldjali, Mutuerjaraera* (1995). Copyright © Lionel Fogarty. Reprinted by permission of Lionel Fogarty and Hyland House. 'Alcheringa' from *Minyung Woolah Binnung: What Saying Says* (2004). Copyright © Lionel Fogarty. Reprinted by permission of Keeaira Press

Richard Frankland: from Josie Douglas (ed.), *Untreated: Poems by Black Writers* (2001). © Richard Frankland. Reprinted by permission of Richard Frankland

Pearl Gibbs: Radio Broadcast, 2GB Sydney and 2WL Wollongong, 8 June 1941. © The Estate of Pearl Gibbs. Reprinted by permission of Anny Druett

Kevin Gilbert: 'People *Are* Legends', 'Redfern', 'Me and Jackomari Talkin' About Land Rights' and 'Tree' from *The Blackside: People Are Legends and Other Poems* (1990). © The Estate of Kevin Gilbert. Reprinted by permission of Hyland House. *The Cherry Pickers* and speech delivered at the Aboriginal Tent Embassy, Canberra. 27 May 1992. © The Estate of Kevin Gilbert. Reprinted by permission of Eleanor Gilbert

Ruby Langford Ginibi: *Don't Take Your Love To Town* (1988). © Dr Ruby Langford Ginibi 1988. Elder of Bundjalung Nation, Female Elder of National NAIDOC Week, Darwin 2007 (50 Years, Lookin' Forward and Lookin' Black). Reprinted by permission of the University of Queensland Press

Stephen Hagan: *The N Word: One Man's Stand* (2005). © Stephen Hagan. Reprinted by permission of Magabala Books

Norman Harris: Public Records Office of Western Australia, AN 1/7, Acc. 993, file A/94/1928, 19 April 1927. © The Estate of Norman Harris. Reprinted by permission of Myrtle Mullaley

Rita Huggins and Jackie Huggins: *Auntie Rita* (1994). © Jackie Huggins. Reprinted by permission of Aboriginal Studies Press

Terri Janke: *Meanjin,* vol. 65, no. 1 (2006), pp. 101–103. © Terri Janke. Reproduced with permission from Golvan Arts Management Pty Ltd

Marcia Langton: '*Well, I heard it on the Radio and I saw it on the Television …': An essay for the Australian Film Commission on the politics and aesthetics of filmmaking by and about Aboriginal people and Things* (Sydney, Australian Film Commission, 1993). © Australian Film Commission 1993. Reprinted by permission of the Australian Film Commission

Kenny Laughton: *Not Quite Men, No Longer Boys* (1999). © K.C. Laughton 1987. Reprinted by permission of Jukurrpa Books, an imprint of IAD Press

Jessie Lennon: *And I Always Been Moving! The Early Life of Jessie Lennon* (1995). © The Lennon Family. Permission given by Emily Betts (née Lennon) on behalf of the Lennon Family

Vincent Lingiari et al.: Petition, 19 April 1967. Reprinted by permission of Sharyn Jerry, Marie D. Jaban, Sabrina Jerry, Sarah Jerry, Jock Vincent, Ronnie Wavehill, Bernard 'Peanut' Pontiari and Ida Malinkya

Melissa Lucashenko: *Steam Pigs* (1997). © Melissa Lucashenko 1997. Reprinted by permission of the University of Queensland Press

Dennis McDermott: *Dorothy's Skin* (2003). © Dennis McDermott. Reprinted by permission of Five Islands Press

Philip McLaren: *Sweet Water ... Stolen Land* (1993). © Philip McLaren 1993 and 2001. Reprinted by permission of Magabala Books

Jennifer Martiniello: *The Imprint of Infinity* (1999), *Southerly*, vol. 62, no. 2 (2002) 'Uluru by Champagne' from *Imprint of Infinity* (Tidbinbilla Press, 1999), 'Emily Kngwarreye' from *Southerly,* vol. 62, no. 2 (2002), pp. 7–8. 'Emily Kngwarreye' also appeared in Jennifer Martiniello, (ed.), *Talking Ink from Ochre* (2002) © Jennifer Avriel Martiniello. Reprinted by permission of Jennifer Martiniello

Maggie Mobourne: National Archives of Australia. From facsimile copy of Maggie Mobourne to D.N. McLeod, 27 February 1900. NAA: series B337, item 507

Romaine Moreton: 'Don't Let It Make You Over' and 'I Shall Surprise You by My Will' from *Post me to the Prime Minister* (2004). © Romaine Moreton. Reprinted by permission of Jukurrpa Books, an imprint of IAD Press. 'Genocide is Never Justified' from 'The Callused Stick of Wanting' *Rimfire* (2000). © Romaine Moreton 1995. Reprinted by permission of Magabala Books

Anna Morgan: *Labor Call*, 20 September 1934

Sally Morgan: *My Place* (1987). © Sally Jane Morgan, 1987. Reprinted by permission of Fremantle Press

Narritjin Maymuru: © The Estate of Narritjin Maymuru. Reprinted by permission of Galuma Maymuru. Methodist Overseas Mission Papers, Mitchell Library, State Library of NSW, MSS MOM 465, March 1963

Bill Neidjie: from Keith Taylor (ed.), *Story About Feeling* (1989). © 1989 Bill Neidjie and Keith Taylor. Reprinted by permission of Magabala Books

John A. Newfong: *Identity*, vol. 1, no. 7 (July 1973). © The Estate of John A. Newfong.

Doug Nicholls: *Age*, 27 May 1963. © The Estate of Sir Douglas Nicholls. Reprinted by permission of Pastor Sir Douglas and Lady Gladys Nicholls Family

Barbara Nicholson: from Kerry Reed-Gilbert (ed.), *The Strength of Us As Women: Black Women Speak* (2000). © Barbara Nicholson. Reprinted by permission of Barbara Nicholson

Oodgeroo of the tribe Noonuccal: 'Aboriginal Charter of Rights', 'The Dispossessed', 'We Are Going', 'Assimilation—No!', 'Integration—Yes!', 'The Dawn is at Hand', 'No More Boomerang' and 'Ballad of the Totems' from *My People*, 4th ed. (2008). Reproduced by permission of John Wiley & Sons Australia. Speech Launching the Petition of the Federal Council for Aboriginal Advancement. 6 October 1962. © The Estate of Oodgeroo Noonuccal. Reproduced by permission of Dennis Walker

Bruce Pascoe: *Night Animals* (1986). © Bruce Pascoe. Reprinted by permission of Penguin Group (Australia)

Noel Pearson: from Peter Craven (ed.), *The Best Australian Essays 2002* (2002). © Noel Pearson 2002. Reprinted by permission of Noel Pearson

Charles Perkins: *Australian*, 8 April 1968. © The Charlie Perkins Children's Trust. Reprinted by permission of Hetti Perkins, Trustee for the Charlie Perkins Children's Trust

Jimmy Pike and Pat Lowe: *Yinti: Desert Child* (1992). © Pat Lowe and Jimmy Pike 1992. Reprinted by permission of Magabala Books

Doris Pilkington: *Follow the Rabbit-Proof Fence* (1996). © Doris Pilkington— Nugi Garimara 1996. Reprinted by permission of the University of Queensland Press

Bob Randall: from Jack Davis, Stephen Muecke, Mudrooroo Narogin and Adam Shoemaker (eds), *Paperbark: A collection of Black Australian writings* (1990). © Bob Randall. Reprinted by permission of Bob Randall

Kerry Reed-Gilbert: *Talkin' About Country* (2002). © Kerry Reed-Gilbert. Reprinted by permission of Kerry Reed-Gilbert

Annie Rich: Letter, 5 April 1882, from Dawn A. Lee *Daughter of Two Worlds* (2002) with the assistance of Tess De Araugo. © Dawn Lee. Reprinted by permission of Dawn Lee. National Archives of Australia. NAA: B313/1, item 42

Archie Roach: *You Have the Power* (1994). © Archie Roach. Reprinted by permission of Archie Roach

Kim Scott: *Benang: From the Heart* (1999). © Kim Scott 1999. Reprinted by permission of Fremantle Press

Alf Taylor: *Overland*, no. 144 (Spring 1996). Also appears in *Long Time Now: Stories of the Dreamtime, the Here and Now* (2001). © Alf Taylor. Reprinted by permission of Magabala Books

Jared Thomas: *Meanjin*, vol. 65, no. 1 (2006). © Jared Thomas 2006. Reprinted by permission of Jared Thomas

Joe Timbery: *Churinga*, vol. 1, no. 10 (December 1968 – March 1969). © The Estate of Joe Timbery. Reprinted by permission of Jeanette Timbery, Lynette Timbery and Joseph Timbery

Pat Torres: *Jalygurr: Aussie Animal Rhymes* (1987). © Pat Torres 1987. Reprinted by permission of Magabala Books

David Unaipon: 'Hungarrda' and 'Narrinyeri Saying' from *Native Legends* (1929). 'Aborigines, Their Traditions and Customs: Where Did They Come From?' and 'The Voice of the Great Spirit' from Stephen Muecke and Adam Shoemaker (eds), *Legendary Tales of the Australian Aborigines* (2001). © The

Estate of David Unaipon. Reprinted by permission of Harold Kropinyeri, eldest son of Melva Kropinyeri

Samuel Wagan Watson: 'Recipe for Metropolis Brisbane' from *Southerly*, vol. 62, no. 2 (2002). 'White Stucco Dreaming', 'For the Wake and Skeleton Dance' and 'Cheap White-Goods at the Dreamtime Sale' from *Smoke Encrypted Whispers* (2004). © Samuel Wagan Watson. Reprinted by permission of the University of Queensland Press

Glenyse Ward: *Wandering Girl* (1987). © Glenyse Ward 1988. Reprinted by permission of Magabala Books

Sam Watson: *The Kadaitcha Sung* (1990). © Sam Watson. Reprinted by permission of Penguin Group (Australia)

Errol West: from Kevin Gilbert (ed.), *Inside Black Australia* (Penguin Books, 1988). © Japananjka errol West; Palawa Warrior; Pairrebeene Clan; Tebrikunna Country. Reprinted by permission of Karan West

Ida West: *Pride Against Prejudice: Reminiscences of a Tasmanian Aborigine* (Revised edition, Montpelier Press, Hobart, 2004). © Ida West 1984, 1987, 2004. Reprinted by permission of Montpelier Press

Herb Wharton: *Where Ya' Been, Mate?* (1996). © Herb Wharton 1996. Reprinted by permission of Herb Wharton

Eric Willmot: *Pemulwuy: The Rainbow Warrior* (1987). © Eric Willmot. Reprinted by permission of New Holland Publishers Australia

Tara June Winch: *Swallow the Air* (2006). © Tara June Winch 2006. Reprinted by permission of the University of Queensland Press

Alexis Wright: *Plains of Promise* (1997). © Alexis Wright 1997. Reprinted by permission of the University of Queensland Press. *Carpentaria* (Giramondo Press, 2006). © Alexis Wright 2006. Reprinted by permission of Giramondo Press

Yirrkala People: Petition, August 1963. Reprinted by permission of Andrew Blake (Manager of the Buku-Larrnggay Mulka Centre, Yirrkala) on behalf of the Yirrkala Community. National Archives of Australia, NAA: series A6180

Galarrwuy Yunupingu: Statement, presented to R.J. Hawke, Prime Minister, at the Barunga Festival, 12 June 1988

Mandawuy Yunupingu: 'Treaty' (Mushroom Music Publishing). Reproduced with kind permission of Mushroom Music and Allen & Unwin Pty Ltd

INDEX

MICHAEL RILEY

Michael Riley (1960–2004) was a member of the Wiradjuri/Kamilaroi people and one of the most significant Indigenous Australian artists of the past few decades. *Untitled* (boomerang) is an image from the series *cloud* (2000), Riley's last and most iconic photographic series, which symbolically explores notions of spirituality, connection to land and Australia's colonial and pastoral past. The *cloud* series has been exhibited internationally and a posthumous retrospective of Riley's work was held in 2006 at the National Gallery of Australia. In the same year Riley was one of eight artists selected to be part of the largest international commission of contemporary Indigenous art from Australia on permanent display at the recently opened Musée du quai Branly in Paris.